¡Speak!
uSpeak!
weSpeak!

AN
INTRODUCTION
TO
CONTEMPORARY
PUBLIC
SPEAKING

JOHN ROSS, JR.
Northeastern Illinois University

Kendall Hunt
publishing company

Kendall Hunt
publishing company

www.kendallhunt.com
Send all inquiries to:
4050 Westmark Drive
Dubuque, IA 52004-1840

Copyright © 2012 by Kendall Hunt Publishing Company

ISBN 978-1-4652-0216-1

Printed in the United States of America
10 9 8 7 6 5 4 3 2 1

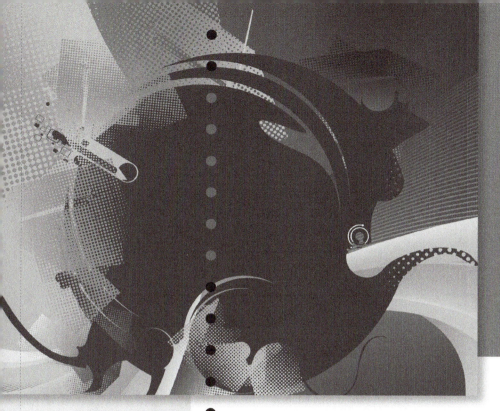

Contents

PART I
Origins of Contemporary Public Speaking

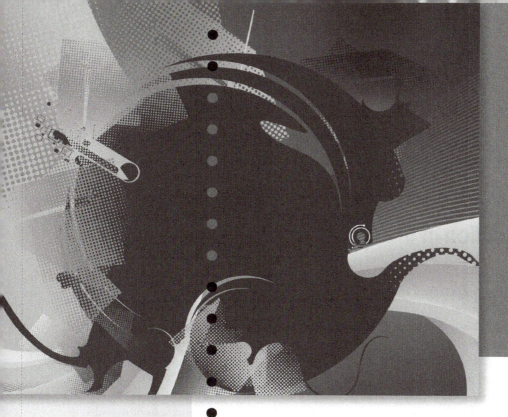

CHAPTER 1

Human Communication in the Digital Age

KEY TERMS
. . . .

digital age

communication

message

classes of messages

nonverbal messages

verbal messages

interpersonal
  messages

written messages

channel

encoding

decoding

noise

feedback

"The digital revolution is far more significant than the invention of writing or even of printing."
—Douglas Engelbart

"What turns me on about the digital age, what excited me personally, is that we have closed the gap between dreaming and doing."
—Paul David Hewson (Bono), lead singer of the band U2

In this chapter we will begin by taking a brief look at the origins of human communication, which date back to prehistory (that is, before the invention of writing), with momentous revolutions in growth and development. Many scholars speculate that human communication reached its pinnacle of efficiency when human speech was first achieved well over 200,000 years ago. Further, they hypothesize that symbolic communication may have been developed somewhere around 25,000 to 30,000 years ago. These changes continuously evolved parallel to changes in political and economic systems and, by extension, systems of tribal power and monarchical control.

Varieties of human communication can range from simple hand waves, quick winks, and morning greetings to seemingly endless, jam-packed conversations in crowded rooms or on cell phones. Writing (a fairly new development) was invented only around 6,000 to 7,000 years ago; and public speaking seems to have its roots in the desire to communicate political and social issues. Public speaking was the central component of human communication in ancient Greece and Rome, where open debates were epitomized through ceremonial and religious expression.

Over the past few centuries alone, there have been major developments in what has been termed *telecommunication*, which involves the transmission of nonspoken signals over long distances for the purpose of sending or receiving messages. Beginning thousands of years ago with smoke signals, horns, drums, and fire torches, humans have experimented with communicating over great distances. In the 1830s electrical communication started to enter into the picture, leading to telegraph, radio, and television, and more recently to computers and camera phones that then ushered in what is now dubbed the *digital age.*

Defining Communication in the Digital Age

The early 19th century introduced new and increasingly efficient forms of transportation and communication to North America. Roads and railways linked many remote communities, providing quick and convenient modes of land-based transportation, while steamships transported mail, freight, and passengers to remote coastal settlements and major cities.

Eventually, the *telegraph* and the *telephone* replaced mail as more-efficient means of electrical communication. Electrical communication was now able to put people in almost instantaneous contact with family, friends, or business associates in other parts of the United States, Canada, and Europe.

North America played an important role in advancing global telecommunications by providing a station for the world's first transatlantic telegraph cable. By the late 1830s electrical communication started to enter into daily life, leading from the telegraph to radio, television, and eventually, in the late 20th century, the introduction of computers. In the early 21st century, it has become quite common for virtually everyone to have use of BlackBerries or iPods as well as camera phones connected to the *Internet* or the *Web.* All this has led into what has now been dubbed the *digital age*—an era of instant information access and instantaneous messages.

The **digital age** is often seen (beginning in the early 21st century) as that "age" where almost all peoples everywhere have the potential or actual capability to communicate and send information in an open free manner. Having virtually immediate access to information is also an important part of the digital age. This sender-receiver relationship would have been impossible in any age prior to it. Since the very dawn when human beings first emerged as highly intelligent creatures, no other era or age has been so rapid in growth alone.

> ▶ Accelerating the swift development of technology in day-to-day life, and in education as well, the "Digital Age" has allowed swift global communications and networking to shape virtually every society as well as how we communicate in public settings.

In spite of our living in a digital age, **communication** in general can still be defined simply as the means by which humans transport information to each other from one location to another. What we actually communicate is termed the message. A **message,** in its most basic form, is the central item of communication. It is a container that provides those who communicate with the means they need to *send* or *receive* information. Yet, at times, the message can be this very information itself. Either way, the desired outcome or goal of any communicational message is namely: *knowledge, understanding,* and *reliability.*

The entire animal world (and a fraction of the plant world as well) sends messages. But for the most part, only humans, primates (such as apes, gorillas, and orangutans), and certain higher mammals such as dolphins, pigs, and elephants are capable of originating and truly comprehending messages.

▶ For we humans, all the more in this new century, being able to access information quickly and communicate messages effectively may be the most important of all life's skills.

Your Public Speaking Connection: Communication is both a very simple and yet at times an extremely complex human phenomenon to describe, particularly now that instant information and handheld devices are at the center of everyday life. Nonetheless, public speaking, like communication itself, is all about *sending, receiving,* and *assessing* messages. Although these are straightforward descriptions, when we actually examine *how* we go about speaking in public and sending messages to gathered groups of listeners, the matter becomes much more involved and complex.

Reflective Questions: Thinking About Digital Communication

We have said that beginning in the 1830s, electrical communication started to enter into modern life, leading from the telegraph, to radio, television, and eventually to iPhones, the Web, and instant messaging. This has given rise to the *digital age.* As you reflect upon the following questions, think about how you assess and evaluate information and how you prefer to communicate when given a choice. Consider how helpful and efficient you think the digital age may really be to you in the end.

You may respond in the spaces provided. For longer responses, feel free to write an extended essay on your laptop, and send it to your class Blackboard account if requested by your instructor.

1. How do I view using the computer in general and the advent of the Web in particular, as being unlike other forms of communication media, such as: TV, radio, DVDs, or the latest movies? Is computer technology my main source for communicating? Why or why not?

   _____

   _____

   _____

   _____

2. What, in my view, are the *strengths* and *weaknesses* of digital communication? Do I feel that there are any dangers involved as digital communication increases exponentially around the world?

   _____

   _____

   _____

   _____

3. In what ways do I see the digital revolution and the Web changing face-to-face connections, culture, and religion, as well as changing the way in which communication relates to them?

   _____

   _____

   _____

   _____

4. With more information resources available, and more Web access offered 24/7, the abundance of information technology makes conducting research uniquely ironic: too many information choices make it far more difficult to conduct research today than doing so was in previous years. What might be the reasons for this surprising paradox? Does having too many information choices cause me frustration?

_____

_____

_____

_____

_____

5. Because of the ease in manipulating digital images with Photoshop or other software applications, many scholars are questioning whether images are real or "doctored" in public presentations. Is it possible to actually believe anything we see anymore? What do you think the ethics should be surrounding the use of images, if any, in the digital age?

_____

_____

_____

_____

_____

6. What is the importance of *motivation* in the digital age? Are data and images being gathered to deceive people or to make the subjects more factually and visually interesting? Is it appropriate for photographers to enhance their images with digital techniques such as contrast and color enhancement? If so, should they inform all those who view them, in the form of public "footnotes"?

_____

_____

_____

_____

_____

7. What is the importance of *honesty* in the digital age? Are data and images being gathered that promote plagiarism, and in turn is a cause for a lack of creativity among those who write research papers and prepare their speeches in universities and colleges? Does digital information cause me personally to be tempted to succumb to minor bouts of plagiarism at times?

_____

_____

_____

_____

_____

Classes of Messages

There are three major **classes of messages** that encompass all forms of human communication: *nonverbal, verbal,* and *written.* The first two are also part of the animal world, particularly of mammals and primates such as gorillas, orangutans, and chimpanzees. These classes of messages include those that encompass body movements, gestures, words, phrases, and even sound signals. Only humans make use of *written messages,* which are fairly late on the communication history timeline. It is difficult to recognize when writing was first truly invented, as numerous cultures developed ways to keep records of crops, taxes, workers' wages, tribe members, and the tracking of other commodities.

Writing was invented multiple times in many places on Earth. The earliest Chinese writing, known as oracle bone script, was inscribed on tortoise shells or ox bones during the Shang Dynasty (ca. 1600–1000 B.C.E). Sacred priests smoldered the shells or bones, then publicly interpreted the fractures as either fortunate or unfortunate prophecies. Another early writing system, which developed in Central America, has been called the *Dresden Codex.* It is one of four surviving pre-Columbian Mayan manuscripts. It is interesting in that it uses written symbols that stand for sounds, for whole words, and at times even for short phrases.

> ▶ For the most part, the Sumerian peoples of Mesopotamia are generally thought to have created the earliest forms of written messages.

The Sumerians used natural reeds to compress symbols into flexible clay, which was then allowed to dry in the sun. This was called *cuneiform,* and the earliest known samples of it date to roughly 4000 B.C.E.

While we keep writing in mind, let's now take a brief look at each of the three general classes of messages: *nonverbal, verbal,* and of course the most recent of all, *writing.* Like writing itself, all three classes have applications for public speaking and connections that date to ages long before speech outlines and instant text messages were even dreamed of by contemporary public speaking instructors.

● ● ● ● ● Nonverbal Messages

Nonverbal messages are those forms of communication, other than verbal (spoken) or written, which create or transmit meaning to others. These messages may include: facial expressions, general body movements, sound, visual signals, and even simple gestures. Nonverbal messages communicate without directly speaking by way of spoken words.

> ▶ In many ways nonverbal messages may be the most important part of human communication; and ironically enough, they make no use of spoken words.

What we do with our face and body while we are speaking oftentimes may say more than what our words may be attempting to communicate. You may say you are not embarrassed, but your face turning red and your voice cracking will not lie to your listeners. Students may say that they are not confused and have no questions after a chemistry or calculus lecture, but their professor will know that half of the class is lost simply by the level of low energy, coupled with confused faces looking back at him or her.

If you have a dog or a cat, it may quite easily follow directions and respond to sounds, or even hand and body movements. Simply open the cupboard where the pet goodies are stored, and your cat may demonstrate sure signs of being restless for a treat; go for the leash in the hall closet, and your dog may begin jumping, wagging its tail, and expressing signs of excitement about going for a morning walk.

General Uses of Nonverbal Messages

There are three general uses of nonverbal messages. The first one is largely for salutations or hellos and good-byes, and for many other forms of greetings. These may include: waves, handshakes, hugs, winks, embraces, kisses, and military salutes.

A second form of nonverbal communication is important for *specific messages*. For example, team members and referees in sporting events may use nonverbal signals as ways to directly communicate without using words. In football, soccer, and baseball, nonverbal signals are very specific and tell those who receive them to move or play left, right, slow, fast, tight, or wide.

Another very important nonverbal operation is *sign language*. This form of communication is used for people who have hearing problems. They use hand signals and lip reading to communicate very detailed information. In fact, American sign language, or ASL, is an authentic language that is quite specific, just as any other type of spoken language might be.

> ▶ Many language scholars say that nonverbal communication may comprise well over 75 percent of the communication messages sent and received all over the world.

A third category of nonverbal messages is *automatic nonverbal cues,* which are signals, movements, and attitudes that show how we may be experiencing the world around us. In most cases these actions are subconscious, and those making them do them automatically without any thought or intention. A head sagged while walking may indicate that a person is a bit depressed, or tears during a speech may indicate that a listener is emotionally moved by the words of a eulogy or sermon. When people yawn or massage their eyes, it may indicate that they are weary, bored, or possibly drained from the demands of a long workday.

> ▶ Since most nonverbal communication is unintended or *subconscious*, in many ways it is more honest and effective than direct speech.

Your Public Speaking Connection: As a public speaker, you need to be aware that nonverbal expressions and gestures are not the same everywhere. Some are local and some are universal. In various parts of Africa, the "thumbs-up" signal is a rude insult, but in the United States and Canada it is a positive sign of approval. Another gesture that can be differently understood is nodding of the head up and down, which in most places indicates yes; but in Bulgaria, and in parts of Macedonia, Greece, and the Middle East, it means a definite no.

• • • • • Verbal Messages

Whenever we use vocal sounds and language to communicate, we are making use of **verbal messages.** Such messages include all communication that can first be spoken and then heard. They help us communicate highly complex information. Verbal messages serve as a powerful means for expressing our thoughts, ideas, inspirations, needs, and impressions. They are fundamental to the development of listening to and understanding information from others. Without verbal messages, no learning or teaching would take place. All education as we know it would be unattainable. Verbal messages have many functions, but their main role is to relay information to one or more receivers. Verbal communication can be used to *inform, question, quarrel,* and *discuss* ideas and topics of all varieties. It is vital to forming bonds and building relationships with other people. Verbal messages are at the foundation of every society.

In combination with *nonverbal* forms of communication, *verbal messages* act as the primary tool for expression between two or more people, or what is termed **interpersonal messages.** An understanding of interpersonal messages is an essential ingredient in fostering good relationships with other individuals or with a listening audience. Interpersonal messages lie at the intersection of our cultural understanding and construction of a world society, due to the complex process by which culture and all forms of communication influence each other. Without them, we would have no digital age that consists of communicating by cell phone calls, instant messages, e-mails, the Web, and texting.

> ▶ Everything from the simple one-syllable sounds of anxious babies to highly complex interviews, discussions, and daily phone calls depends upon verbal messages to communicate complex thoughts and ideas.

Although all animals, from tiny insects and flying birds to fish and mammals, are able to communicate, verbal messages *per se* are largely a human event. They allow for more accuracy and greater detail than any form of communication found in the animal world. Many animals do communicate by *smell messages*: they discharge chemicals, called pheromones, into the air in order to send information to one another. These play an important role in reproduction and other social behavior.

Both smell messages and nonverbal messages are used by many animals, including bees, crabs, deer, gorillas, and of course we humans. For instance, the scout bee will boogie in the hive, and its dance instructs other bees to the exact location of the nectar. Male fiddler crabs signal by their larger claw to attract their favorite female fiddler crabs across the way; white-tailed deer demonstrate panic by brushing up their tails; and gorillas will extend their tongues in public to show others their disapproval or even resentment toward smelly humans gawking at them in the zoo.

Your Public Speaking Connection: When it comes to public speaking, *verbal messages* can bring a host of challenges; and the possibility of miscommunication can never be completely avoided. It is possible to increase your chances of communicating successfully by appropriate preparation and giving careful detail to anything you might say in public. Strongly give attention to *what* you hope to say and *how* you hope to say it. Speaking loudly and enunciating your words clearly is essential when speaking to a group of listeners, since there are many more pairs of ears out there waiting to misinterpret anything you might say in public.

• • • • • Written Messages

Written messages include any type of communication that makes use of written words and written language. Since no speech is involved, written messages do not have to be delivered on the spur of the moment. As an alternative, they can be corrected and revised numerous times before they are sent to those who will receive them. The advantage of all written messages is that they provide for us a permanent record that may be set aside for later study and review. Written forms of communication also enable recipients to take more time in reviewing the message and then providing appropriate *feedback.* For these reasons, written forms of communication are often considered more appropriate for complex business, legal, medical, and scientific messages, since each of these include essential facts, figures, and significant details.

> ▶ Unlike verbal communication, where responses and reactions may be exchanged within a live setting, the sender of *written messages* (in most cases) may not receive immediate feedback from his or her message.

Receiving little or no feedback may cause a bit of discouragement and uncertainty in communication situations in which a swift response is desired. Since written messages frequently take more time to compose, because of their highly informational nature, there is often a challenge involved in preparing a successful and well-received written document. In turn, receiving any response from those who have received it, may also take some time.

> ▶ Sometimes you may have to wait one or two days before you get a response from an e-mail you worked so hard to send to your professor about a speech topic.

Your Public Speaking Connection: It is important to use written messages when presenting a speech, especially if you are new to public speaking. The key to written messages lies in *written notes* on your laptop or on traditional *note cards.* Using notes effectively helps you to have a conversation with your listeners. When presenting a speech, the less written material you have, the better for both you and your audience. Nonetheless, you do need to rely upon written messages to remind you of ideas, facts, transitions, examples, and perhaps even a joke or two.

Your **A, B, C**s for Recalling the Classes of Messages

NONVERBAL MESSAGES

Remember:

A *Nonverbal* messages are those other-than-verbal (spoken) or written ones that create or transmit meaning to others.

B They include facial expressions, general body movements, sounds, visual signals, and simple gestures. They always communicate either directly or indirectly without the need for spoken words.

C Most nonverbal communication is unintended or *subconscious.* In many ways it is more honest and effective than direct speech.

VERBAL MESSAGES

Remember:

A *Verbal messages* include all communication that can be spoken or heard. They help us communicate highly complex information. Without verbal messages, no learning or teaching could take place.

B They serve as a powerful means for expressing our *thoughts, ideas, inspirations, needs, and impressions* and are fundamental to the development of listening to and understanding information from others.

C Verbal messages are unique because they can be used to inform, question, quarrel, and discuss ideas and topics of all varieties.

WRITTEN MESSAGES

Remember:

A *Written messages* include any type of communication that makes use of written words and written language or symbols. Since no speech is involved, written messages do not have to be delivered on the spur of the moment.

B As an alternative, they can be corrected and revised numerous times before they are sent to those who will receive them. The advantage of all written messages is that they provide a permanent record so that they can be set aside for later study and appraisal.

C Written forms of communication also enable recipients to take more time in reviewing the message and then providing appropriate and detailed *feedback*.

INTERPERSONAL MESSAGES

Remember:

A *Interpersonal messages* act as the primary tool for expression between two or more people and are at the center of all human communication in the digital age.

B An understanding of interpersonal messages is an essential ingredient in fostering good relationships with other individuals and with a listening audience.

C They form the complex process by which culture and all forms of communication influence each other. Without them, we would have no *digital age* consisting of cell phones, instant messages, e-mails, and the like.

Message Channels

The means by which we go about sending and receiving messages is often termed a **channel.** There are multiple channels available to us early in the 21st century—everything from simple *face-to-face* conversations in restaurants and cafes, *telephone* calls, *text* messages, and *e-mail*, to all forms of *social media* found on the Web, such as *Facebook* and *Twitter*. Before the advent of social media, the dominant channels of technology were radio and television. Before those, the channels were postcards, letter writing, flyers, advertisements, and various types of memos and reports.

▶ Deciding upon the right *channel* is vital for successful communication, since each offers different advantages and disadvantages, depending upon your communication needs.

When offering news concerning a school arts or sports event, a written e-mail may be the best channel for your message, but perhaps only to a handful of friends or neighbors, at best. Most likely it will not be very efficient, nor as cost effective, as making good use of a local TV or radio broadcast as your main channel of communication. Since reaching a large number of people is the ultimate goal, a mass media channel is by far the better choice.

In other cases, written or printed material may be the best channels when the situation calls for highly analytical or complex information. By providing printed documents and bound materials for close analysis, you will permit those who read them to highlight important points, in order to read and reread them at their own pace at a later time. A written channel may even help them to interpret the information by way of charts and diagrams that they may need to more fully understand what needs to be understood.

Written communication is also a useful way of recording what has been said: for example, taking notes during a college lecture or dictating notes during an interview for a newspaper column or a book. In some cases students may prefer a voice recorder as their channel for collecting information. In short, choosing the appropriate channel helps make communication more efficient, as it is the means through which a message is transmitted to its intended audience. These channels may include sound, visual, print, broadcast, or electronic means.

Your Public Speaking Connection: Speaking before a live audience is still very much a powerful communication channel. It is an immediate way of communicating messages to both small groups and large auditoriums full of listeners. Public speaking is the most intuitive and earliest form of *message channel*. As for religious or political information, even a recorded live sermon or speech is far more effective, when hoping to inspire others, than anything electronically written, printed, or distributed by hand. From the earliest beginnings of communication history, public speaking has been at the forefront of passing vital information from person to person.

Encoding and Decoding Messages

If messages are to be successful, they must be sent *via* a form that can be conveyed by the communication channel best chosen for that given message. This is referred to as **encoding**. We all encode information on a daily basis by transferring our complex ideas and thoughts into spoken words or into an e-mail or a Twitter response. Various communication channels entail different forms of encoding. Effective communicators *encode* their messages with their intended audience in mind as well as the communication channel that they feel will work best. This involves the correct use of a code that may be the words, the phrases, or the language used in general. *Encoding* involves sending information simply and clearly, while anticipating and eliminating likely causes of confusion and misunderstanding. Successful encoding of messages is a vital skill in effective communication. If you do not fully understand someone, it is most likely because the code is not fully clear to you.

Once a message is sent and then received, the receivers need to decode the message. Successful **decoding** is also very important all on its own. Receivers will decode and understand messages in different ways, based upon any "noise" that they may experience in the process.

> ▶ Writers, TV broadcasters, and public speakers are all encoders. Readers, TV watchers, and audience members are all decoders.

Noise includes any obstacles to communication that might be at hand to obstruct the message intended by the encoder. These obstacles may include any barriers to listeners' experience and understanding of the context of the message, their psychological state, and the time and place of reception, as well as many other potential factors. Understanding how the message will be *decoded*, and anticipating as many of the potential sources of misunderstanding as possible, is the art of a successful communicator.

Receivers of messages are likely to provide what is termed **feedback.** Feedback is a clear indication that receivers have understood the messages through both verbal and nonverbal reactions.

> ▶ Keep in mind that the extent and form of feedback will vary, according to the *communication channel* used. Feedback while face-to-face or during telephone conversations will be immediate and direct, but feedback from messages conveyed *via* TV, radio, and movies will be indirect.

Oftentimes feedback may be delayed, or even conveyed through other media. With films and videos, the possibility for feedback may be through printed reviews, internet blogs, e-mails, and even in some cases public protests outside the movie theater where a controversial film may be playing. A perfect example of *immediate feedback* on the radio is when live callers are invited to comment or ask questions on the air. Radio sports channels offer call-in feedback opportunities for fans, while some religious broadcasters offer scriptural question-and-answer sessions to live listeners.

Your Public Speaking Connection: When offering presentations in public, speakers should pay close attention to *audience feedback*. For them as public speakers, feedback is the only way to assess whether their message has been understood as intended; and it allows them to correct and adjust for any confusion. The energy level of the audience is vital as a form of feedback. Any laughter, occasional applause, amen's, boos, heckles, restlessness, smiles, and the like, are all forms of feedback that will can help the public speaker assess his or her success from start to finish.

Always
Rules

Using Written Messages for Public Speaking

Written messages are a useful way of recording what needs to be said. The key to using written messages properly lies in composing clear and concise notes.

As we have mentioned, it is important to use written messages when presenting a speech, especially if you are new to public speaking. The following are helpful rules to keep in mind when using *laptop* computers, *handheld* devices, and *iPads*. Of course, good old-fashioned *note cards* are still preferred by many, and never seem to fail you when you need to give a well-organized speech.

We will go into greater detail in Chapter 7 about how to organize and outline your speeches. The following are just a few simple reminders of how written messages in general will help you as a public speaker to be more powerfully verbal in public.

- *Always* remember that your notes should *not* include the entire script of your speech. If you write every word, you will fail to have an honest conversation with your audience. If you then read a speech to them, you will rarely make eye contact since your attention will be focused on your written words and *not* upon your audience.

- *Always* remember that it is fine to write out your opening line and the goals for your speech. With practice, you should be able to deliver what is on your note cards or computer screen without depending upon them. It is always a great idea to have notes in front of you in case you get nervous and forget. Having strong opening lines written out can build your confidence, but the bulk of what you have to say should come from notes.

- *Always* write out phrases or key words for each *main point, subpoints,* and any supporting material. Always separate main sections in your notes with blank lines, indentation, or whatever will signal to you to pause, regroup, and then move on to the next major point of your speech.

- *Always* write down your summary and closing lines, for the same reason that you wrote down your opening words—just as a backup plan. In your closing notes be sure to restate your message and restate the purpose of your speech.

- *Always* keep in mind that the size of font you use (in printed notes) should be large enough so that you can see things quickly and clearly. You should be able to glance at your note cards or screen and quickly find your place and the appropriate phrase you need. The size of your font depends upon your eyesight, whether you wear glasses, and of course the light level of the room. If you need to, be sure to adjust the brightness of your computer screen so that things are crystal clear.

- *Always* remember the importance of practice. It will be almost impossible to deliver a successful presentation with notes if you do not orally practice what you have written down. It is not essential to memorize every word of your speech, but it is important to get comfortable presenting it in a variety of ways, using your notes to remember the important words, phrases, and significant transitions.

Summary

In this chapter we have explored what it means to be a part of the digital age: namely, the idea that the 21st century is largely distinguished by the capability of people from all over the globe to quickly transfer information freely, and to have immediate access to it in a manner that would have been impossible to develop in any previous era. Apart from the digital age, communication in general can be defined simply as the means by which humans transport information from person to person, and also from one place to another. What we actually communicate is termed the *message*, which, in its most basic sense, is the fundamental item of all communication.

There are three major *classes of messages* which encompass all of human communication. They are *nonverbal, verbal,* and *written.* The first two are also part of the animal world, particularly among primates and higher mammals. Nonverbal messages include body movements, gestures, and even sign language. Verbal messages include all communication that can be spoken or heard. Verbal messages serve as a powerful means for expressing our thoughts, ideas, inspirations, desires, and impressions; and they are fundamental to the development of listening to and understanding information from others.

Only humans make use of written messages, which are fairly late on the communication history timeline. These include any type of communication which makes use of written symbols, words, and written language. Since no speech is involved, writing does not have to be delivered instantaneously. The advantage of all written communication is that it provides for us a permanent record of the message so that it can be set aside for later study and review.

An understanding of *interpersonal messages* is an essential ingredient in fostering good relationships with other individuals and with a listening audience. They lie at the intersection of our cultural understanding and construction of a world society, due to the complex process by which culture and all forms of communication influence each other. Without them, we would have no era embracing the use of cell phones, instant messages, e-mails, the Web, and texting.

By bringing about a speedy evolution of communication technology in daily life, as well as in educational life, the *digital age* has permitted swift communications and networking to shape both our global society and how we communicate in public settings. All the more in this new century, being able to access information quickly and to communicate messages efficiently may be the most important of all life skills.

Discussion Questions

1. Discuss what is meant by the term *communication*. What are the main types of advancements brought about by communication in the digital age? In what ways are both time and distance essential to the digital age?

2. What do we mean by the term *nonverbal?* In what ways are animals able to make efficient use of nonverbal messages? What do you think it means when we say that nonverbal messages may be more honest than verbal messages?

3. Why do you think that writing, as powerful as it is, has the shortest of communication histories, roughly only 4,000 to 5,000 years at best? Which do you think is more powerful and efficient in the end, verbal messages *or* written messages?

4. What are meant by the terms *encoding, decoding,* and *noise?* How might noise be connected to verbal messages when giving or listening to a speech in public?

5. The *digital age* has permitted swift global communications and networking to shape both our global society and how we communicate in public settings. Do you think that there is a limit to its progress? Will the digital age bring communication eventually into the realm of what many scholars refer to as an age of science-fiction, with robots and computers that may have minds and thoughts of their own?

● ● ● ● ● Quick Quiz

Match the following capsule sentences with the correct letter of the term which best describes the key terms or phrases discussed in this chapter.

1. _____ Any barriers to communication that might obstruct the encoder's message.

2. _____ The information we hope to send and then have successfully received by others.

3. _____ Verbal and nonverbal responses by those who receive information from others.

4. _____ The item of communication that provides communicators with information.

5. _____ The actual means by which we go about communicating a message.

6. _____ The process by which a message is received and then interpreted.

7. _____ Subconscious actions that are done automatically without thought or intention.

8. _____ Means by which we transport information from one location to another.

9. _____ Era in which the transfer of information is instant and available with access for all.

10. _____ The use of actual sounds and language to communicate with others.

A. Encoding	**B.** Feedback	**C.** Channel
D. Verbal messages	**E.** Automatic nonverbal cues	**F.** Communication
G. Decoding	**H.** Digital age	**I.** Noise
J. Message		

KEY TERMS

rhetoric

Aristotle

sophistry

genres of rhetoric

liberal education

orator

canon

fine arts

visual arts

auditory arts

performance arts

rhetorical analysis

rhetorical appeals

rhetorical purpose

rhetorical situation

"In making a speech one must study three points: first, the means of producing persuasion; second, the language; third, the proper arrangement of the various parts of the speech."
—Aristotle

"As soon as a boy has made sufficient progress in his studies to be able to follow what I have styled the first stage of instruction in rhetoric, he should be placed under a rhetorician."
—Quintilian

Humans have explored and studied rhetoric (or speaking in public) since the early days of writing, and possibly even before. Both the Mesopotamians and the ancient Egyptians highly valued the talents and acquired skills needed to offer presentations and speeches in public. Presentations with fluency, wisdom, and the ability to captivate an audience were the ambition of everyone who hoped to be successful in the ancient world. It was the early Greeks, along with their democratic principles and ideals about government that actually molded rhetoric into an institutionalized form of art. For them, it amounted to an almost athletic level of skillfulness.

For both early Greece and the Roman Empire to follow, the study and practice of rhetoric evolved into a form of high art that was studied and developed systematically. To be successful and to improve one's place in life, mastering rhetoric and being a skilled public speaker was a necessity.

It was this Greco-Roman world that gave us both the awareness and the presentation skills we know and study today as: *volume, pitch, rhythm, diction, eye contact,* and *body gestures.* These ancients were very much attuned to the *do's* and *don'ts* of how a public speaker could make a powerful impression in order to inform and persuade an audience. First by emphasizing how the speaker must look and sound before a group of listeners, and second by having speakers pay attention to the details of *what* is to be said and *how*, the Greeks and Romans gave us the foundational directives that we follow to this very day.

Rhetoric in Ancient Greece: Plato and Aristotle

From a small gathering to a large auditorium, **rhetoric** is the ancient art of using language honestly and effectively to inform and persuade an audience. It traditionally incorporates what are known as modes of *appeal,* and can be effectively divided into five categories, or *canons,* as well. It is important to realize that rhetoric has a long and fascinating history beginning with the *sophists* of ancient Greece. Later adapted by the Romans, the art of rhetoric continued to evolve further on through to the Enlightenment, the Renaissance, and eventually our own 21st century. Today most *rhetorical analysis* has become focused upon discovering creative approaches to using rhetoric, developing personal styles, and making effective use of current digital technology to develop and enhance public presentations.

● ● ● ● ● Sophistry

Most historians credit the ancient city-state of Athens as the source of classical rhetoric. Athenian democracy helped incorporate every free male citizen into politics, and consequently, every adult man had to be adequately prepared to stand in the political assembly and present powerful words to persuade his fellow citizens to vote for or against a specific piece of legislation. All success and influence in ancient Athens depended upon one's rhetorical talents. As a result, small schools dedicated to teaching rhetoric began to form. The first of these schools began in the 5th century B.C.E. among an itinerant group of teachers called *sophists.* The sophists were traveling professional teachers and intellectuals who frequented Athens and other Greek cities in the second half of the 5th century B.C.E. In return for a high payment, the sophists offered young, wealthy Greek men an education in persuasive techniques and general world knowledge. The goal of the sophists was to help these young men achieve further wealth and even fame, which frequently was won at the cost of arousing hostility and trouble in Greek society.

Due in large part to the influence of both Plato and Aristotle, the term **sophistry** has come to signify the deliberate use of fallacious reasoning, intellectual deceit, and ethical corruption. Plato is largely responsible for our contemporary view of the sophist as a greedy instructor who manipulates his or her language in public settings in order to deceive or to support misleading or misdirected reasoning. The sophist is not concerned with what is helpful, truthful, or virtuous, but rather seeks to achieve power and control by public means.

> ▶ Both Plato and Aristotle challenged the philosophical foundations of sophistry, which later gave rise to *rhetoric* and consequently the morals and ethical responsibilities surrounding those who speak in public.

● ● ● ● ● Aristotle

The grand philosopher **Aristotle** (384–322 B.C.E.) was the first to passionately disapprove of the ideals and practices of sophistry. He was very displeased at the exploitation of speech and was able both to see the great and powerful potential it had in helping those gathered in large crowds to understand informational truths, and to pursue honest means of persuasion. In his famous dissertation entitled: *The Art of Rhetoric*, Aristotle established the first system of understanding and teaching rhetoric in a fashion that influenced everyone who came after him. His powerful legacy gave rise to how public speaking courses are taught to this day in colleges and universities.

In *The Art of Rhetoric*, Aristotle roughly defines rhetoric (paraphrased) as: "the skill to examine the means by which one can first inform then persuade others." For him, rhetoric helped provide people with the necessary weapons to separate those who willfully deceive from those who use knowledge for more truthful means.

> ▶ According to Aristotle, the best way to fight *destructive* words and language is by using *constructive* words and beneficial language.

● ● ● ● ● Genres of Rhetoric

Aristotle identified three types or **genres of rhetoric**: *forensic,* or judicial, was concerned with determining the truth or false nature of events as understood historically; *deliberative,* or political, which was concerned with determining whether or not particular actions *should* or *should not* be undertaken in the future; and *epideictic,* or ceremonial, which was concerned with either honoring or faulting others, and with acclaiming right and wrong, as revealed in each present age.

After establishing the need for rhetorical knowledge and skills, Aristotle set forth a foundational structure for effectively applying rhetorical skills in a systematic and practical manner. His pioneering work still endures.

> ▶ *The Art of Rhetoric* further continued to have a remarkable influence on the growth of the study of public speaking for the next two centuries.

Today when we speak of *rhetoric* we usually mean the art and skill of informing or persuading others within a public setting. Your college or university course in public speaking is directly linked to the ancient world by way of Aristotle, and afterward by the Roman rhetoricians Cicero and Quintilian.

Rhetoric in Ancient Rome: Cicero and Quintilian

Rhetoric was slow but sure to develop beyond ancient Greece. The Roman rhetoricians frequently spoke about and taught Aristotle's principles throughout the Roman Empire. Roman rhetoric started to flourish when the empire conquered Greece and began to be influenced more directly by Greek traditions. While the Romans incorporated many of the rhetorical elements established by the Greeks, they diverged from those customs in many ways. Public speakers, lecturers, and even writers in ancient Rome depended more on stylistic elements, storytelling, and the more vivid use of words and language in general. They were less concerned with logical reasoning and highly persuasive skillfulness. In short, the Romans developed a more artful approach to rhetoric.

The first virtuoso performer was Marcus Tullius Cicero (106–46 B.C.E.). He was a revered statesman and the model for all rhetoricians who followed him. Like Aristotle in Greece before him, Cicero wrote three classic dissertations on the subject: *On Invention, On Oration,* and *Topics.* His writings on rhetoric were utilized by universities on the subject well into the time of the Renaissance, and then flourished throughout Europe. Cicero's approach to rhetoric was foundational to how we view not only public speaking, but all of education and learning to this very day. In many ways, Cicero is the father of what is termed **liberal education**. Such an education entails being equally acquainted with world history, politics, ethics, the basic sciences, and finally, both literature and the arts.

Cicero believed that by having a liberal education anyone who spoke in public would be able to emotionally bond with any audience at any time or location. For him a liberal education was the key to being a successful public speaker and to benefiting all of society.

> ▶ For the Romans, public speaking became an important part of public life, and Cicero was the grand leader among them all. Today, he still remains the best-known ancient public speaker who not only spoke frequently but also produced helpful teachings on the subject.

After Cicero, Marcus Fabius Quintilianus (35–100 C.E.), simply known as Quintilian, was the second great Roman thinker to influence the history of rhetoric and, consequently, public speaking. His principles and skills have their origin in the great courts of the Roman Empire. Later in his career, Quintilian founded what became a public school devoted to the exclusive study of rhetorical principles and the art of public speaking. This school was unique in that it guided each student through various levels of beginning, moderate, and highly advanced rhetorical training. Quintilian preserved his principles in a twelve-volume textbook entitled *Institutio Oratoria.* This is perhaps the first textbook on public speaking, one that covers all aspects of the art of speech-making: organization, use of quotations, incorporating anecdotes, and many other advanced rhetorical principles. Quintilian highly advocated being equally acquainted with world history, politics, ethics, law, and the sciences; and of course literature and the arts. As did Aristotle before him, Quintilian advocated a rhetorical education and stressed that being a well-rounded citizen benefited all of society. Both men taught that powerful speaking in public was the best way to go about achieving it.

> ▶ For Quintilian, rhetorical education begins (if possible) not long after a baby is born and then progressively focuses on more-developed principles throughout childhood, and eventually should be continuous throughout adulthood.

Quintilian's approach encompasses not only the art of rhetoric, but also the formation of the perfect orator. An **orator** is an individual who delivers an eloquent *oration* (or speech), especially a person distinguished for his or her skill and power as a public speaker. Cicero is famous for having said, "*Great is our admiration of the orator who speaks with fluency and discretion.*" For the Romans, the proper rhetorical education should create a politically active, public-minded citizen who was both confident and distinctive. They emphasized the moral application of rhetorical training and the formation of adults into virtuous people.

In his *Five Canons of Rhetoric,* Quintilian establishes the foundation for all public speaking, one that is embraced in textbooks to this very day: A **canon** is a basic rule or foundational principle to be memorized and then put into regular practice. Quintilian's standard notion of rhetoric included the following five canons: *Invention, Arrangement, Style, Memory,* and *Delivery.* Each of these canons is still pertinent today, and serves as the core around which the majority of college and university professors construct their public speaking course designs and syllabi.

Still Alive Today: Quintilian's *Five Canons of Rhetoric*

The following is a brief description of each of Quintilian's *Five Canons of Rhetoric,* followed by a few commentary notes on their contemporary application. We will go into further detail by applying each of these canons in various forms and manifestations covered throughout Chapters 4 through 9 of this book.

Invention: This is the careful procedure for developing and refining both the *purpose* and the exact *goals* of your speech. More important, it includes the various arguments for any and all levels of persuasion, with an emphasis upon credible information.

> ***Note:** Quintilian uses the Latin term for *invention* as the very first canon in planning a speech. Inventiveness and creativity were very important to Roman rhetoricians back then, and still are today. By being creative in your approach to your speech, you are taking the first step in becoming an *orator.*

Arrangement: This is the process of *arranging* and *organizing* your main points (and subpoints) and any informative elements or persuasive arguments in a progressive order which will result in having maximum impact on your audience.

> ***Note:** Quintilian is concerned about being *organized* and not jumbled or haphazard. He is interested in *what* is to be included as well as *when* and *where* to place it in your speech.

Style: This is the careful approach to determining exactly *how* you present your main points (and subpoints) and any arguments you offer, using colorful words, figures of speech, and other symbolic language, or employing presentation techniques that will captivate your audience.

> ***Note:** Quintilian was concerned with style *or* approach and how the choice of words and phrases are an important element to public speaking. Style is key to becoming an orator.

Memory: This is the developmental process of learning and memorizing the contents of your speech in order to able to deliver it without the need for directly *reading* it to your audience. This consisted of basically memorizing the entire *outline* of the speech, and then memorizing powerful anecdotes, humorous stories, and quotations as well.

> ***Note:** For Quintilian, memorization included preparing impactful quotations, as well as literary references and other startling facts that could be used on the spot, should the audience appear to drift or lose interest at any point.

Delivery: This is the disciplined process of practicing *how* you present your speech, using gestures, proper pronunciation, eye contact, and calculated levels of volume and and word emphasis.

> ***Note:** For Quintilian, not only *what* is said but also *eye contact, gestures,* and *body movement* were equally vital.

Rhetoric During the Middle Ages (or Medieval Times)

After the fall of the Roman Empire, the study of speech and rhetoric continued to be significant to the study of speech and literature, but eventually it weakened into decline for several centuries thereafter. There began at this time a gradual rise in formal education, evolving into what became the rise of medieval universities such as the those founded in Bologna and Paris; and later Oxford and Cambridge universities in England. During the Middle Ages (roughly the 5th century C.E. to the 15th century C.E.), rhetoric shifted from an emphasis upon law, politics, and war-expansion speeches to one focused upon religious ideals and Christian themes. Instead of being merely a tool to lead the nations, forge political agendas and even foment wars, rhetoric was seen as a means to gather spiritual followers and even bring about eternal salivation.

Church fathers such as Augustine of Hippo (354–430 C.E.) and Thomas Aquinas (ca. 1225–1274 C.E.) investigated ways in which they could use the nonreligious art of rhetoric to advance the Christian teachings of Jesus to the unethical, materialistic, and unconverted pagans. They became spiritual orators and preachers who used rhetorical principles largely for religious means. Rhetoric took on the role of structured preaching. To be a great orator often meant to be a great preacher amid large as well as small gatherings, not unlike the myriad preachers seen today on broadcast television or cable channels.

Toward the end of the medieval period, universities began forming all over continental Europe and Great Britain. In France, Italy and England, students were required to take compulsory classes on grammar, logic, and rhetoric (just as in ancient times). These students also studied the texts of Aristotle and Quintilian to learn rhetorical theory, and they spent countless hours repeating written and oral exercises, in both Greek and Latin, to improve their oratory skills, especially content and delivery. The study of religion and theology was a common educational goal.

▶ Although stress and emphasis were placed upon the classics of Aristotle, Cicero, and Quintilian, somehow medieval teachers and philosophers rarely made any new or innovative contributions to the further development of rhetoric and oratory as a growing discipline.

Rhetoric During the Renaissance

As with literature, music, sculpture, painting, dance, medicine, and the sciences, the study and focus of rhetoric also experienced a rebirth during the Renaissance. The Renaissance is understood as a historical age that was preceded by the Middle Ages and followed by the Protestant Reformation in Europe. According to most historians it began in Italy in the 15th century, and spread throughout the rest of the continent from there. It is unique in that it represented a reconnection of Western Europe with the ancient classical world of Aristotle, Cicero, and Quintilian. During the Renaissance all fields of knowledge (above all, mathematics and science)—ranging from the Arab world, scientific experimentation, and a general blossoming of knowledge brought on by printing and innovative techniques in art, poetry, and architecture—led to a fundamental change in the style and substance found in the arts and literature. The Italian Renaissance is often labeled as the era when the early seeds of the modern era began to take their early root.

During this period the classical texts of Aristotle, Cicero, and Quintilian were rediscovered, emphasized, and used in rigorous courses of study. Quintilian's *De Inventione* (Concerning Inventions) quickly became a standard rhetoric textbook at all European universities in France, Italy and Spain, as well as in England at the universities of Oxford and Cambridge.

> ▶ Renaissance scholars began producing new treatises and books on rhetoric, many of them emphasizing the application of rhetorical skills to one's own vernacular language, as opposed to the original Latin or Greek.

In a sense, there was an updated or "neo-classical" approach to rhetoric which emphasized the basics as founded in ancient Greece and Rome but which in turn were made more relevant to the life and times of the blossoming ideals and thoughts congruent with the Renaissance. Both rhetorical thinking and oratory were influenced by literature and the arts, and thus took on a more artistic identity.

Rhetoric During the Enlightenment

The rejuvenation of rhetoric continued through the Renaissance and on into the Enlightenment, a period in Western thought and culture stretching roughly from the mid-17th through the 18th centuries. This period was greatly typified by innovative revolutions in science, philosophy, politics, and society in general, revolutions that continued to brush away medieval thoughts and societal norms and eventually gave rise to our contemporary Western world of today. Enlightenment thought is also very historically rooted in the rise of the French Revolution during which monarchical, political, and social orders (including the dominant power of the Roman Catholic Church) were strongly challenged and in some cases destroyed. Most political, social, and religious institutions were restored by a political, social, and religious foundation that was informed by the *Enlightenment ideals* of: freedom, democracy, and equal-rights movements at all levels of society. Here human reason took reign as the guiding principle for societal and political progress, and monarchical and autocratic control was seriously challenged, if not directly obliterated.

In many ways, the Enlightenment reached its summit with the scientific revolutions found in the 16th and 17th centuries. The rise of the scientific age progressively undermined not only the classical earth-bound conception of the universe, but with it the entire set of presuppositions that had served to constrain and guide all philosophical inquiry rooted in doctrinal religion and the Bible.

As notions of free government, new attitudes toward science, and the rise of democracy began to spread throughout Europe and the young American colonies in Philadelphia and Boston, rhetoric shifted back once gain from a religious and spiritual emphasis to that of governmental and civic duty. For a second time, rhetorical studies and the words of their trained orators took on highly political, even revolutionary themes.

> ▶ Political philosophers and revolutionary idealists used public speaking as a weapon in their campaign to spread liberty and freedom. It was a source of spiritual discourse away from aristocracy, theocracy, and monarchy.

As in the past, colleges and universities were at the forefront. During the 18th and 19th centuries, both Europe and the newly formed United States of America began devoting entire academic departments to the study of rhetoric. Many universities such as Harvard, Yale, and Princeton proliferated with rhetorical scholars, speech teachers, and oratory specialists, along with academic writings that reflected the importance of how to powerfully communicate in public.

One of the more influential books on rhetoric that came out during this period was published in 1783, entitled *Lectures on Rhetoric and Belles-Lettres,* by Hugh Blair. It became the standard textbook on rhetoric and speech at colleges and universities across Europe and America for more than a century. To this day, it is considered a major historical resource in most graduate programs in rhetoric and advanced public speaking.

Rhetoric During Modern and Contemporary Times

The 20th century has been dubbed the age of technology and the 21st century as the age of communication. There has been an incredible explosion of technology and mass media in both centuries which has caused yet further alterations in the study of rhetoric since the Enlightenment.

At some point in the 19th century, scholars began more and more to emphasize differences between what was termed a science and an art. Eventually the term **fine arts** came to mean anything that had been created to please the human senses. After separating from the sciences, fine arts came to include *music, dance, opera,* and *literature,* as well as forms which we most often consider pure art, like: *painting, sculpture, architecture,* and the *decorative arts.*

It was during the 20th century that colleges and universities started to separate the fine arts into what are today known as the **visual arts.** These have been more basically listed as *drawing, illustrating, diagramming, painting, sculpture, computer graphics and images,* and so on.

In the early 21st century what are termed the **auditory arts,** namely all forms of *experimental sound, music, acoustics, theater, spoken narratives,* and *sound literature,* have now taken on new roles that go beyond the visual. Each of these art forms can today be effectively incorporated into public presentations and speech formats. These days, computers and multimedia technologies help rhetorical studies in a manner that those in the past could never have dreamed would be a part of rhetorical history.

Performance arts, which can be visual, auditory, or a combination of the two, are those that are performed live before an audience and are unique to the late 20th century and have been further developed into the 21st century as well. Performance art blends rhetorical history and theory with movement and performance, to explore how information and persuasive techniques can communicate meaning to audiences. These audiences now share a more diverse and global outlook on politics, religion, science, and the arts in general.

Today *contemporary rhetoric* examines bringing information and persuasive meaning not only through traditional public speaking, but also through visual language, sound technology, and embodied performances. As they were in the past, colleges and universities are once again at the forefront in developing and promoting rhetorical growth. All over the world, speech departments are offering sophisticated courses with titles like *visual-rhetorical analysis, rhetorical theory and performance studies, rhetoric and social action, virtual persuasion and argumentation,* and *rhetoric and popular culture.* There are even courses at American universities with titles such as "*High-Tech Images: The Art of Debate*" and "*Rhetoric, Sound, and Performance.*" In many ways, the 21st century presents its own renaissance by way of computers, technology, and pioneering explorations of images and sounds.

▶ Contemporary rhetoric now includes the elements of multimedia and sound resources as viable components for public speaking. Colorful and powerful images in photography, film, satellite television, and the Internet have now become impressive rhetorical tools.

By supplying information and arguments for persuading audiences to understand or believe what the speaker wishes, contemporary orators and rhetoricians have expanded their academic and scholarly interests. Today they incorporate not only traditional academic principles and methodologies from Greco-Roman times, the Renaissance, and the Enlightenment, but also contemporary performance, virtual, visual, and graphic-based elements as well.

Your **A**, **B**, **C**s for a Better Recall of Rhetorical History

CLASSICAL/GREEK

Remember:

A *Plato* is largely responsible for our contemporary view of the *sophist* as a greedy instructor who manipulates his or her language in public settings in order to deceive, or to support misleading or misdirected reasoning

B *Aristotle* (384–322 B.C.E.) was the first to passionately disapprove of and help eliminate the ideals and practices of sophistry.

C Aristotle roughly defines *rhetoric* as "the skill to examine the means by which an individual can first inform, then persuade others."

CLASSICAL/ROMAN

Remember:

A Roman rhetoric flourished when the empire conquered Greece and began to be influenced by Greek traditions. The Romans incorporated many of the rhetorical elements established by the Greeks, but they diverged from the Greek customs in many different ways.

B The first virtuoso orator was *Cicero* (106–46 B.C.E.). He was a revered statesman and the model for orators and rhetoricians who followed him.

C *Quintilian* (35–100 C.E.) was the second great Roman thinker to influence the history of rhetoric and, consequently, public speaking. His principles have their origin in the great courts of Rome.

MEDIEVAL

Remember:

A After the fall of the Roman Empire, rhetoric continued to be significant to the study of speech and literature, but eventually weakened into decline for several centuries thereafter during the Middle Ages.

B No longer a tool to lead the nations, political agendas, and even wars, rhetoric was seen as a means to gather spiritual followers and even bring about eternal salivation and spread the teachings of Christianity. For the most part, all orators were preachers.

C Although stress and emphasis were placed upon the classics, somehow medieval teachers and philosophers rarely made any new or innovative contributions to the further development of rhetoric as a growing discipline.

RENNAISSANCE

Remember:

A As with literature, music, sculpture, painting, dance, medicine, and the sciences, the study of classical rhetoric experienced a rebirth during the Renaissance period.

B During this period the texts of *Aristotle, Cicero,* and *Quintilian* were emphasized and employed in rigorous courses of study. Quintilian's *De Inventione* (Concerning Inventions) quickly became a standard rhetoric textbook at all European universities.

C Rhetoric emphasized the basics, as founded in ancient Greece and Rome, yet its principles were made more relevant to the life and times of the blossoming ideals and thoughts congruent with the Renaissance.

ENLIGHTENMENT

Remember:

A The Enlightenment stretches roughly from the mid-17th century through the 18th century. It was greatly typified by innovative revolutions in science, philosophy, politics, and society in general. These revolutions brushed away all medieval thoughts and helped welcome in our contemporary Western world as we know it today.

B Philosophers and revolutionary idealists used rhetoric as a weapon in their campaign to spread liberty and freedom. It was a source of spiritual discourse away from aristocracy, theocracy, and monarchy.

C American universities such as Harvard, Yale, and Princeton proliferated with rhetorical scholars and speech teachers, along with academic writings that reflected the importance of how to communicate for the good of public freedom.

MODERN/CONTEMPORARY

Remember:

A The 20th century has been dubbed the age of technology and the 21st century as the age of communication. There has been an incredible explosion of mass media in both centuries that has caused yet another alteration in the study of rhetoric.

B Early modern rhetoric started including the elements of photography, film, and television as viable components for public speaking.

C Contemporary rhetoricians have expanded their academic and scholarly interests to incorporate academic principles and methodologies surrounding performance studies and various experimental visual, computer, and sound-based art forms.

Contemporary Rhetorical Analysis

As stated earlier, the study of rhetoric in contemporary colleges and universities has made a comeback with the advent of computers and multimedia resources. Particularly over the last ten to fifteen years or so, rethinking and analyzing the principles of rhetoric (first initiated in ancient Greece and Rome) has become a more recognized part of courses offered in formal debate, persuasion, argumentation, and public speaking in general. While rhetoric is still first among the liberal arts, it experienced a bit of downsizing when the study of all literature began placing less emphasis upon traditional rhetoric and public speaking, giving instead more focus upon the history and analysis of short stories, novels, poetry, drama, essays, and literary criticism.

Today there is a renewed interest in **rhetorical analysis**. This is essentially a constructive awareness of the relationship between rhetoric and civic responsibility, and its connection to all of literature in general. This seems to have helped unite the learning of public speaking skills with the broader humanistic tradition of how we as students, teachers, and citizens in general address our shared desires and goals in a highly diverse and information-driven society.

> ▶ By preparing to speak to a particular audience in a specific situation, or with a focused demographic and profile, public speakers can make information more comprehensible by being responsive to audience needs.

Proper *analysis* makes informing and persuading audiences more effective, and communication in general more analytically and critically connected. By being sensitive to *rhetorical appeals*, today's public speakers can help connect their presentations to public needs and issues by fostering the sort of reflective and engaged sensitivity that first helped fight against the abusive tactics of the sophists long ago in ancient Greece.

Rhetorical Analysis I: Rhetorical Appeals

Using the four *reflection questions* that follow and the audience needs they engender, you will be taking part in an exercise focusing on the basic elements of classical rhetoric rooted in ancient Greece and ancient Rome, as well as those who were influenced by them up to this very day. The goal of rhetoric is to both inform and persuade your audience that your ideas are valid, or more suitable than alternatives offered by others. Aristotle and other ancient Greeks and Romans referred to these needs as **rhetorical appeals**. They are designated here as *pathetic, logical, ethical,* and *stylistic.* In a later chapter we will speak about rhetorical appeals in more detail. Consider the following general questions when you are assigned to give a Speech in class.

1. What societal values and needs will directly benefit my audience by my topic choice? The Greeks and Romans labeled this as a *pathetic appeal,* but it can be more broadly concerned with values or ideal standards for the betterment of a particular group or society in general.

   _____
   _____
   _____
   _____

2. What helpful facts, researched information, and honest arguments (*logical appeals*) have been or could be made about my chosen topic that will interest and affect my audience in a practical, direct manner?

   _____
   _____
   _____
   _____

3. What academic, personal, and practical experiences and claims to authority (*ethical appeals*) qualify me as a speaker to honestly inform or persuade my audience about my chosen topic in a manner that is not grossly manipulative or intimidating?

    _____
    _____
    _____
    _____

4. What language, word choices, images, sounds, and multimedia technology (*stylistic appeals*) will most effectively keep my audience curious about and engaged with my chosen topic?

    _____
    _____
    _____
    _____

Critical Engagement

One of the oldest ways to learn rhetoric is to argue both for and against a position. While ancient Greek and Roman philosophers were notorious for failing to respect integrity and honesty by their sophistry, early rhetoricians like Aristotle and Cicero enabled people to assess the weaknesses and gross assumptions in their own thinking and to anticipate honest responses to them from those who listened to them. More than just a means to appease an audience, *critical engagement* can also help foster reflections on why your audience thinks and behaves the way they do. It can help you to become a more reflective speaker, and perhaps more critical and less apt to accept things the way they are, and in turn be more receptive to societal changes around you which may be present in your listeners themselves.

Further, critical engagement helps public speakers think through the experiences, assumptions, and purposes of others. It helps shift your focus from *what* to *how*, and away from what has happened to how an action or argument arises from a set of experiences that led others to think and behave in the manners and actions they seem to uphold. Critical engagement enables you to begin to understand the experiences, beliefs, and purposes of your audience, which can be valuable if for no other reason than to reflect before overreacting or offending others. And, more than that, it can help prepare you to speak better when offering your next speech.

At its best, critical engagement is best done right after you have given your speech. It can be in the form of questions and answers (Q and A) directly from your audience, or it can be a way in which you, the speaker, conduct a Q and A with your audience. It may be as simple as: *What did my speech mean to you today? What did you learn that you did not know? Did you find anything provocative or personally offensive? Were there times when I was confusing or spoke too quickly for you to follow?* As with rhetorical appeals, *critical engagement* helps publicly reveal and even solidify what is known as the *rhetorical situation*.

The Rhetorical Situation

In addition to rhetorical appeals, contemporary thinkers speak of what is termed the rhetorical situation. In his classic 1968 work entitled *The Rhetorical Situation,* Lloyd Bitzer announced that basically a public conversation is always called into existence by its situation. He defined the **rhetorical situation** roughly as a multifaceted gathering of persons, events, objects, and relations presenting an actual or potential rhetorical dialogue with each other. For Bitzer, the rhetorical situation dictates the significant physical and verbal responses as well as the sorts of observations to be made by you, the invited speaker.

Essentially, only you can honestly determine the very *situation* in which you find yourself as the public speaker. By analyzing your rhetorical situation you can better give sense and meaning to your chosen topic; and determine how best to present it to your audience in a manner which meets their focused needs as well as your own. The rhetorical situation often uses questions that examine points in *time, place, demographics, sexual orientation, religious affiliation,* and even *political tendencies* that operate within a particular gathered audience. These analyses become the ideological basis of the social experiences, cultural assumptions, and political purposes in the area of your chosen topic. By analyzing and reflecting your *situation*, you become better informed as to how to help communicate your chosen topic with your audience.

Rhetorical Analysis II: Your *Situation* for Speaking

Using the five *reflective questions* that follow and the *situational considerations* they engender, you will be taking part once more in an exercise focusing on the basic elements of classical rhetoric, partially rooted in ancient Greece and Rome, as well as those developed further by Lloyd Bitzer, a contemporary rhetorical thinker who has influenced rhetoric to this very day.

1. **Who are my listeners, specifically?** What is the general demographic of my audience, and how can I be sensitive to who they are as both separate individuals as well as a gathered community of listeners?

   _____
   _____
   _____
   _____

2. **Who am I?** How do I see or define myself politically, socially, religiously, ethnically, sexually, and so forth? How may I honestly help and inform my audience, based upon my own self-understanding and self-image?

   _____
   _____
   _____
   _____

3. **Where are the resources for my topic being generated from?** Are they credible, and are they verifiable for others to reference for their own further study? Are they available to fact-check, if necessary? Are some of my resources already familiar to my audience? How can I make them more fully relevant?

_____

_____

_____

_____

4. **What makes me uniquely connected to my audience?** In what helpful ways can I speak to them about my chosen topic? If I am an outsider, not a professional, nor even an expert on my topic, how may I honestly make myself credible to speak in public about it?

_____

_____

_____

_____

5. **When and where will I be speaking to my audience?** What time of day will I speak to them? Have any significant events occurred recently that either they or I should be sensitive to, or that may affect how we communicate with one another?

_____

_____

_____

_____

Rhetorical Purpose

Public speaking, whether done for a class assignment, marketing a product, a scientific lecture, or even a religious teaching, must be designed to accomplish some clear goal. Trained professional speakers spend a great deal of their time thinking and planning how to reach their goals by making their chosen topic engaging, appealing, and, if necessary, capable of persuading their audience for or against a position. At other times, they may be interested in proposing a solution to a particular problem or analyzing a specific case or issue at hand. These rationales—attracting and enticing an audience, persuading them, or solving a particular crisis—were also at the center of classical, Renaissance, and Enlightenment rhetoric. The educated classes in each era believed that understanding your **rhetorical purpose** was necessary to succeed in politics, religion, war, and certainly in order to maintain a viable democratic society.

Even before classical literature was developed, professional philosophers in ancient Greece taught merchants, doctors, lawyers, clergy, and loyal citizens how to master the principles of rhetoric and speech. Beyond eloquent oratory, classical rhetoric encompassed the art of touching both the rational mind and the emotions of a gathered audience.

As with the Greeks, your _rhetorical purpose_ will begin to develop and evolve as you continue to do research and think about your topic and its relationship to your audience. In fact, without adequate research and considering the diverse attitudes and opinions you may expect from your audience, it will be difficult to find a truly engaging rhetorical purpose for what you need to say.

As a speaker, you must make an effort to find an actual connection to your audience if you wish to present a successful speech. Understanding each and every purpose which you hope to offer in your presentation will distinguish what drives your words and what makes them meaningful both to you as a speaker and in turn to your listeners.

Rhetorical Analysis III: Your *Purpose* for Speaking

Following are five classically based elements used to help you reflect upon your overall *purpose for speaking* on a topic in public. Below each heading, spaces are provided to add any notes or commentary which you may feel are necessary to help you focus upon the classical notion of *purpose*.

Informative: Is my purpose to fairly and honestly inform my audience of a topic that fascinates and interests me, and hopefully them as well? Am I approaching my topic from a basic *informational standpoint* or from an exclusive or more advanced standpoint for those more familiar with my topic?

_____

_____

_____

_____

Persuasive: Is my purpose to honestly build a fair and sincere argument either in favor of or against some position. Is it a position that I feel passionately about, and is not for personal profit or gain? Am I planning to be as unbiased as possible?

_____

_____

_____

_____

Creative: Is what I am presenting in public a form of my own creative spoken art? Is it essentially a unique expression of my own imagination and inspired need to express myself openly and honestly? Is it a distinctive approach to research and public presentation, or am I heavily borrowing from the work of others?

_____

_____

_____

_____

Self-expressive: Is my speech an expression of my own literary, dramatic, or poetic momentum, or that on behalf of another's work? Am I in complete harmony with my topic, or in some cases am I in opposition to it or struggling to reconcile myself with it?

_____

_____

_____

_____

Literary: If what I am presenting in public is an expression of the literary, dramatic, or poetic achievements of the work of others, am I clear about this? Am I offering appropriate attribution and credit to those who first inspired or originated it?

_____

_____

_____

_____

Summary

In this chapter we have explored what it means to define and understand the basic *principles of rhetoric,* and have demonstrated that it was the early Greeks, along with their democratic principles and ideals about government, that molded public speaking into an institutionalized form of art. For them it amounted to an almost athletic level of skillfulness as a truthful response to *sophistry.* Due in large part to the influence of Plato, the term "sophistry" has come to signify the deliberate use of fallacious reasoning, intellectual deceit, and ethical corruption. Plato was largely responsible for our contemporary view of the sophist as a greedy instructor who manipulates his or her language in public settings in order to deceive.

It was Aristotle who established the first system of understanding and teaching *rhetoric* in a fashion which influenced everyone who came after him. His influential legacy first gave rise to how public speaking courses are still taught today in colleges and universities. These days when we speak of *rhetoric* we usually mean the art and skill of informing or persuading others within a public setting. Rhetoric is rooted in honesty, integrity, and a concern for the public good.

The first virtuoso public speaker was Cicero, a revered Roman statesman and the model for all rhetoricians who followed him. He, like Aristotle before him in Greece, wrote several enduring dissertations on the subject that lasted well into the time of the Renaissance, then flourished throughout Europe and the Enlightenment, to reach us in the 20th century and beyond.

Today there is a renewed interest in the relationship between rhetoric and civic responsibility. This seems to have helped unite the learning of public speaking skills with the broader humanistic tradition of how we as students, teachers, and citizens in general, address our shared desires and goals in a highly informational-driven society. *Rhetorical analysis* makes informing and persuading audiences more effective, and makes communication in general more analytically and critically connected. By being sensitive to *rhetorical appeals,* today's public speakers can help connect their presentations to public needs and issues by fostering the sort of reflective and engaged sensitivity that first helped fight against the abusive tactics of the sophists in ancient Greece.

Discussion Questions

1. What do we mean when we declare that someone is a sophist? Do you think that sophistry is still alive in the 21st century? If so, where might it be found in our midst today?

2. Quintilian established the foundation for all public speaking, a standard notion of rhetoric, in his five canons: *Invention, Arrangement, Style, Memory,* and *Delivery.* Which of these do

you think are the most important, and why? Can any of them be omitted in a speech and still have the speech not be considered a form of sophistry?

3. What is meant by the term "liberal education," first conceived by Cicero in ancient Rome? Do you think in this age of specialties that a liberal education is dying out in the 21st century? If so, why or why not? Is a liberal education really valid anymore in order for one to succeed as a public speaker in an informational age comprised of highly specialized individuals?

4. We said in this chapter that *rhetorical analysis* should focus on how to achieve a logical rationale by using the resources of a given *situation* in order to present a speech in public. What are the dangers of losing sight of this notion? Is it possible for us to fall into sophistry and not even be aware of it, if we lose sight of honest *rhetorical appeals?*

5. Why are the *Five Canons of Quintilian* still critical for being effective as a public speaker in the 21st century? Which of the various elements of his canon do you feel could be updated today? Why or why not? Or is each one equally complete and important?

● ● ● ● ● Quick Quiz

Match the following capsule sentences with the correct letter of the term which best describes the key terms or phrases discussed in this chapter.

1. _____ Arts that are simply listed as: drawing, painting, sculpture, computer graphics, and the like.

2. _____ The classical art and skill of public speaking to both inform and persuade others.

3. _____ A foundational principle to be memorized and then put into practical use.

4. _____ Conscious use of fallacious reasoning and intellectual deceit in public speaking.

5. _____ The father of what today may be termed: liberal education.

6. _____ Ways in which listeners can become informed and persuaded about a given topic.

7. _____ He established the first system of understanding and teaching rhetoric to the world.

8. _____ All forms of experimental sound, music, drama, and spoken narratives and literature.

9. _____ Being equally familiar with history, politics, science, literature, and the arts.

10. _____ He wrote the first textbook on public speaking, covering all aspects of the art.

A. Rhetorical appeals	**B.** Rhetoric	**C.** Auditory arts
D. Canon	**E.** Liberal education	**F.** Quintilian
G. Cicero	**H.** Sophistry	**I.** Visual arts
J. Aristotle		

CHAPTER 3

Understanding Your Contemporary Audience

KEY TERMS

- audience
- collaboration
- audience assessment
- speaker-audience bond
- civic duty
- audience adjustment
- culturally perceptive
- ethnocentrism
- gender
- stereotypes
- class status
- economic status
- convictions
- attitude
- values

"All the world's a stage,
And all the men and women merely players;
They have their exits and their entrances,
And one man in his time plays many parts,
His acts being seven ages."
—William Shakespeare, *As You Like It* (Act 2, scene 7)

"I miss performing before a live audience—the energy and
excitement; there's nothing to compare with it!"
—Rita Mero, film and stage performer

When William Shakespeare announces that *"All the world's a stage . . . ,"* this also includes each of us as individuals, while others all around us watch and listen to what we *say* and *do* on a daily basis. Like all actors, singers, dancers, and other types of performers, the public speaker is also on stage. But for public speakers, the audience takes on a special meaning, since successful speakers must adapt their messages to more closely bond with their audiences. Assessing your audience to fit your speech involves you getting to know those whom you will be addressing. It requires anticipating your listener's needs, interests, and any particular curiosities; it also includes understanding their level of familiarity with your chosen topic.

The nature of audiences has changed since Shakespeare's time, evolving from a highly energetic and participating throng of bystanders, to an assembly of people sitting behind a designated boundary line, silently observing and listening to actors, dancers, and public speakers. The nature of audiences is still a growing, and changing social phenomenon to this very day. Since there has always been a need for human beings to communicate their wants, needs, perceptions, and disagreements to others in a public setting, no one knows exactly when this whole public relationship first started. The need to communicate *openly* is the foundation of performance, and in turn is the basis for all public speakers to offer their words within a setting involving both small and very large groups of people. In most cases they are gathered to be informed or persuaded with regard to some designated topic—a distinctive one, chosen by you as the performing speaker.

Exploring the General Nature of Your Audience

As a public speaker, it is essential that you explore the *nature* of your audience. In short, an **audience** is a group of people gathered together to experience an event in a public setting. For public speakers, this simply means the live assembly of people gathered together to see and hear what you have to say about your chosen topic. Successful and conscientious speakers should take the time to get to know the nature of their audience by first viewing them as communal collaborators. **Collaboration** refers to the mutual process of working together as a team. Achieving positive results begins and ends with understanding the collaborative nature of your audience. Through **audience assessment**, you learn how to approach your speech and then tailor it to the specific, time, place, and gathered population. Often speakers make the oversight of focusing a large amount of preparation on the *content* of their speeches, without taking out enough time to consider the nature of their listeners, and also *when* and *where* they will be speaking to them.

> ▶ Failure to understand your audience properly can result in unpleasant results for all involved. Remember, a speech is a *collaboration*, and involves a sense of give-and-take from both you and your audience.

In order to collaborate with your audience, you must keep in mind that audiences bring diverse expectations to a speaking occasion: some desire to be there, others do not; some wish to be entertained, while others are seriously hoping to be informed. Some may be very susceptible and willing to be persuaded. Others may be quite unwilling to modify their opinions about anything. Others may expect a very polished presentation involving PowerPoint, while others may be looking for a more casual or conversational presentation. All of these various audience expectations help shape the nature of your speaking situation—one that only you can assess.

● ● ● ● ● The Time and Location of Your Speech

Like other forms of performance, public speaking takes place at a precise time and a given location. Keep in mind that your speech can be affected by events that have very recently occurred just weeks prior, the very day before, or even the actual day of your speech.

> ▶ An impending holiday, the day's tragic or triumphant news, even a local event may be fresh in your audience's mind as they gather to hear you speak. Always be aware of the adjacent news surrounding your speech.

Also be aware that the actual time of day can have an impact on both your attitude and energy level (as well as that of your audience). A speech offered at 9 a.m. on a rainy morning in February will be quite different from one offered just after everyone has had a satisfying warm, summer lunch; and again quite different from one given at around 8 p.m. after the sun has set over the Pacific Ocean.

The location of your speech matters as well—different-size rooms have an effect on the perception of visual aids, on sound levels, on general acoustics, and on how far you the speaker may be located from the very last row of the audience. Diverse locations make a difference in how audiences perceive intimacy with you as their speaker. Speaking in a mid-sized classroom, a very large auditorium, or in a small house of worship all help determine the energy level and nature of your speaker-audience bond. Your **speaker-audience bond** is in essence the emotional and reliant connection you make with your audience. This involves trust, intimacy, and the level of openness involved for communication. It is like a two-way boulevard, going in both directions.

There is, of course, always a reason why your speech is being given in the first place, namely the occasion for which your audience has gathered. Are you speaking at the wedding of close friends or relatives, or at a memorial of someone who has passed on? At a more information-centered lecture or at a public meeting of concerned citizens involving the garbage-collecting problems in your city? Each of these occasions involves different expectations from your audience, calling for both you and they to communicate in different modes—from ceremonial and formal to unceremonious and informal, from more humorous to serious, from conversational to highly solemn and reverent.

● ● ● ● ● Your Classroom Audience

The time and location for a college or university speech class differs from those of most public speaking events. In many ways, as a student taking a course in public speaking, you have many convenient advantages. In most cases you will have already formed a strong speaker-audience bond with many of your classmates, especially for your second speech within the same friendly classroom environment. You also have the advantage of instructional lectures, listening and learning from other members of the class, as well as the advantage of being evaluated on your weaknesses and strengths as a public speaker. Even though you may be within an artificial classroom setting, it is still necessary that you be aware of these advantages and make wise use of them. Lastly, there is, of course, the element of your grade. Always remember:

> ▶ What is important is that you improve with each subsequent speech you offer. It is far better to start with a grade of C or B, and eventually end up with A-level speech skills by the end of your term or semester.

It is important that you improve over time. Keep in mind that even though your required speech assignments must be tailored to your instructor's meeting *time* and *place*, as well as to your *given audience*, your speech still needs to be tailored to the students present in your course. Diversity is common among contemporary college and university populations.

By preparing your words, actions, sound, and visual resources appropriately, you still must make your speech accessible and appropriate for your classroom instructor and class audience. In many ways it is an artificial public speaking scenario in a contrived location, since the classroom offers you a safe and controlled environment, one that you may explore, make a few mistakes in, and hopefully use to discover who you are as a public speaker. So eventually, when you are not required to speak before a nonclassroom audience, you will be confident, well prepared, and not intimidated.

Always Rules — Exploring the General Nature of Your Audience

- *Always* be familiar with the actual location in which you will speak. Arrive early, walk around the speaking area, and practice using the microphone and any visual aids.

- *Always* be sure to greet some of your audience as they arrive to take their seats. It's easier to speak to a group of acquaintances than to a group of complete strangers.

- *Always* practice your speech in the actual location where you will speak, if at all possible. If you're not familiar with your location or are uncomfortable with it, your nervousness will be more likely to increase.

- *Always* keep in mind that your speech can be affected by events that have very recently occurred, whether weeks before, the previous day, or even the very day of your speech. If necessary, find a clever way to tie in any such events to create a better *speaker-audience bond*.

- *Always* consider how the actual time of the day can have an impact on both your attitude and your energy level, as well as that of your audience. If you need a quick morning coffee, or need to encourage your audience to recognize the time of day or evening, adjust accordingly.

- *Always* be sure to take some time at your designated location to ease any speaker tension by doing a few physical or breathing exercises at a nearby setting.

Exploring Beyond Your Classroom Audience

As we have discussed, the time and location for a college or university speech class differs from those of most public speaking events. A keen awareness of your audience's needs beyond the classroom is most likely where you will be speaking as you continue forward in life beyond your college or university years. As such, you must keep in mind the concerns, opinions, previous knowledge, and overall demographics of your audience, beyond the safe classroom environment. These concerns make you more than merely a public speaker or a performer; they make you one who is sharing in a civic duty. A **civic duty** involves helping to enlighten, educate, and promote a more just and fair society by performing some sort of public action—in this case, speaking before a live audience.

A civic duty need not be a lofty mission. Indeed, if you choose to speak about the health dangers of poor eating habits, the need for prompt garbage collection in your city, or even choose to promote awareness about saving for retirement, you help society and promote its betterment. As such, it is essential that you adjust your ideas, thoughts, information, and research to your specific intended audience. This process is termed **audience adjustment**.

▶ Through *audience adjustment* you tailor your speech to offer a message by which your intended audience can identify, one that will resonate with them and speak to their special needs and interests.

Being aware of *race, ethnicity, gender, sexual orientation, age, experience, religion, creed, class,* and even *economic status* will help you better identify with your audience. It will also give you the tools you need to create a strong and satisfying *audience bond.*

● ● ● ● ● Race and Ethnicity

Because both race and ethnicity are growing realities in our increasingly diverse society, it is important to have an awareness of these issues when speaking to virtually any audience, apart from a visibly multicultural one. Chances are that both your class audience and any audience beyond your classroom, will have a fundamental multicultural or multiethnic dimension. As a public speaker, you need to be keenly aware that the point of view which you may hold on any given topic may not automatically be mutual by some or even most of the listeners in your audience. Therefore, it is imperative that you become a speaker who is culturally perceptive.

Culturally perceptive speakers develop the capability to appreciate other cultures and acquire the necessary skills to speak successfully to audiences with diverse racial, ethnic, and nationalistic backgrounds. It is not uncommon for those new to public speaking to succumb to a perspective that their culture is dominant and that other cultures are not quite as significant or well-developed. This unspoken (and in most cases subconscious) attitude is referred to as **ethnocentrism**. Multicultural and multi-ethnic audiences at times may be a challenge for some public speakers.

> ▶ In the end, being *culturally perceptive* offers you an opportunity to examine people, issues, and ideas from various perspectives, and in turn further distributes these perspectives throughout society.

● ● ● ● ● Gender

In most cases, the members of your listening audience will be classified as either male or female, something largely determined by biology, and will be mirrored in their anatomical and reproductive systems. Most individuals are born either male or female, and in very rare cases have both types of genitals; such individuals usually undergo surgery and choose one set of genitals over the other, and thus have either male or female gender in the end.

It is important to be aware that **gender** is in reality a culturally constructed and psychologically based perception of oneself as being either *feminine* or *masculine*. An individual's gender-role identity, which wavers on a sliding scale from highly masculine to highly feminine, is learned or socially reinforced by one's surroundings, as well as by one's own personality and life experiences. Of course, inherited genetics will also help determine and shape an individual's gender role identity. Although you can certainly make some fair assumptions about speech topics that might interest your listeners of each gender, it would be quite out of place to assume that all males in your audience are particularly interested in hunting, sports cars and the latest sports teams; and all your female listeners enjoy an evening of dinner, dancing, and going to the latest movies.

> ▶ Always try to ensure that your speech reflects sensitivity to gender diversity in your overall points of view.

Finally, in general, be cautious of **stereotypes**. These are, as you may already be aware of, *fixed beliefs* or *opinions* about people of any particular group: political, intellectual, economic, sexual, or regional. Stereotyping neglects individual differences, and often causes people to make decisions based on flawed reasoning. The best way to avoid stereotyping is to learn as much as possible about an audience by using a bit of research, instead of relying on preconceived notions of any given race, culture, gender, or sexual orientation.

Sexist Perspectives

A *sexist perspective* stereotypes or prejudges how someone will react based on his or her gender identity. Be sure to take a moment to instruct yourself about which words, phrases, or perspectives are likely to offend or may create distance from your audience. Think carefully about the insinuations of words or phrases you take for granted in your own cultural perspective. Always be sure to be cautious about jokes and humor. Some forms of humor may be considered offensive to one sex or the other. Avoid stereotypes in your stories and examples as well.

> ▶ Try to use more gender-neutral terms, and steer away from such stereotypes as female doctors or lawyers, male flight attendants, male nurses, and female chefs.

Age and Experience

Knowing the average age of your audience can be very helpful in choosing both a topic and your way of researching and finally presenting it. Although you must use caution in possibly stereotyping from the perspective of age alone, considering age as a central factor can be an opportunity in many fun and interesting ways. Anecdotes, humor, quotations, rhetorical questions and even various types of visual and sound materials in your speech, can be retailored to reflect a sense of age consciousness.

Keep in mind that many students in your public-speaking class will most likely be recent or post–high school graduates. More than likely, their age range will be from late teens to the early or mid-twenties. Increasingly, however, many students are entering colleges and universities at later ages in life. These older students offer a wonderful dimension of life experience to the classroom. Many students today have gained experience as working professionals, parents, and even grandparents. In many instances these were individuals who were denied higher education in the past (for various reasons) and are now taking the opportunity to catch-up. As a result, many less-mature students may be more keenly aware of computer and digital technology, for example, whereas more-mature students may not be as familiar with fancy software, virtual games and everything from "twittering" and sending intermittent text messages throughout their day. Do not assume that everyone is a member of our contemporary youth culture.

Keep in mind that if you are going to give a talk on heavy metal rock, popular reggae, or the latest rap or hip-hop stars, you will have to explain who the various performers are and describe or demonstrate their style if you want all the members of your audience to understand who and what you are talking about. On the other hand, if you are from a previous generation, you must also be aware that many of your listeners may not be aware of or remember the fads and fashions in America when Ronald Reagan, say, or Jimmy Carter lived in the White House.

> Be as *age inclusive* as possible. If you are speaking to a mixed audience, make sure your speech relates to all your listeners, not just to the older or the younger generation.

• • • • • Religion and Creed

Some of your listening audience may be devout members of the Church of Jesus Christ of Latter-day Saints (LDS), or Mormons. Other may be adherents of religious or spiritual practices ranging from Buddhism, Taoism, and Shinto to perhaps Dianetics, Scientology, or even atheism. To each of these adherents, their religious fervor most likely will be as central to them as the sacred principles based on the Koran, Torah, and Bible will be to serious Muslims, Jews, or Christians.

If, for instance, you find yourself planning to speak before a more Christian evangelical-centered audience, you must be aware that more fundamental Christian churches would more likely view Buddhism or Mormonism as heretical, and might consider Scientology or Dianetics to be a religious cult. You should be consciously aware of your audience's religious beliefs as you prepare and eventually present your speech, no matter the time or the location.

When touching on religious beliefs or creeds, you should use enormous care in *what* you say and *how* you say it in public. Continually remind yourself that some members of your audience will not share your own beliefs, creed, or faith perspective. Not everyone believes or worships the same way, even among Christian, Jewish, and Muslim denominations.

> Few convictions are held as deeply as religious ones. If you do not wish to offend your listeners, plan and deliver your speech with much attention and sensitivity to the diversity of religions and creeds in your audience.

• • • • • Class and Economic Status

Class and economic status is your audience's perceived worth and sense of social power, based on such factors as: income, occupation, location of residence, and even level of education. In various parts of Europe, Asia, the Middle East, and other areas of the world (including Africa), early traditions of recognizing class distinctions may still be an important feature of both their culture and society. In North America, and to a larger degree in Europe, most people today prefer not to publicly discuss or recognize class distinctions or economic status differentiations.

In most parts of the world influenced by democratic ideals and free-market principles, the belief that human rights and economic opportunity should be an all-pervasive ideal tends to infuse all forms of thinking, ideology, and even opportunity. Class consciousness and economic status still do exist in both the United States and Canada, but they are often more understated and are not often in the forefront of most public dialogue. Keep in mind that what people do to earn their living may indeed have both class and economic status implications for various audience members, nonetheless. This can offer some possibly useful information to you about how to adapt your message to include all of your listeners. This may also include their more popular interests as well.

Keep in mind that speaking to die-hard sports fans and health professionals gives you an opportunity to use different examples and illustrations that may be of interest to them, as opposed to an audience of, say, musicians, artists, politicians, or religiously affiliated listeners.

Although most college and university students may not yet have established careers, being aware of their academic majors and future career plans can aid you in modifying your chosen topic and tailoring your speech content to their future professional interests.

> ▶ Being aware of your intended audience's incomes, occupations, and even education levels can be helpful as you develop a message that connects with each of them in a more personal way.

TWIN RULES

Centering Your Speech on Your Audience, and *Not* on You

Be perceptive: with the diversity of your audience

A. Remember: Many people gathered in most audiences speak different languages and use different expressions and jargon as well as different slang terms and phrases.

B. Your goal: If you are translating words or phrases, make sure that your translations are accurate and that you are using concrete language instead of slang or jargon from your own culture or age group, as it can be baffling to your listeners.

Be mindful of: the way other cultures may go about their thinking

A. Remember: Different cultures have different cultural ways of thinking and processing information, as well as different ways of understanding and perceiving, than those from your own culture.

B. Your goal: Engage everyone; and communicate with your entire audience. Therefore you must be perceptive and measure your audience as to their diverse ways of thinking, and be sensitive to the differing ways of approaching reason, logic, and judgment.

Be open to: performing live for your diverse audience

A. Remember: Most audiences feel affection for a live performance. If you can sing a song, play a musical instrument, or even recite a poem or significant text which relates to a diverse number of cultures or religions, you will be far more appreciated than you may understand.

B. Your goal: Offer yourself as a culturally diverse and engaging visual-sound resource. The more you give of yourself, in addition to commonly used videos or even sound recordings, the better you will connect. Remember, you can become a living multicultural artifact for your audience.

Be willing to: avoid ethnocentrism at all costs

A. Remember: Never assume that your own culture is dominant or better than other cultures. Ethnocentrism is *the belief that one's own culture or ethnicity is superior.*

B. Your goal: Bring yourself into an immediate connection with your diverse audience. Remember that, in many cases, you will be appealing to a diverse group of listeners. Subconscious ethnocentric viewpoints offer the strong possibility that you will obstruct any audience-speaker bonding that could take place.

Speaking Beyond Your Own Principles and Viewpoints

In addition to exploring the general nature of your audience, which may include everything from *race, gender,* and *sexual orientation* to *religion* and *economic status,* it is quite useful to be aware of just what principles and viewpoints your audience may hold about your chosen topic. Recognizing given standards beyond your own, helps you to understand the deeper nature of your audience. It will help you foresee whether members of your audience are likely to be open-minded enthusiasts, ardent supporters, vehement opponents, or in many cases, simply neutral about your topic. Being aware of your audience's principles and viewpoints can help you to hit upon the most useful ways to either inform or attempt to persuade them.

Your chosen speech provides an opportunity for you to become aware of your audience's *convictions, attitudes,* and *values.* It is constructive to know how your listeners actually feel about your topic. You should become aware of how interested, knowledgeable, or even apathetic they may be about the topic. If the topic tends to be on the controversial side, it is quite helpful to know if they are largely *pro* or *con* to your own position.

> ▶ Knowing the answers to where your audience stands on your topic helps you adjust your message accordingly.

● ● ● ● ● Audience Convictions

Convictions are deep-rooted *beliefs, opinions,* or *ideologies* to which an individual or group may strongly adhere, to the point of little negotiation or discussion. A public speaker needs to be aware of audience convictions, whether those opinions or ideologies are accurate or not. True or untrue, obstinate convictions can be a major barrier to your audience's treatment of you, and even to their eventual reception of your overall message.

Keep in mind that most ideals can be made into convictions by simply believing them to be true—profound belief is all that is required. Any thought or opinion can be fashioned into the form of a conviction. For instance, you may believe in anything from flying saucers, to ghosts, to reincarnation. You may ardently believe that your favorite sports team or your native country is the best that ever was or ever will be. Each of these can become strong convictions—and none of them are rooted in any provable facts. Either way, there is a *conviction* in operation that drives these beliefs forward.

Let's take a look at a few common convictions that audience members or audiences, as a whole, may hold strongly: *"the world as we know it was created by only a single God as revealed in the Bible and found in the Book of Genesis"*; *"smoking marijuana is an immoral activity and a serious gateway drug to cocaine and heroin"*; *"evolution is a clear scientific fact, not fiction, and creationism is largely a medieval superstition"*; and finally: *"homosexuality is an unnatural orientation and, if not rectified, such individuals will not be accepted by God, nor inherit everlasting life."*

As frightening as it may be, each of the above statements is a verbatim quote from various printed resources and consequently is being upheld by the communities that promulgated them.

> ▶ If you have to give a speech of any variety, and your audience is strongly convinced about an issue, you must be prepared to adjust your speaking approach accordingly, otherwise you run the risk of serious failure.

• • • • • Audience Attitudes

When we speak of someone having a bad *attitude* about something, it most often connotes a negative outlook about a given subject, or maybe even about life itself. In general, an **attitude** is, by and large, a learned disposition and not one we are genetically born with. It is an outlook that regularly subscribes to a consistently constructive or fault-finding temperament. This temperament may be with respect to an *individual,* a *thing,* a specific *idea,* or even a particular *incident.* Attitudes come in a variety of different shapes and appearances.

You are very likely to know that serious attitudes are in attendance when someone from your audience announces during a question-and-answer (Q and A) session that they are pro–gun control or anti–Wall Street, feel opposed to gay marriage, or genuinely feel that all global warming is a liberal hoax. Again, each of these attitudes was spoken by actual audience members at live Q-and-A sessions following student speeches in Chicago. The small virtue about attitudes is that they are largely teachable and subject to adjustment. With a bit of time and after a well-presented speech or two, attitudes can be adjusted. It is important to appreciate, as a public speaker, that both individual and group attitudes are learned and are not in any way automatically set in stone.

Attitudes can transform into broader and more-progressive dimensions, or even into more narrower ones, over time. In most cases, however, *convictions* will not evolve quite so straightforwardly. Now let's quickly examine a few possible individual and audience attitudes: *"I am a pro-choice woman on every front"; "I am anti-affirmative action"; and "I am against all forms of war, no matter what the reason";* and finally: *"I am for free enterprise at every corner; anything less is socialism."* While each of these statements may appear sensationalized or even over-the-top, each one was actually taken from a videotape recording during various post-discussion public speaking events in the Chicago area.

> ▶ Remember, attitudes are not as durable as *convictions* and *values.* Nonetheless, they are first-rate indicators of how certain people in your audience may view the persons, ideas, or events that shape their view of the world in which they live.

• • • • • Audience Values

In addition to having convictions, audiences also have what are termed values. **Values** are long-term thoughts and perceptions; they are usually strongly embedded and have been formed over a long period of time. In essence, values are what an individual or group understands to be good or bad, correct or incorrect. In the end, values constitute a sensibility about what is to be considered as virtuously *right* and innately *wrong.* They are very ingrained feelings, are more stable than attitudes or even convictions, and are therefore more challenging to oppose or change. Values are at the center of both religion and politics.

Values most often help sustain attitudes and bolster convictions. For example, if you choose to exercise several days per week, it is because you believe that studies are correct in promoting physical training, and also because regular exercise is more healthful and life sustaining. Even though oftentimes you may not enjoy exercising at times, you do it because of your attitude and conviction about what constitutes good health. You, of course, might hold the conviction, as most people do, that murder is evil and wrong. Further, say you believe that all embryos, from conception to birth, are humans; such a conviction prepares you to value all forms of life as human, and thus you are vehemently against all forms of abortion.

> ▶ As with convictions and attitudes, a speaker who has some understanding of an audience's *values* is more likely to feel connected, as well as more likely to succeed in connecting with his or her audience in the end.

Six Helpful Tips for Speaking Beyond *Your Own* Principles and Viewpoints

The following are six general principles that every speaker should keep in mind when seeking to connect with an audience beyond his or her own personal attitudes, values and convictions.

1. A public speaker needs to be aware of audience *convictions.*
   Remember: Whether those strong opinions or ideologies are accurate or not, *they do exist,* and as a speaker you must be aware of them.

2. An *attitude* is, by and large, a learned disposition, and not one that your listeners are genetically born with or must be bound to for life.
   Remember: Attitudes can transform into broader, more liberal or more conservative ones over time; if you as a speaker have a positive attitude toward your listeners, you may change their minds.

3. *Values* are long-term perceptions, are deeply rooted, and have been formed over extended periods of time.
   Remember: Values are challenging to oppose or change, so you should be cautious about them. It is best to not directly confront values unless absolutely necessary.

4. It is constructive to know how your gathered listeners actually feel about your topic in general.
   Remember: You should be aware of how interested or apathetic they may be, or how knowledgeable they may be about it in the first place. Always begin by meeting them where they are.

5. Recognizing given principles, beyond your own, helps you to understand the deeper nature of your audience; and in turn helps transform them into respecting your viewpoints as well.
   Remember: Their viewpoints will help you foresee if they are likely to be open-minded enthusiasts, vehement opponents, or simply neutral about your topic.

6. Your chosen speech always provides an opportunity for you to become aware of your audience's *convictions, attitudes,* and *values.*
   Remember: All people believe differently—the more you understand these three aspects that comprise the viewpoints and principles of your listeners, the more likely you are to succeed and be invited back as a speaker.

Exploring Your Audience *During* and *After* You Speak

Always keep on exploring your audience. Audience exploration continues even after you start speaking. As a public speaker, you should observe any feedback that audience members present. If you begin to regularly notice various individuals appearing puzzled, then you may have over-valued the level of your audience's background and knowledge of the topic, or simply not made yourself clear enough. Always be sure to explain technical terms, define new words and phrases; and supply basic background information. If your audience appears uninterested or inattentive to you, then you must make adjustments to enliven the speech—either with more audience connection or more enthusiasm and energy on your part.

> ▶ Your speech will have the maximum chance for success if you treat your audience members as partners in an on-going communication process.

Audience Reactions

In most cases you will not have a direct communicational exchange with your audience unless there is a brief question-and-answer session (Q-and-A) or discussion opportunity to follow. Nonetheless, once the speech is in actual progress, you the speaker must continually rely upon *reactions* from your listeners to accurately moderate how they are receiving your message.

Oftentimes beginning public speakers may find it quite challenging to not only have the responsibility of presenting a speech they have regularly practiced, but then also to adjust or modify their speech while they are indeed giving it. Keep in mind that with minimal experience you can develop the skills needed to adapt to your audience in a very responsive way. Just as you subconsciously adjust in a classroom discussion or perhaps in a job interview, you can adapt regularly to those to whom you are offering your speech.

It is important to analyze and adapt to *audience reactions* which will in turn boost the effectiveness of your overall message.

> ▶ It is very important to keenly be aware of all unspoken reactions that your audience either is hanging on your every word, or is unfortunately bored stiff.

Nonverbal Reactions

Possibly the first indication which establishes whether your listeners are retaining interest in your speech, is to be aware of their eye contact. The more they establish eye contact with you, the more likely they are listening to your prepared message. If you discover they are frequently looking down at objects, closing their eyes, or continuously gazing at the wall clock (or their own wrist-watches), you can reasonably assume that they have lost interest in what you have to say about your chosen topic.

Another important reaction is to observe facial expressions. Interested and attentive listeners not only make frequent eye contact, but also have conscientious facial expressions. Be on the lookout for cold, insensitive faces. Heads held at tilted angles, and dim, frozen smiles, accompanied by hands holding up chins, will always point to a sense of polite boredom.

In most cases your listeners will be courteous, and will offer you the *false appearance* of giving you their undivided attention. They are more than likely daydreaming or thinking about what they will have for dinner, or perhaps focusing on a romantic interest sitting a row or two in front of them—anything but your speech topic.

Keep in mind that an interested audience most likely does not twitch and squirm; they usually are quite comfortably planted in their seats. Early signs of lack of interest in your speech include: fidgeting, swaying, constant foot movements, leg wagging, and any fingers or arms wiggling.

> ▶ Seat-squirming, foot-shuffling, and habitual head and body movements are sure indications that your listeners have lost attention to your message.

● ● ● ● ● Speaker Reactions

The value of identifying nonverbal reactions from your audience is that you have the opportunity to also respond to them as needed. If your audience clearly seems engaged in what you have to say, frequently smiles and nods, and visibly appears sympathetic toward your topic, it is obvious that you have taken the right approach in preparing and also delivering your speech.

If your audience is visibly agitated, looking everywhere but at you the speaker, and you visibly suspect audience members are drifting off into their own thoughts, or at odds with what you have to say, you must adjust accordingly. If you suspect they do not comprehend your message and are quickly approaching boredom, you then need to definitely make some quick adjustments while delivering your message. Do not be afraid to ask them if you are clear, or if they are lost or confused.

> ▶ A few spontaneous adjustments can do wonders. It takes awareness and spontaneity to make on-the-spot changes in your speech.

● ● ● ● ● After You Have Spoken

After you have spoken, it is not uncommon to over hear comments among audience members themselves. If you had an effect upon them, there will be a buzz in the audience about your topic. It some cases they may come and speak to you face-to-face, ask for clarification on some points, or even speak to you directly about what your message meant to them personally. Such comments as *"I really enjoyed what you had to say,"* or *"What an inspiring topic that was!,"* or *"I felt at various moments that your speech was what I personally, really needed to hear"* are good for your confidence; they also further connect you to your audience. Both general and more-specific comments can point toward areas where you succeeded in your objectives; and also areas where at times you may have not communicated as you had hoped. Direct comments help prepare you for speeches in the future, and let you know that you have been appreciated. Speaker comments also help you realize that you have communication potential for further public speaking.

If the purpose of your speech was to persuade your listeners to change their minds about a topic, you will want to learn whether they ultimately reconsidered or adjusted their viewpoint. For instance, if you wanted them to consider the possibility of the existence of intelligent life beyond planet Earth (as related to your presentation regarding the phenomena of unexplained UFO sightings), you might attempt to discover what audience members feel about your topic now that they have background information from your speech.

▷ Audience reactions and comments after you are done speaking are the very best indicators of your public speaking success.

Your A, B, Cs for Better Exploring Your Audience
Before, During, and *After You Speak*

Before presenting a speech, you should *always be sure to:*

A Learn as much as possible about your listeners *before* you speak to them.
B Remember that audience *attitudes, values,* and *convictions* can help you connect.
C Never permit your own viewpoints to get in the way of your communication.

While actually speaking to your audience, you should *always be sure to:*

A Take the time to look for nonverbal reactions, such as eye contact and fidgeting.
B Pay close attention to faces for indications of confusion or boredom.
C Make spontaneous adjustments to win back your audience's attention.

After your speech has concluded, you should *always be sure to:*

A Listen for any buzz about your speech among your listeners.
B Offer an opportunity (if possible) for a quick Q-and-A session with your audience.
C Be prepared to speak face-to-face, and welcome comments and feedback.

Remember: The best indicator of your speaking success *before, during,* and *after* your speech is whether your audience is actually able to respect and consider your viewpoint; and genuinely be willing to follow your advice to them.

▷ Last of all: the best compliment you can receive as a speaker, is that your audience *actually remembers what you have presented to them.*

Summary

In this chapter we have explored what it means to be keenly aware of your audience *before, during,* and *after* you speak to them. Through *audience assessment,* you learn how to approach your speech and then tailor it to the needs of your gathered listeners. This includes not focusing a large amount of preparation on what you want to say without taking enough time to consider the nature of your audience. Part of your preparation should include your focus on *when, where,* and *how* you will approach speaking to them.

Even though you may be within an artificial classroom setting, and your required speech assignments must be tailored to your classroom's meeting *time* and *place,* your speech still needs be tailored to the students present in your course. Remember that diversity is not uncommon to college and university populations these days. As such, it is essential that you adjust your information and research to your specific, intended audience. This process is termed *audience adjustment,* which means that you tailor your speech to offer a message that identifies with your intended listeners, one that will resonate with them, and will speak to their needs and interests long after you have spoken.

Being aware of *race, ethnicity, gender, sexual orientation, age, experience, religion, creed, class,* and even *economic status* will help you better identify with your audience. It will also give you the tools you need to create a strong and satisfying *audience bond.*

Recognizing principles and viewpoints beyond your own helps you to understand the deeper nature of your audience. It will help you foresee if your audience is likely to be open-minded enthusiasts, ardent supporters, vehement opponents, or, in many cases, simply neutral about what you have to say. Being aware of audience principles and viewpoints can help you to hit upon the most useful ways to either inform or attempt to persuade them in favor of your way of looking at things. Tailoring your speech to fit your audience involves you getting to know those whom you will be addressing. It requires anticipating their needs, interests, and any particular curiosities; and it includes understanding their level of familiarity with your chosen topic.

Discussion Questions

1. What is meant by the term *audience assessment*? Why is it essential to evaluate your audience in order to feel comfortable in front of them? What do you think might be the dangers, if any, of speaking without any audience assessment beforehand?

2. Do you think the size and energy of the location where a speech may be offered has any actual impact on either you the speaker or they the listeners? When may it actually be important to seriously consider the size and location of your speech? In what possible ways might the time of day you present your speech affect both you and they as listeners?

3. What do we mean when we say that a public speaker must be aware of his or her *civic duty*? Do you believe that a public speaker can truly help enlighten, educate, and promote a more just and fair society by speaking before a live audience? Why or why not?

4. Why is it essential to analyze and adapt to audience reactions *during* and *after your speech has been presented*? How may any adjustments to the speech while giving it, or comments you receive afterward, be advantageous to any future speeches you may offer?

5. What are the advantages involved in making a *speaker-audience bond*? Is the emotional and trustful connection you make with your audience of any real help to your speech succeeding as you planned? In the first place, why should we care about connecting with an audience during a speech that is unlikely to last for a prolonged period (such as a play, concert, or movie) is likely to last?

● ● ● ● ● Quick Quiz

Match the following capsule sentences with the correct letter of the term which best describes the key terms or phrases discussed in this chapter.

1. _____ Adjusting your ideas, information, and research to your specific, intended audience.

2. _____ *Beliefs, principles,* or *ideologies* that an audience may strongly uphold and defend.

3. _____ Approaching your speech and then tailoring it to your gathered audience.

4. _____ The perspective that your culture is dominant and other cultures are not as significant.

5. _____ The emotional and communicational connection you have with your audience.

6. _____ Valuing other cultures, and being able to speak to those with diverse ethnic backgrounds.

7. _____ Cultural and psychological perceptions of persons as either *feminine* or *masculine.*

8. _____ A group of people gathered together in a public setting to experience an event.

9. _____ An audience outlook that subscribes to a constructive or fault-finding temperament.

10. _____ To enlighten, educate, and promote a just and fair society by a public action.

A. Speaker-audience bond   **B.** Gender   **C.** Audience

D. Civic duty   **E.** Audience adjustment   **F.** Audience assessment

G. Ethnocentrism   **H.** Culturally perceptive   **I.** Audience attitudes

J. Audience convictions

PART II
The Basic Anatomy of Your Speech

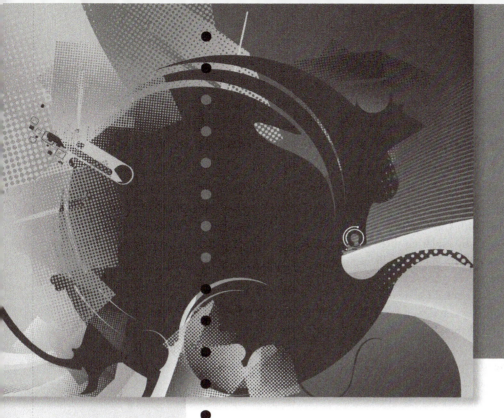

CHAPTER 4

Content: *What You Choose to Speak About*

KEY TERMS

brainstorming

great noun

noun inventory

search engine

event

topic goals

goal

broad goal

narrow goal

thesis statement

"What this country needs is more free speech . . . worth listening to . . ."
—Hansell B. Duckett

"Why doesn't the fellow who says 'I'm no speechmaker' let it go at that, instead of giving us a demonstration . . . ?"
—Kin Hubbard

The first major assignment for you as a public speaker (before all else) is to select the appropriate topic for your anticipated assignment, and consequently your audience. For many, this can be the most challenging part of taking any university public speaking course; and at any age. Essentially, the very fact that you may not even know what to speak about could be the source that fuels all your fears and anxieties about speaking in the first place. For others the major question is: will my audience really even care about what I have to say to them? Truth be told, just as you are fearing your audience, so too are they anxious about you. Everyone wants to be a successful, engaging, and at times even entertaining speaker. The good news is that we all have something to say and offer to the class and, in turn, perhaps to the public. We all have needs, wants, desires, and passions about things. It is all a matter of reflection, intent, and focus in the end.

In order to find an appropriate topic, we must first *think* about it. We all have interests, ethnic backgrounds, religious affiliations, travel experiences, and even unusual hobbies and skills that others may have no knowledge about at all. This chapter is designed to help you get started on *what* to speak about—namely, your *content*.

Answering the *What?* Question:
Finding the Content of Your Speech

It is quite possible in a speech class (and beyond) to approach a topic that will be interesting and definitely connect with your listeners. In order to even think about the great "*What?*" question, it is helpful to begin by exploring three basic topic objectives. In most cases, everything else will begin to flow from them, and hopefully begin to fall into place.

No matter what you choose to speak about, you must always consider your audience. After all, your speech is intended for them; and you must of course design your speech around their needs, possible interests, and even some basic expectations that they may have for any speaker at large. As such, this chapter is designed to help you to select an appropriate topic for your speech; and hopefully will assist you in relieving any major anxiety issues from the very beginning. As with attempting to generate great ideas, about anything ranging from marketing ventures to moneymaking investments, we usually begin by *brainstorming*.

● ● ● ● ● Brainstorming

It is common in public speaking courses to talk about the process of creating enjoyable ideas for speech topics, or **brainstorming**. This is a general technique that encourages free association of thought in a fun, gamelike manner. Brainstorming encourages you to seek out an interesting, informative topic not only for yourself, but also for your intended audience. But before we begin brainstorming in a more guided and structured manner, consider *reflecting* upon the following three topic objectives. Even though there is space provided below each of them, you do not have to answer any of the questions in written form if you so choose. What is important is to take some quiet time to think about yourself and your interests. You may simply wander about in thought for a while. Then reflect on and think about the notion of goals, or, more importantly, what we will eventually label in this chapter as the *objectives* of your speech: namely, what you hope to achieve in the end.

Reflective Questions: Your Three Topic Objectives

Keep in mind that, of the various speeches that have been given since the days when humans first started offering words in public, all generally surround three major *topic objectives (or goals)*. Understanding clearly what you want to say, and why you need to say it, is vital to both your motivation and your success as a public speaker. Every speaker must have clear goals for his or her audience. When those goals are finally achieved, giving your next speech will be a welcome endeavor.

▶ Selecting your topic is really a matter of stopping a moment to *reflect*, and then asking yourself a few very basic, practical questions.

All you need is a bit of enthusiasm, coupled with your own imagination. But first, always ask yourself these three quick, basic questions:

1. What topics or subjects really interest and excite me? What are those things which I would choose to talk about at a party, or maybe at an important job interview?

   _____

   _____

   _____

   _____

2. Of the many topics that interest and excite me, which are at the top of my list? Which of them makes me feel confident when I discuss them with others?

   _____

   _____

   _____

   _____

3. Considering my top interests, which would be most appropriate for my intended audience? Which would be the easiest to explain and present in a public setting?

   _____

   _____

   _____

   _____

Exploring the "Great Noun"

As you continue to reflect, you may now begin by directly asking yourself which topics or subjects *most* interest you. You may now think about the **great noun**! As you might recall, a noun is a *person, place, thing,* or *idea.* As you begin to think about nouns which interest you, you can devise for yourself a **noun inventory**. Your list should consist of simple broad nouns which first interest you, and then will be of appropriate interest to your intended listeners.

To begin, think about some of your favorite *persons,* both living and dead. Think about the countless possibilities throughout history: sports figures, celebrities, film stars, political heroes and heroines, and even perhaps local personalities from your hometown area, or maybe even out-of-the-ordinary relatives of yours.

Listing nouns can be as simple as sitting in the library with your laptop and recording all of the various nouns that interest you. Exotic or interesting *places* you may have visited, topics from past term papers you have written, favorite types of animals, or hobbies—all are great noun categories to begin your general inventory.

> ▶ At first it may take a little time to come up with some general noun topics, but after a while thoughts and ideas will begin to flow.

Of course, noun categories may be more inclusive and defined beyond simply the categories of *persons, places, things,* or *ideas,* and may include such expansive notions as natural wonders, world problems, common procedures, and even public policies. Again, the possibilities are virtually endless. You may even consider connecting some topics together as a form of narrowing down your topic to a more specific focal point of presentation. We will discuss this process later in the chapter.

You, of course, may choose to make use of electronic technology to help you further brainstorm your possible topic ideas. Always take advantage of the Internet, and uncover topics by browsing a **search engine** for a subject index. *Lycos, Yahoo!, Ask.com, Infospace, WebCrawler, AltaVista, GoodSearch, Excite,* and of course *Google* are all popular and fun places to explore. Search engines are online sites that help you find a word, topic, or idea available by simply entering data *via* that given site.

The following are actual listings of representative noun inventories for students from both Northeastern Illinois University and Roosevelt University in Chicago. Each is typical of public speaking students hoping to make a general noun listing:

<**PERSONS**>: Madonna
Snoop Dog
Steve Jobs
Homer Simpson
Eleanor Roosevelt
Kathy Rigby
Warren Buffett

<**PLACES**>: England
Disney World
Washington, D.C.
Mexico
The Caribbean
China
Africa

<**THINGS**>: Chocolate
UFOs
Sharks
The *Titanic*
Cats
Sushi
Skateboards

<**IDEAS**>: Communism
Human rights
Religion
Capitalism
World peace
Vegetarianism
Cubism (art)

The following are more-extensive renderings of the noun that are a bit beyond the simple notion of person, place, thing, or idea. These are more elaborate notions of the *great noun* and can offer an even further element of curiosity and spice to any hopeful speaker in search of an interesting topic.

<NATURAL WONDERS>:   Geysers
Avalanches
Falling stars
The Northern Lights
Waterfalls
Rainbows
Caves

<GLOBAL PROBLEMS>:   World famine
The Eurozone
Anti-Semitism
Racial profiling
Human trafficking
Identity theft
Neo-Nazism

<COMMON PROCEDURES>:   Making beer or wine
Baking birthday cakes
Taking photographs
Bird watching
Setting up an aquarium
Pet grooming
Designing greeting cards

<PUBLIC POLICIES>:   Socialized medicine
Home schooling
Balancing the budget
Immigration rules
Same-sex marriage
Public school curricula
Separation of religion and state

● ● ● ● ● Your Own "Great Noun" Word Search

Now, using your own approach to things, in each of the blank spaces provided below, list *three* general topic nouns that most interest you. These should all relate to nouns of which you personally have general knowledge or experience at this point in your life. You should feel currently connected to each of your choices, and also feel *confident* that you can effectively present information about each of them to your gathered audience:

<PERSONS>:   1. _____
2. _____
3. _____

<PLACES>:   1. _____
2. _____
3. _____

\<THINGS>: 1. _____
              2. _____
              3. _____

\<IDEAS>: 1. _____
              2. _____
              3. _____

The following are more-extensive renderings of the great noun that are a bit beyond the simple notion of *person, place, thing,* or *idea.* See if you can come up with a least three such nouns that will be of interest not only to you, but also to your prospective audience. Remember: you should already have some minimal connection to the noun topics you choose; and feel reasonably confident about them as possible topics. The key to finding a good topic is related to how much previous knowledge and experience you already possess concerning your possible choices. The less time and research required, the better!

\<NATURAL WONDERS>: 1. _____
              2. _____
              3. _____

\<GLOBAL PROBLEMS>: 1. _____
              2. _____
              3. _____

\<COMMON PROCEEDURES>: 1. _____
              2. _____
              3. _____

\<PUBLIC POLICIES>: 1. _____
              2. _____
              3. _____

Keep in mind that you may also wish to use a recognized event as the foundation for your topic. An **event** is most often a historical happening that has made a mark in either U.S. or world history, and is formally or informally recognized (as well as commemorated) by others. The most simple and informal of events may simply be your own birthday, whereas Abraham Lincoln is on a much more commemorative and public scale. A few are listed below for your convenience:

\<EVENTS>: The Nobel Prize Ceremony in Sweden
Jewish, Christian, or Muslim holidays
The 9/11 disaster, or the recent earthquake in Haiti
Earth Day, or World Peace Day
The World Series, or the Super Bowl
The Olympics, or the NBA Play-offs
The Chinese New Year, or the festival of *Diwali*

Now, consider choosing three of your own important *events*. Again, these should be events in which you have a clear interest, or some level of connection to your previous experience, and which will be of similar interest to your prospective audience:

<EVENTS>: 1. _____
  2. _____
  3. _____

Once again, using your computer to assist you, can be a great source of inspiration. You should feel uninhibited to freely combine your thoughts, as if composing an abstract poem or a fun short list of nouns for a hidden-word game.

Oftentimes, placing your broad ideas on a blank screen allows you the stimulus of speedy uninhibited ideas, in quick, creative succession. If considering the great noun doesn't work well for you, we invite you to think further about the following *Six Topic Considerations Beyond the "Great Noun."* These are listed below for your convenience, as an alternative starting point for finding your appropriate topic.

Six Topic Considerations Beyond the "Great Noun"

1. To help make your topic more *tangible* and *immediate* for your audience . . .
 Consider: using current events from newspapers or 24-hour news channels.

2. To help add a sense of *variety* and *diversity* to your overall topic . . .
 Consider: speaking about a very unusual or unique experience you've had.

3. To help create a more *general interest* for your university or college audience . . .
 Consider: your hobbies, leisure pursuits, or pastime interests at your school.

4. To help connect your *topic to your life*, speak about your current or past job . . .
 Consider: speaking about what would be useful to people *not* in your line of work.

5. To help generate more *popular audience interest* about best sellers on the market . . .
 Consider: speaking about a fascinating book or film you may have read or seen recently.

6. To help address a *multiplicity of learning methods* and other possible approaches . . .
 Consider: speaking about the best way to do or *not* do something, such as losing weight.

Formulating Your Topic Goals

As with most things in life, in order to be successful you must formulate a few conscious objectives, or what are more commonly identified as *goals*. In this case, these will be your **topic goals**. Your topic goals may be simply your two main objectives for wanting to speak about your chosen topic in the first place. Always keep in mind that ultimately these goals should be rooted in your own individual motivation, inspiration, and level of personal experience.

▶ You must genuinely desire to speak about your topic; and must recognize that what you choose to speak about is not merely something deemed an assignment to be proudly placed in your professor's grade book.

Ideally, your motivation must be rooted in both a *broad* goal and a *narrow* goal or goals, combined, to give you an overall purpose and inspiration for speaking. When you have goals, you then have an end point in sight. A **goal** is simply a target you want to reach or achieve. It is a focused objective that nudges you to move on and reach it, with some form of satisfaction.

The **broad goal** of a speaker is, in essence, to convey the speech's *general intention*. Perhaps the goal is to *enlighten, inform,* or even *persuade* your audience. It may be to *motivate* them into taking some form of action. Or it may be to solemnly persuade them of your environmental views. It may be as simple as *introducing* a speaker for an important public presentation, or to *memorialize* a significant event. Further, the broad goal of a speech may also serve as the occasion for someone to *accept* an award, or a *public recognition* of achievement.

The **narrow goal** of a speech, by contrast, has a more-specific and focused purpose, one which identifies precisely what a speaker wants to accomplish with his or her speech by its final conclusion.

▶ In short: your broad goal is your general *focus,* and your narrow goal or goals is your overall *rationale* or purpose.

Further, it is important to keep in mind that when thinking about your topic, you will be successful according to how much careful planning and preparation you put into the process, far more than from any natural speaking talents you may naturally possess.

▶ Although advance preparation and searching for the appropriate topic ensure careful thought and hard work, *understanding your goals* will continually guide you throughout the duration of your speech.

The worst thing any speaker can do is attempt to wing it or improvise and pad a speech by ad-libbing or making things up along the way. Remember: your *broad* and *narrow* goals should be clearly *understood*, be clearly *stated*, and never diverge from your original intentions.

● ● ● ● ● A Brief Guide to Your Broad Goals

IF you are planning to INFORM >>> then you should be certain to:
    <<< DEFINE, JUSTIFY, DESCRIBE, and EXPLAIN your overall topic to your gathered audience.

IF you are planning to INTRODUCE >>> then you should be certain to:
    <<< PRESENT, FAMILIARIZE, HOST, and LAUNCH your overall topic to your gathered audience.

IF you are planning to PERSUADE >>> then you should be certain to:
    <<< INFLUENCE, CONVINCE, SWAY, and IMPACT your overall topic to your gathered audience.

IF you are planning to COMMEMORATE >>> then you should be certain to:
>>> TRIBUTE, VENERATE, REMEMBER, and HONOR your overall topic to your gathered audience.

IF you are planning to ACCEPT AN AWARD >>> then you should be certain to:
>>> RECOGNIZE OTHERS and OFFER GRATITUDE, with a sense of HUMILITY, as you present your overall topic to your gathered audience.

Narrowing Your Topic Goals

After you have clearly established the broad goal of your speech, you must now consider the narrower aspects of your chosen topic. Namely, you must determine what precisely you specifically wish to communicate to your audience. A narrow goal accurately affirms what you hope to achieve in the speech.

> ▶ When you declare your narrow speaking goal, you must state it clearly, first to yourself, and then to your audience.

Then you must remain centered on it and also intentionally focused upon your audience. Your speech must remain directed, focused, and always aimed at arriving toward your final broad goal. The following two examples should serve to help get you started in this process.

Example 1: *Broad Goal*

To effectively *inform* my audience about Benjamin Franklin as one of America's great patriots and founding fathers, and tell why he never became president of the United States.

Example 1: *Narrow Goals*

1. I will first introduce my audience to a basic yet concise biography of Ben Franklin's life, from his birth in Boston, to his celebrated career in Philadelphia.

2. I will then inform my audience about Franklin's extensive contributions to science, and his further contribution to the world by way of his time-honored inventions.

3. I will briefly discuss Franklin's successful formation of our first national university, post office, and diplomatic corps.

4. I will then inform my audience more explicitly about Franklin's role in the American Revolution, and the consequent American Declaration of Independence.

5. I will lastly inform my audience as to why Franklin was so popular as to be almost virtually drafted to become U.S. president, and why he choose not to run a national campaign for that highly coveted office.

Notice how each of the first four narrow goals, informed first by the *broad goal*, focuses upon clear, informed choices about Ben Franklin, ones which eventually lead up to the *finishing* goal (the fifth one) of declaring why he choose *not* to run for national office. Oftentimes we refer to the final goal as a: **thesis statement.** This statement should be succinctly articulated in perhaps no more than one clearly detailed sentence.

Your *thesis statement* should be a few words, in a verbal nutshell, telling exactly what you hope to speak about, and how you propose to do it. Your thesis statement should be established early in the speech itself, and be noticeably articulated to your audience. In many ways, your thesis statement is similar to a topic sentence or a central statement in a written essay or perhaps a term paper, which reveals the general direction and content of your paper. Depending upon your *broad goal,* your thesis statement can have virtually any possible avenues of approach. Let's take a look at a second example. This time the broad goal is persuasive, and for the most part it is indeed the overall *thesis statement.*

Example 2: *Broad Goal*

To *persuade* my audience that there is a very strong, yet unproven possibility, of the existence of intelligent life beyond planet Earth; and to convince them that the existence of genuinely unexplained sightings of unidentified flying objects (UFOs) may contribute toward the truth of this phenomenon.

Example 2: *Narrow Goals*

1. Define for my audience the precise definition of a UFO, both as viewed in popular culture and as viewed by the U.S. Pentagon, the U.S. Air Force, and the majority of scientists worldwide.

2. Present a brief yet concise history of UFOs dating from ancient prebiblical times, to our current 21st century.

3. Honestly inform my audience of the many UFO hoaxes, the eccentric personalities seeking attention; and the bad press these hoaxers often stir up about more-unexplained and more-respected UFO phenomena.

4. Inform my audience of the small yet profound number of UFOs that remain unexplained; and which in turn have perplexed serious scientists worldwide, government officials, and the U.S. Pentagon.

5. Bear witness to my audience the many highly trained scientists, astronauts, and even elected national figures who claim to have seen or experienced UFOs themselves.

6. Lastly: state that scientists around the world are very open to the mathematical possibility of life beyond planet Earth; and that this in turn would explain, to some degree, how our expansive universe is not so apparently empty as we so often perceive it to be.

Once again, notice how the *broad goal* is quite *persuasive* in nature; and how each of the first five narrow goals lead toward the *thesis statement* (the sixth goal) of convincing the audience that the possibility of life beyond our planet is not so crazy an idea after all. As with any good preparation, the *setting of goals* is vital to relieving anxiety, will ease fears about speech delivery, and in the end will help make gathering facts and figures a smoother and more-enjoyable process.

As you begin to organize your speech goals, write your broad and narrow statements of purpose in the tear-away page provided below.

Note: You may first photocopy this page as an unused page, so as to use it over and over again for as many speeches as may be needed, for your own future convenience.

Writing Your Own Broad and Narrow Topic Goals

Broad Goal

My speech goal is to effectively: _____
_____
_____
_____
_____
_____

Narrow Goals

1. _____
_____
_____
_____

2. _____
_____
_____
_____

3. _____
_____
_____
_____

4. _____
_____
_____
_____

5. _____
_____
_____
_____

Once again, your *thesis statement* should be succinctly articulated in perhaps no more than one clearly detailed sentence. There are several ways in which a thesis statement can be articulated. Consider the following other possibilities for a general speech topic centered on UFOs.

Possible Thesis Statements for the General Topic: UFOs

1. Scarce yet plain evidence suggests that UFOs are real, and may indicate intelligent life both deep within and well beyond our solar system.

2. Overwhelming evidence suggests that UFOs are largely a hoax, and have become a source of quick celebrity and notoriety; for fameseekers both in the U.S. and around the world.

3. I hope to introduce two highly reputable astronomers who will each speak about the evidence for and against UFOs, respectively. In the end, you the listener must decide.

4. UFOs have been a social-historical phenomenon from ancient times. Even now they continue to cause controversy about the possibility of life within and beyond our solar system, just as they did thousands of years ago.

5. UFO sightings represent a tendency toward sensationalistic thinking, and help foster a growing culture of science fiction and pseudoscience in our global society.

6. The growing phenomena of UFO sightings represent the possibility of the existence of the supernatural, our yearning for the divine, and our need as humans for religion.

Notice how each of these thesis statements is clear, directed, and well-focused. For each one there is a sense of *purpose* rooted in clearly thought-out goals, both broadly and narrowly.

> ▶ A thesis statement should be a focused proclamation rather than a problem, description, or even a question.

Your thesis statement should be a clear, complete, concise sentence and not a fragment or a grouping of intentions. It should avoid flowery language and strive for unambiguous and literal wording. It is designed to answer questions, not ask or subtly supply them to your intended audience. Now we will consider some poor examples of thesis statements.

Poor Examples of Thesis Statements on the General Topic: UFOs

1. Showing that UFOs are fascinating and interesting.

2. People who claim they've seen UFOs proves that there's life beyond planet Earth.

3. UFOs are silly and do not exist; those who claim they've seen them are crazy.

4. A few UFOs are actually genuine UFOs.

5. Have you ever seen or thought you witnessed a UFO in the sky?

6. Would you like to meet someone who has actually seen or been on board a UFO?

Notice how each of these statements is vague, highly assumptive, and at times not even a complete thought or sentence. Some even ask the audience an unfair question. Based upon our discussion of the meaning and importance of a thesis statement, ask yourself how these poor examples may be transformed into effective ones; write your response in the spaces provided underneath each restated example.

Correcting a Poor Thesis Statement and Making It Effective

In the spaces provided below, attempt to correct each of these poor examples, to the best of your ability. Remember to be clear, to be concise; and have a sense of both a broad and a narrow purpose or goal which, when combined, make one overall clear statement.

1. UFOs are fascinating and interesting.

_____
_____
_____
_____

2. Scientists and Pentagon officials can truly know about real UFOs.

_____
_____
_____
_____

3. UFOs are silly and do not exist; those who claim they've seen them are crazy.

_____
_____
_____
_____

4. A few UFOs are possibly genuine UFOs.

_____
_____
_____
_____

5. Have you ever seen or thought you've seen a UFO?

_____
_____
_____
_____

6. Would you like to meet someone who has actually seen or been on board a UFO?

_____

_____

_____

_____

Be aware that, in order to speak fairly and ethically, your thesis statement should reveal your specific purpose or goal, and not disguise or attempt to conceal it from your audience.

It is important to note that sometimes speakers choose to hide their agenda. Oftentimes cult organizers, political leaders, religious crusaders, and even militant atheists, humanists, and scientists may intentionally (or unintentionally) conceal their goals before an audience, and consequently attempt to quietly seduce them. Always keep in mind that:

> ▶ The greater the distance of honesty and openness between your thesis statement and your hidden agenda, the greater the risk of ethical deception and audience resentment.

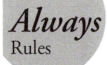

Always Rules Selecting Your Topic

- *Always* be sure to seek a topic with which you are already familiar, and have at least a minimal level of knowledge and experience.

- *Always* survey topic ideas by: first *brainstorming* all possibilities. You should permit yourself to explore topics, without any hidden purpose or agenda.

- *Always* consider, initially, a general *noun listing* of simple persons, places, things, or ideas. Then you may continue narrowing down your general nouns more specifically. You may, for example, begin with cats and then work your way toward exotic Persians, wild bobcats, or possibly even the hit Broadway musical: *Cats.*

- *Always* be sure that your topic has a *broad goal*, such as: to *inform, persuade, introduce,* or even recall or memorialize an event. Your broad goal is, in essence, your overall approach.

- *Always* be sure that your broad purpose is imbued with smaller, narrower goals. In short, your narrow goals are how you will go about achieving your main broad goal: to inform, persuade, introduce, and so on.

- *Always* be sure to formulate a clear and concise *thesis statement*. This should combine both your broad and narrow goals; and be explicitly stated in one well-focused sentence. Never have an unspoken agenda hidden within your thesis statement.

Connecting Your Audience to Your Topic

Collecting information about your listening audience can be more or less significant, depending upon the availability of the time, energy, and regular access you may have *before, during,* and *after* the speech itself.

In most cases, you will be in a classroom setting and already have a good idea of not only the composition of your audience, but also the style of the instructor. Nonetheless, you may still need to make an educated and fair assessment in order to feel more comfortable when speaking in front of them both. In most cases your analysis will be indirect, and for the most part intuitive as well. You will need to infer as much as possible from your experience at lectures, classroom activities, and the various speeches and reactions from others who may have spoken before you. It is all a matter of keeping your eyes and ears open to the clues all around you.

Every audience has a set of *attitudes, beliefs,* and *values.* In most college and university settings these days, there is a great diversity among each of these commodities. You will gain audience awareness with each subsequent speech you give. Always be sure to keep your intended audience in mind, and then craft your speech to suit their needs by clearly defining all terms, ideas, and arguments in your speech. Never assume anything.

> ▶ Always keep things relevant to your audience at all times. Avoid focusing exclusively on your own curiosity and admiration for your topic.

TWIN RULES

You, Your Topic, and Your Audience

Sense of authority: be modest

A. Remember: Be loud, be clear, and never pretend to be a complete authority. You too are always learning about your topic as well, and no one likes an "expert snob." Modesty is a powerful tool that attracts listeners and keeps them listening.

B. Your goal: Be heard clearly and emphatically. Be sure to consider how your speech topic must continually relate to your listeners; never speak only on behalf of yourself and your own interest in your topic

The way you approach your topic: be mindful

A. Remember: When speaking about your topic, consider the demographics of your listeners. It is a diverse classroom? Always be sensitive to both sexes, as well as to age levels, religions, and even sexual orientations. Keep in mind that not everyone in the class is interested in the opposite sex, is a Christian, or was born in North America.

B. Your goal: Engage everyone, and help to generate new interest in your topic. You are there to help your audience focus on the unique way you love and approach your topic before them, in a live setting. Your unique take on the topic is your contribution to your audience.

Summary

In this chapter we have explored what it means to set goals for an effective (and eventually) successful speech; and how first-hand personal knowledge and experience should inform the eventual selection of your speech topic. Your personal experience adds *credibility, authenticity,* and *audience interest* to your speech.

You should begin searching for a topic by reflecting upon what interests you personally. Such topics will, in turn, interest your audience as well. By the use of *brainstorming,* a general technique that encourages free association of thought in a fun and gamelike manner, you will then be prepared to seek out an interesting and informative topic, not only for yourself but also for your intended audience.

As you think about *general nouns* that captivate you, you can devise for yourself a *noun inventory,* which in turn is a simple, broad listing of nouns that primarily interest you and will also be of possible interest to your listeners.

You should begin by thinking about some of your favorite *persons, places, things,* and *ideas.* Listing nouns can be as simple as sitting in the library with your laptop and recording all of the various nouns that appeal to you. Noun categories may be more wide-ranging and include such expansive notions as natural wonders, world problems, common procedures, and even public policies. Topic possibilities are virtually endless.

After you have clearly established the *broad goal* of your speech, you must now consider the more *narrow aspects* of your chosen topic. Namely, you must determine what precisely you want to fully communicate to your audience. A narrow goal affirms accurately what you hope to achieve in the speech. When you declare your narrow speaking goals, combined with your broad goal, you then have a *thesis statement* that must be stated clearly, first to yourself and then to your audience.

Discussion Questions

1. Discuss what is meant by the term *thesis statement.* Why do you think it is essential to have clear, concise objectives for any speech to really be effective in the end? What elements do you think make a clear and concise thesis statement?

2. What do we mean by using a *noun inventory* when searching for a topic to present in public speaking class or even beyond? What are some of the other dimensions, outside the common definition of a noun that may be excellent areas for topic consideration?

3. When considering your personal interests in a speech topic, why is it also essential to reflect upon how your corresponding audience may welcome the topic as well? What measures can you take to help those who may not care about your topic, or are unfamiliar with it, to become interested in what you have to say?

4. Why is Kin Hubbard's comment at the beginning of this chapter so important? What do you think he means when he boldly asserts: "*Why doesn't the fellow who says 'I'm no speechmaker' let it go at that, instead of giving us a demonstration . . . ?*"

5. What is it essential to be personally connected to your topic before you even select it? Do you feel that it is ever appropriate for a speaker to research and talk on a topic about which he or she has no previous knowledge or experience? Explain why *or* why not? Do you think it would be a risky venture to speak about a topic that is new to you, the speaker?

● ● ● ● ● Quick Quiz

Match the following capsule sentences with the correct letter of the term which best describes the key terms or phrases discussed in this chapter.

1. _____ Special topics about animals, plants, phenomena, and usual occurrences.

2. _____ A precise and concise one-sentence description of your speech intentions.

3. _____ Searching, then listing: general persons, places, things, or ideas.

4. _____ Looking at *Google, AltaVista,* or other various web capabilities for topic ideas.

5. _____ A relaxed and free-association method for searching out a speech topic.

6. _____ Considering all *persons, places, things,* or *ideas* as possible speech topics.

7. _____ The basic intent and purpose of your speech, such as to *inform* or *persuade.*

8. _____ The general and overall reasons for choosing your topic.

9. _____ Any important historical occurrence as a means for a speech topic.

10. _____ The restricted elements of a speech topic that guide its overall purpose.

A. Events	**B.** Thesis statement	**C.** Natural wonders
D. Brainstorming	**E.** Search engine	**F.** Topic goals
G. Narrow goals	**H.** Noun inventory	**I.** Great noun
J. Broad goal		

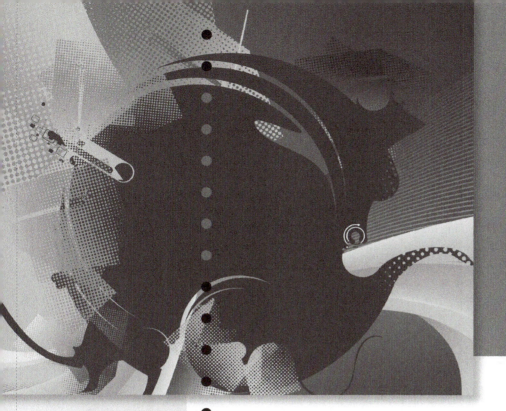

KEY TERMS

delivery

communicational relationship

timbre

totems

memorized delivery

shooting from the hip

extemporaneous delivery

impromptu delivery

manuscript delivery

speech dynamics

attire

eye contact

vocal fluency

vocal projection

vocal pitch

monotone

rhythm

gestures

interrupters

"When you deliver a lecture you get good pay, but when you deliver a good speech you don't get a cent."
—Mark Twain, political speech, Republican rally, Hartford Opera House, October 26, 1880

" . . . that speech is most worth listening to, which has been carefully prepared in private; and tried on a plaster cast, or an empty chair, or any other appreciative object that will keep quiet, until the speaker has got his matter and his delivery limbered up so that they will seem impromptu to an audience."
—Mark Twain, speech in New York City, March 31, 1885

When any audience gathers to hear a speech, they are prepared to listen to a live individual before their very eyes. For them, the event it not only about *who* is speaking (and perhaps even their level of celebrity), but also about *what* is going to be said. Perhaps most importantly, they will care even further about *how* the speaker hopes to go about saying what her or she came to hear. *How* we choose to speak is called *delivery.*

In this chapter we will learn what it means to powerfully and effectively *deliver* a speech. The best public speakers make their delivery look effortless and, for the most part, trouble-free. They do so by preparing well in advance and practicing their speech until they know it well in both content and sequence—until they know it like the alphabet.

Practicing and focusing on how your speech will be delivered will make you look dignified, feel confident, and appear to your audience as if in a very conversational manner. Your objective is to make your speech comfortable for you and for your audience. The objective of good delivery is to make your speech tasty and digestible to the point that your audience will feel that you are speaking in conversation *with them*, and not simply lecturing your information *at them.*

This chapter will help you discover ways in which you can utilize both the *verbal* and *nonverbal* features of delivery, including volume, pitch, rhythm, diction, eye contact, and body movement (gestures). Ultimately you will make an impression by how well you look and sound before your audience. Everything lies not in the story, but ultimately in the telling of it. Not unlike a hilarious joke, an effective speech consists not only of *what* you are telling, but of *how* you go about telling it. The goal of this chapter is to help you acquire the appropriate attitude and skills to successfully deliver an energetic and inspiring speech, one that will make a memorable impression upon your listeners.

Delivering Your Speech

A speech before a live audience is far more than the words of information, or the arguments you may provide to persuade them of beliefs or positions which you support on your chosen topic. A successful speech should provide your audience with an honest sense of **delivery**. Your delivery entails the way you look, sound, and move your body, along with the very level of confidence and preparation which you offer before your live audience. Delivery involves giving the impression that you know you are on stage and enjoy being there! It involves both your wants and your needs to be seen and heard, as a confident and prepared speaker.

Not unlike an actor, how you deliver your speech on stage must create a **communicational relationship**. It must create an honest sense of give-and-take between you and your audience. This relationship in turn may cause them to laugh, cry, chuckle, moan, applaud, or even be respectfully silent. Your communicational relationship must be maintained throughout the duration of your speech.

It is imperative that you never lose your audience. Your face, voice, body, and overall energy must keep them in constant communication with you. In turn, their eyes should be frequently focused on you, and their smiles, and occasional laughter, should be a regular reinforcement of your mutual relationship with them. At times even their unexpected applause will supply you with the force and confidence you will need to sustain your communicational relationship with them. Keep in mind:

> ▶ As you continue to grow in knowledge and skill, you should observe how highly experienced speakers all around you, both live and recorded, deliver their messages to the public.

Stop for a moment and reflect upon those elements of delivery which keep you connected to the radio, the television, or an engaging comedian or storyteller. In turn, imagine how you may also begin to acquire some of these skills to keep your audience connected to you throughout your own speech. You should then consider your unique natural voice and the innate elements that you already have placed before you—perhaps ones which you are not even aware you may have in the first place.

• • • • • Thinking About Your Own Natural Voice

Consider those elements of your personal vocal pattern that you most admire, those that perhaps others have told you they like about your voice. Of course there are those elements that may tend to please both yourself and others a bit less, as well. Think about how you hear yourself, and about how others may perceive your voice.

> ▶ Your voice, like your fingerprint, defines your own unique vocal identity. It is the thing which makes you recognizable to others.

We refer to this unique vocal sound and pattern as: **timbre**. Timbre is the very tones, qualities, and vocal characteristics that are unique to you. Homer Simpson, Mickey Mouse, and your favorite celebrities each have a timbre that is quickly identifiable at an instant. Your voice is what makes you (among others things) a unique communicator. Consider the following questions about your own *timbre*, as you explore your own vocal inventory.

> ▶ Paying attention to your own voice is the first step in beginning to improve and polish it up for an audience.

You should expand upon what you like about your voice and work at constricting those vocal habits that may not be to your own betterment as a public speaker. You already have all you need to deliver a powerful and engaging speech. You simply have to *stop, listen,* and *think* about your own voice. You may begin by writing in the spaces provided, as you take your personal voice inventory.

• • • • • Your Personal Voice Inventory

1. Do you generally speak with a softer voice or with a more direct and louder voice?

_____

_____

2. Are you an even-measured speaker? Or do you vary your voice regularly?

_____

_____

3. Do others often tell you to slow down in conversation? Are you sometimes hard to follow?

_____

_____

4. Is your pitch often in the higher register? Or are you a more low-voiced speaker?

_____

_____

5. Do you tend to end your sentences as if everything is a question? If so, why?

_____

_____

6. Do you often interrupt yourself with phrases like "um," "eh," or "you know?" If so, why?

_____

_____

7. Do you look directly at others when you speak, or do you tend to look away? Why so?

_____

_____

8. Do you nervously laugh or giggle when you speak? If so, why do you laugh?

_____

_____

9. Do you always sound too serious, or do you most often sound glib and fun when you speak? Why do you think this is so?

_____

_____

10. Do you offer long-winded or short, quick answers to questions in conversations?

_____

_____

We all learn by imitation. As we observe and *listen to, watch,* and *emulate* others, we tend to pick up their habits as well. Speech habits are no different. Most children will end up speaking like one or both of their parents to some degree. Everything from accent to pitch, pace and volume, influence us as children when listening to our parents speak on a daily basis. When we watch television, listen to the radio, or stream information on line, we are continually absorbing and then imitating communicational delivery cues.

Take a moment to focus upon listening to a newscast on either the television or the radio. The information you hear should be ancillary and for the most part extraneous. Try to listen to the *delivery* of the speakers. Listen to *volume, speed, emphasis of words,* and *changes in both speed* and *loudness* or *softness* of the information being presented. Now consider the following reflective questions about those you have heard from a broadcast delivery, and consider in some cases how they may relate to how you will deliver your own speech.

Reflective Questions on the Speech Delivery of Others

1. What comfort or trust level have I reached by listening to or watching others broadcast *via* TV, radio, or the Internet? What makes me intrigued about what I've heard in their delivery?

_____

_____

_____

_____

2. If I am also to intrigue my listeners, what basic skills must I acquire to at least approach being as engaging as a speaker on the TV, Internet, or the radio?

_____

_____

_____

_____

3. Was I ever bored by a public broadcast? What things tend to bore me personally when I am listening to someone else speak?

_____

_____

_____

_____

4. Do I personally like to listen to more soft- or more hard-sounding voices, or does it make no difference to me as long as the speaker is prepared and competent?

_____

_____

_____

_____

4. Do I understand and appreciate the pauses and uses of emphasis that I hear in public broadcasts? Why are pauses so crucial for a speaker?

_____

_____

_____

_____

5. What negative qualities, if any, did I hear during the broadcast? Was there a continual engaging energy with everyone who spoke?

_____

_____

_____

_____

6. What emotional elements seem to excite me personally, and motivate me specifically, when listening to others?

_____

_____

_____

_____

7. In what new ways can I be inspirational and passionate by using a style which will permit my speech to be something more than just the information I offer my audience?

_____

_____

_____

_____

8. In what ways does _loudness_ versus _softness,_ and _fast_ versus _slow_ speech patterns, help keep me personally engaged when listening to the radio or watching someone on television?

_____

_____

_____

_____

Your personal answers to the eight reflective questions about others, as well as about yourself, should help you begin to think about and plan how to deliver your speeches in a manner that will provide your listeners with a higher awareness of your topic. Remember, there is a level of expectation for you as a public speaker, namely to be conversational and engaging about the information you deliver to your audience.

> ▶ A successful speech that has energy and a sense of anticipation; and it should cover as many nonspoken performance elements as is possible.

Your delivery should offer additional information far beyond what you actually have to say. This should begin with regularly practicing your speech, speaking as clearly as possible, maintaining eye contact, and avoiding distracting mannerisms and nervous hand movements.

When speaking in public it is important to avoid the use of **totems.** Totems are nervous (and oftentimes unconscious) movements such as bouncing up and down, playing with your glasses, tapping a pencil, or even swaying back and forth during your speech. Totems, of course, cause distractions for your audience. Keep in mind that the goal of your delivery is to enhance, _not_ distract from, your speech. Every move you make and every word you pronounce will either _improve_ on or _detract_ from your speech. Further, you should:

> ▶ Always be certain to pronounce foreign words, personal names, and technical terms correctly.

Basic Forms of Speech Delivery

As continually mentioned throughout this text, we live in a digital-driven society—a world often governed by cell phones with high-resolution cameras, iPods, tweets, instant e-mails, and those omnipresent laptops and flat-screen TV sets. Because of this, the importance of keeping your audience at constant attention can hardly be overemphasized. Listeners are quite used to being engaged. The flow of constant communication is now rooted in our very nature as members of the human species. As such, when we speak in public we need to be aware of the four basic forms of delivery. These forms have been used for thousands of years, in virtually every age and time since humans first started speaking in public.

The classic forms of delivery are: (1) *memorization*, and its direct opposite (2) *extemporaneous;* (3) the unrehearsed or *impromptu* delivery; and lastly, the use of a guided text or (4) *manuscript.* Each of these approaches depends upon the nature of your chosen topic, the character of your gathered audience, and, in the case of your classroom assignments, even what your instructor may require of you as a part of his or her teaching approach to each project. We will now take a brief look at each basic form.

● ● ● ● ● Memorization

The **memorized delivery** is one that is common throughout the history of public speaking. This involves having memorized *everything* about your speech. Not only everything in the sense of word-for-word, but also your gestures, pauses, and even when and where to look up and make eye contact. This also includes your smiles, frowns, and dramatic use of loud and soft volume. For the most part, everything is planned and memorized.

The lecture circuit of ex-presidents, famous authors, and celebrities are occasions where you will find speech memorization as the main form of delivery. Also, introducing an invited speaker or speaking at a special ceremony where you are not expected to speak for very long, gives you an excellent reason for memorizing your delivery.

As you might expect, during congressional, presidential, and local campaign season, politicians subscribe to using *careful, safer, memorized* speeches and comments. For most politicians, every word is previously thought out, measured, and analyzed for public consumption. Occasionally they will speak off their prepared and memorized words. When this happens, more often than not, they get themselves into trouble. This is called **shooting from the hip** and often makes the headline news.

For politicians and public servants, shooting from the hip sometimes leads them to offering a public apology. When they go off their script, they run the risk of putting their foot in their mouth and saying something that was not well thought out beforehand. These kinds of statements can be quite revealing about what goes on in the speakers head, about their personality, morals, and ultimately their worldview.

There are several advantages and disadvantages of memorization. You should choose to offer a memorized speech only if you feel that your advantages clearly outweigh your disadvantages. This should be based upon your topic choice, the reason for the speech, and your corresponding audience.

> ▶ The central *advantage* of memorization is that it permits a *powerful, dramatic delivery.* You can control every word and moment of your speech. You can become a classic orator before your audience in the fashion of a JFK or an Abe Lincoln,

TWIN RULES

Delivering by Memorization

Things are set in stone

A. **Remember:** There is little or no room for changes or adaptations. You are limited by what you have committed to memory—not unlike an actor in a play.

B. **Also,** if you feel your audience is confused or even lost, it becomes very difficult to go back and clarify or explain a point or idea over again.

If you are new to public speaking

A. **Remember:** You run the risk of looking and sounding robotic or memorized, and will most likely appear to your audience as a well-rehearsed speaker and a contrived spokesperson.

B. **Always be sure** to keep in mind that if you forget or leave out a point or idea, you have to search for your place, and you run the risk of panicking if you become confused or lost in your speech.

If you are required to use memorization

A. **Remember:** Use it for commencement addresses, campaign speeches, public policy announcements, or at some form of commemoration event or ceremony, and generally not for your own free thoughts and personal ideas.

B. **Always be sure** to keep everything simple, concise, and to the point. A memorized delivery always runs the risk of becoming stale if it must be endured for too long by an audience.

Extemporaneous (*Ex Tempore*) Delivery

The **extemporaneous delivery,** sometimes designated as *ex tempore,* is one where the speaker presents his or her speech from an *outline,* from *note cards,* or from *an assemblage of key words, phrases,* or *concisely written comments* or *a series of short sentences.* Extemporaneous speaking often sounds very conversational and unrehearsed. It can be very engaging with an audience, and creates an atmosphere of authority within the context of informality.

> ▶ Extemporaneous delivery is the preferred mode of *most public speaking instructors.* It is most often used for guest speaking events, and is the delivery form generally preferred by most audiences.

The extemporaneous speech is *not* something ever to be memorized. In most cases the speaker never gives the same speech twice. The hallmark of this type of delivery is to keep both content and delivery adaptable and quite flexible for each new audience. The speaker may offer new information and delivery elements, and the speech may continue to grow and evolve, not only from audience to audience, but also (even within the speech itself) before a single given audience. The speaker may even stop and welcome questions or comments in the midst of the speech, and then continue on, undisturbed by a break in his or her speaking pattern.

A *conversation* with the audience is the main communicational characteristic of the *ex tempore* speech. The speaker may occasionally glance down at notes or an outline, but in the end he or she never loses eye contact or the attention of the audience.

Speaking *ex tempore* requires considerable preparation and effort; it is far from winging things from the top of your head, or from your note cards or an outline. You must carefully select your topic, and then outline your introduction, conclusion, main points, and any other supporting materials or any argumentative departure points. And most importantly, you must *practice your speech*. Each time it may be different, but the overall message and approach will remain the same when you offer it before any live audience.

> ▶ With appropriate preparation and suitable practice, delivering an *ex tempore* speech is a free and enjoyable experience for both the speaker and the audience

TWIN RULES

Delivering Extemporaneously

Things are never set in stone

A. Remember: There is always plenty of room for changes or adaptations to your speech, both in your practice sessions and when speaking before your audience.

B. Always be sure you know your audience is with you at every moment. Should they grow confused or even lost, it becomes very simple to stop, step backward or forward, and adjust to your audience's needs and desires right then and there.

If you are new to public speaking

A. Remember: You never run the risk of looking and sounding robotic, since your *ex tempore* speaking will most likely appear to your audience as a *conversational* and fresh experience. Feel free to plan some elements on the spot as needed.

B. Always be sure to keep in mind that if you forget or leave out a point or idea, you do not run the risk of panicking if you become confused or lost in your speech. There is always room to breathe and go either forward or backward with some measure of reason.

If you are required to use ex tempore delivery

A. Remember: Use it for selecting a topic that interests you greatly and for which you already have some level of expertise. You are in control throughout the entire presentation before your audience. Let yourself maintain control using your own natural voice, energy, and any inspiration you may feel at any given moment.

B. Always be sure to keep everything natural and honest by your motivated use of eye contact, bodily movements, volume, and pauses. Each time you practice or give the same speech, all these may change according to time, place, and the energy of the moment.

• • • • • Impromptu

The **impromptu delivery** involves giving a speech with the least amount of notice, and consequently the least amount of homework or formal preparation. Most often, minimal planning and research is involved or required for this mode of delivery. You may be asked to give an impromptu speech based upon your knowledge, expertise, and extensive background in an area of professional skill or understanding. The solution to impromptu delivery is centered on simply taking the time and focus to organize your thoughts and to efficiently arrange important points and goals without concern for "how?," "what?," "when?," or "where?" you are going to speak.

Most of us already have at least minimal experience with impromptu speaking. Anytime you respond to a question in class, in public, or even in an interview, you are in the impromptu delivery form. Facts, notions, and ideas about your thoughts, your ideas, and even about class assignments you may have read, are all the negligible preparation you need to respond to such questions.

When someone invites you to introduce yourself, clarify something at a meeting, or perhaps give an explanation of a misunderstanding of a subject you know quite well, you are offering your response in an impromptu delivery manner as well.

Impromptu delivery provides you with the chance *to think on your feet*, be spontaneous, and offer yourself in a fresh, unplanned manner. It actually makes public your ability to deal with unintentional situations and circumstances; it is a great test of your ability at being able to speak "out-of-the-blue." Your skill at being impromptu during a job interview (or even on the job itself) may tell your employers (or potential ones) far more about your capabilities and skillfulness than if you were subjected to more traditional question-and-answer sessions.

Also in the classroom, impromptu delivery can be a great advantage to your overall grade in a university course. Offering an accurate yet all-embracing answer to a challenging question within a classroom setting, displays comprehension not only of a given concept, but perhaps of the very field itself. Not having planned answers and being required to operate out of what is already in your head, is quite revealing about who you are, and what you actually *do* or *do not* know.

Of course, there are a few disadvantages to this mode of delivery as well. It takes skill and experience to make impromptu approaches work in your favor. You always run the risk of actually looking, sounding, and conveying that you are unprepared, unskilled, or simply winging it in the presence of your audience. Oftentimes spontaneity can offer the impression of unplanned research or lack of detail, and may even discourage audience analysis and participation.

▶ Always use the impromptu delivery style with caution. If you choose to speak, as it were, without a net, remember there may be no one to catch you, and you may fall hard.

TWIN RULES

Delivering by Impromptu Means

Things are never set in stone

A. Remember: There is considerable room for creativity or adjustment to your agenda. Always be sure to slow down, pause, and reflect when at all possible. Always take time to think in public—this is not uncommon and is even expected of you.

B. Also, if you feel your audience is confused or even lost, it becomes very easy to go back and clarify or explain a point or idea over again. Do not be afraid to ask those who question you to repeat their queries.

If you are new to public speaking

A. Remember: You run the risk of looking and sounding unprepared, or very confused, and will most likely appear to your audience as an individual who likes to wing it, or impress others as an expert.

B. Also be sure to keep in mind that if you forget or leave out a point or idea, you can resort to a dialogue and ask those questioning you for any further clarification which may in turn guide you and fuel you on to further success.

If you are required to use impromptu delivery

A. Remember: Use it with confidence, humility, and a genuine request by which you are willing to welcome help from others present if necessary.

B. Always be sure to keep everything *simple, concise,* and *to the point.* An impromptu delivery always runs the risk of becoming vague and formless if it is endured for too long. Don't ramble on; be sure to end when you run out of inspiration or any informational steam.

● ● ● ● ● ## Manuscript

The classic **manuscript delivery** involves offering a presentation in public with a fully written-out statement—virtually word for word. In essence, it is a skilled and authoritative manner of reading in public, yet it is *not* memorized, although the speaker must be very familiar with its entire contents. A manuscript is appropriate when the information being offered must *be specific, be accurate, avoid all error*; and in the end the speaker must be *accountable* for every word offered in public. A manuscript is a very careful, exact, and well-thought-out presentation of communal or even public information.

Many teachers and university professors lecture from a manuscript, as do many preachers, public office holders, heads of state (such as presidents, prime ministers, and royalty), management representatives, and also diplomats.

A manuscript always offers the impression of professionalism, importance, and a no-nonsense attitude. In turn it offers no surprises from the speaker, and always prevents any shooting from the hip. It most often prevents wobbly word choices, vocal blunders, and any overall communicational distortion.

When you choose to read a letter in public, present sections from a short story or novel, or recite poetry from a collection, the skills of the manuscript mode must be at the center of your delivery. Speaking by way of a manuscript offers the great security of a net to catch you: everything you need to say is always right in front of you. You would of course never change the words of another's letter or a published piece of literature.

As for giving your own speech, your words may even be printed ahead of time for public archival preservation. For instance, many preachers have their sermons printed up in advance for those who may be unable to attend services, long before they offer the sermon within a live church, mosque, or synagogue setting.

> ▶ Unfortunately manuscript delivery has numerous disadvantages, and is often a forbidden delivery strategy in most public speaking courses.

Manuscripts greatly reduce eye contact, and offer distance from your audience. Essentially a manuscript forces the speaker *to read* in public. This is a "no-no" in most all public speaking courses. Manuscripts do not permit you to respond to audience reactions, and for the most part *do not* afford you the opportunity of countering your audience. Feedback becomes very difficult. Vocal variety can become very weak, and gestures are often kept to a bare minimum.

In most public speaking courses, manuscript delivery *sounds read*, or at best lacks any vital sense of a conversation with your audience. Oftentimes the speaker appears bound to the podium, and can appear like an authoritative speaker who is talking at, and not talking with, his or her audience.

Lastly, since the speaker is more in *reading mode* than in *speaking mode,* he or she runs the risk of simply being an information machine without any real passion, soul, or communicational inspiration. Unless specifically instructed to do so, public speakers should *never* resort to the manuscript delivery style.

> ▶ Without proper training and experience, using a manuscript will bore your listeners, and most likely make public speaking an unpleasant experience for both speaker and audience.

TWIN RULES

Twin Rules for Delivering with a Manuscript

Things are very much set in stone

A. **Remember:** There is *absolutely no room* for creativity or adjustment to your agenda. You are required to always stay on course, as written. Your manuscript is your only map—and changing your route is forbidden.

B. **Also, if you** feel your audience is confused or even lost, it becomes impossible to go back and clarify or explain a point or idea over again. You must continue to present your speech as if your audience understands and accepts every word.

If you are new to public speaking

A. **Remember:** You will run the risk of wanting to use a manuscript. It is a *safe, secure* approach to speaking in public. You simply follow your written text—but you run the risk of boring everyone within hearing distance, not to mention garnering a low grade from your instructor.

B. **Also be sure** to keep in mind that if you forget or leave out a point, you may not go back and continue where you accidentally made your departure. There is no room for amending your words or ideas. All is written in stone and is accountable as written.

If you are required to use manuscript delivery

A. **Remember:** Use your manuscript with confidence, power, and a genuine approach by which you avoid looking and sounding as if you are reading. Regularly hold your place and look up at your audience. Attempt to connect with your audience as much as possible within the confines of your frozen manuscript. Reading in public is a great skill, and takes years of practice.

B. **Always be sure** to speak everything *as written*, making no on-the-spot adjustments of ideas or important points. Attempt to be as relaxed as possible, and adjust both your body and your voice regularly so as not to look stiff and sound *monotone*.

Always Rules — Powerful Speech Delivery

- *Always* let your audience come away from your speech feeling as if you just had a public conversation with them and not a lecture.

- *Always* be sure to look and feel spontaneous at all times, appearing effortless and never as if rehearsed or staged.

- *Always* be sure to keep an even level of regular eye contact with your audience, and never be afraid to pause and smile occasionally.

- *Always* be sure to remain focused on your central topic, thus avoiding the temptation to go off on a related or interesting digression.

- *Always* be sure to remain confident and assured that you are in command of your speech. If you make an obvious slip-up, or need to adjust yourself, remain self-assured.

- *Always* pay close attention to the faces and general *awareness level* of your audience. If they seem puzzled or lost, take time to ask them if you are being understood.

Speech Dynamics

As with music, the use of *dynamics* is important when you are giving your speech. In our case, **speech dynamics** refers to how you regulate your eyes, voice, and body movements while delivering your speech—namely, how you control every aspect of your speech except for the actual words and content themselves. Speech dynamics involves everything that is *nonverbal* about how you communicate. Speech dynamics is concerned with everything from eye contact and suitable attire to your exact pitch and volume. It is important to keep in mind that if *what* you have to say to your audience is significant, then also *how* you go about it is equally important in order to fulfill your ultimate goal of communication.

> ▶ Remember that *content* and *delivery* complete two sides of the same speech coin.

Not only is *what* you say important, but also *how* you dress, gesture, move, and generally sound. Delivery helps complete your speech as an effective and pleasant listening experience for your audience. Now we will examine *eight important elements* of speech dynamics: *suitable attire, eye contact, vocal fluency, vocal projection, vocal pitch, rhythm and tempo, gestures and movement,* and *interrupters.*

Eight Elements of Speech Dynamics

Suitable Attire

Your choice of **attire** and overall physical appearance have an effect on the final impact of your speech, both inside and outside of the classroom environment. Therefore your attire options should be adjusted to your audience and *not* to your own needs. You should always dress in a manner which is characteristic of your audience, unless you wish to wear clothing which is directly relevant to your speech. For instance, if you are speaking about a particular ethnic tradition or culture, you may choose to wear clothing unique to that set of traditions.

Be sure to remember to avoid wearing accessories such as body ornaments, hats, sunglasses, or ostentatious jewelry which could possibly divert your audience from keeping their attention upon your speech. Remember that you, the speaker, are at the center of your speech, and *not* what you are wearing.

> ▶ Your attire and accessories should contribute to your credibility; always try to avoid provocative or revealing clothing, unless it is directly related to your speech topic at hand.

Eye Contact

Essentially your **eye contact** is the manner by which you monitor your audience while speaking to them. As they watch you, so too must you watch them. *Eye contact directly connects you with your audience.* Generally speaking, making good eye contact is a skill that tends to grow with public speaking experience. It is a way of letting the audience know that you are having a conversation with them and not offering a lecture. It lets them know you are interested in them, as well as in your words to them. Audiences want to be *spoken to*, not *spoken at*, and maintaining good eye contact builds a relationship of audience attention and trust in you as a speaker.

Keep in mind that the better you know your speech (by frequent practicing), the more comfortable you will be with making eye contact. When you are rusty with your material you are more likely to be focused on your notes or manuscript, and *not* on your audience. Do not be afraid to scan your audience at frequent intervals. At times, address various sections of the audience more directly to see if they are connecting with you. Every smile, laugh, nod, or unconscious signal they send to you, is a way not only of connecting to you, but also of indicating how you are coming across to them in your speech.

At times, you may find it helpful and encouraging to regularly focus upon various individuals who tend to offer you various forms of positive feedback. Responsive faces and frequent nods help build confidence, and assist you in monitoring the progress of your speech.

> ▶ If your eye contact is weak or too infrequent, your audience may become offended by your lack of direct interest in them as a conversational partner.

● ● ● ● ● Vocal Fluency

We often speak about someone as being fluent in a foreign language. Fluency is often perceived to be the *ease* or *confidence* a person maintains while speaking. In terms of speech delivery, **vocal fluency** refers to the smoothness of your words, and the ease with which you speak. A fluent public speaker never stumbles over words or phrases. When you are smooth in your speech, no one notices or even really cares, but when you frequently stumble, everyone notices, everyone cares, and you then risk becoming a nuisance.

Vocal fluency can also be accomplished by practicing the correct pronunciation of foreign words and phrases; checking on the correct pronunciation of technical, scientific, and medical terms; and also being sure how to articulate words which are new to your vocabulary. In short, *fluency* is the relative energy and comfortable flow of your speech. Vocal fluency helps make your speech devoid of awkward pauses, and frequent stumbling over unfamiliar words and phrases.

> ▶ As with eye contact, fluency comes with being confident about what you have to say to your audience. Practice and preparation breed strong vocal fluency.

● ● ● ● ● Vocal Projection

When communicating, being heard is everything. *"Can you speak up?"* and *"We can't hear you back here!"* are not reactions from your audience which you should ever look forward to hearing. *Remember: being heard is everything to a speaker, just as being seen is everything to a dancer.* **Vocal projection** (or volume) means knowing how to properly adjust your volume to both your audience, and the situation at hand. Management of your volume can be a powerful communicational tool. Controlling your voice can convey solemnity, stress certain important points, and even add a level of humor to your speech.

Remember, your voice must carry at all times. You must be aware of your audience's need to hear. If you want to be heard, then you will be heard. Even if you have a microphone, you still must strive to be heard by everyone. If your voice is soft and quiet in front of a mike, it will also be soft and quiet when amplified. Always speak loudly and strongly, and do not be afraid to ask your audience if you are being heard by all, as they will be grateful for your concern in the end.

> No matter how great your speech may be, if you are not clearly heard by everyone in the audience, your efforts will for the most part be in vain.

Vocal Pitch

When we speak of **vocal pitch**, we are speaking about the relative highness or lowness of your voice, your downward or upward intonation. In many ways, vocal pitch is the musical nature of the spoken voice. A competent public speaker is never monotone, but explores the variations in pitch at various points in his or her presentation. Pitch illustrates the difference between a question and a declarative statement. It conveys the difference between being gravely serious about a topic, and simply speaking about it in a light or joking manner.

Controlling vocal pitch creates honesty, sincerity, and focus in a public presentation. The best public speakers know how to control their pitch. They know when to whisper, shout, and be quite serious. They keep an audience from being uninterested and bored to tears. They never resort to being monotonous.

> When you know and understand what you are saying, your pitch should naturally follow your emotional intentions. The opposite of pitch is **monotone**. Nothing is more boring to an audience than being held hostage to a speaker who is monotone.

Rhythm/Tempo

As with music, **rhythm** suggests the tempo of a presentation. In a speech, the rhythm most often starts out measured and oftentimes quite slowly, then begins to build as the speaker becomes more involved in his or her topic. Oftentimes we refer to tempo, rhythm, and *pace* as the same commodity—namely, the speed of your speech.

During the main points of a speech, your pace tends to quicken with verbal pauses and emphasis, indicating what is central and what is not to your listening audience. After a while, the speaker finds his or her "sailing speed" for the speech, a tempo or pace which is natural and comfortable for both speaker and audience.

As the speech works its way toward coming to a close, as in the beginning of the speech, things may begin to slow down toward a theatrical ending. The use of *pauses, planned silences,* and even measured *whispering* can add spice and intrigue to both your pacing and your emphasis of important points.

▶ Be aware that you run the risk of *racing* when you are not prepared, or unsure of what you want to say. Being unprepared can also cause you to *drag* your speech as you grapple for what to say, or attempt to buy time.

Gestures/Movement

You speak not only with your appearance and your voice, but also with your body. **Gestures** are the actions of the arms and hands as well as the body as a whole. When you speak, *how you move is very powerful to how you are being heard*. Efficient gestures make a distinction between outstanding and dynamic speaking, and boring or commonplace speaking. Oftentimes your gestures may be unconscious and distracting to your audience.

If you are not careful, you could find yourself swaying back and forth or even tapping your hands on the podium without even being aware of it. We referred to these nervous movements as totems in an earlier chapter. Totems are for the most part an unconscious use of the body. They include the following: constantly straightening your tie or necklace, excessively adjusting your glasses, fixing your hair continuously, tapping your feet, scratching your nose, and even bobbing up and down behind the podium. Totems are distracting and show your audience that you are not prepared, unfocused, and not really in full control of your speech. To say the least, they may indicate a high level of nervousness as well.

Body movement and gestures fluctuate with the size of the audience and the occasion of the speech. With smaller audiences your gestures are often identical to daily conversation, while with larger, more formal audiences, your gestures should be grand and more noticeable.

Gestures should be *natural* and never *choreographed* or overly intentional. If they are too rehearsed, then you run the risk of appearing staged or even robotic and planned. It is important that you are conscious of your body movements and gestures, but at the same time you should always permit them to be *natural* and *honest* to you as an individual. Sincere gestures create credibility and trust in your audience; and they identify you as a real, true-to-life person having a conversation in front of them.

▶ The best way to monitor your gestures, is to practice in front of friends or, better yet, in front of a video camera, to then reveal where all your unconscious movements or secret *totems* may lie.

Interrupters

Lastly, a quick word about interrupters, or what many additionally refer to as "garbage words." These include everything from poor grammar usage, an abundance of slang terms, swear words, and even street lingo. Always avoid things which interrupt either yourself or your audience's focus with a jarring intrusion.

More specifically, **interrupters** are words or phrases you may unconsciously use to interrupt yourself. We often interrupt ourselves in daily informal conversation with filler expressions such as: "yah know?," "uh-huh," "ummm," "uhhhh," "let's see now," and "Okay, okay?" These may be fine for daily informal conversations, but not for a more prescribed conversation with an audience within a public setting.

Rather than resort to such phrases as "well . . . let's see now" and "where were we?," it is better to take a moment and *pause, collect yourself,* and then move on. Most audiences are kind and patient when speakers need to keep their focus. They are grateful for your willingness to speak to them. It is better to pause and refuel your thoughts, than to buy time using interrupters and "garbage terms."

Remember that interrupters often cause your audience to experience a disconnection, and may even make both they and your speech itself, appear insignificant or even trivial. Some refer to interrupters as "lazy-speech" and, as mentioned earlier, consider them to be a way of buying a little time for thinking about what you need to say next.

Many first-time public speaking students appear behind the podium just as they do in front of their friends in the university cafeteria. If you subscribe to lazy-speech in class, you will then most likely do it in a more formal setting when you are asked to speak outside of the classroom. Always be conscious of your words. *Just as totems are with movement, so too, interrupters are with words.*

▶ The worst type of interruption is the one caused by you yourself, the speaker. Always be sure *not* to resort to garbage words, lazy-speech or slang when speaking in public

Your **A**, **B**, **C**s for Better Delivery Dynamics

ATTIRE

IF you *know how to* adjust your physical appearance to your audience, then you should be able to:

A Wear *attire* that establishes your credibility.

B Avoid being adorned with distracting accessories.

C And, if possible, directly relate to your topic.

EYE CONTACT

IF you *know* your topic well and are seriously prepared, then you should regularly:

A Maintain genuine *eye contact* throughout your speech.

B Scan at regular intervals; equally focus upon various sections of the room.

C Make eye contact with those who offer positive feedback.

VOCAL FLUENCY

IF you *know* you are going to introduce foreign and technical terms or speak proper names, then you should:

A Explore accurate pronunciations of all foreign words, names, and phrases.

B Research the pronunciation of all technical, medical, legal, and scientific terms.

C Avoid being choppy, and attempt a smooth, free-flowing delivery.

VOCAL PROJECTION

IF you *know* your audience will be basically on the larger side (that is, more than 10 to 12 persons), then you should:

A Be sure to project your voice so that everyone present may hear you.

B Make your volume consistently audible at all times, and never lose vocal "steam."

C Never hesitate to ask if you are being heard by all present.

VOCAL PITCH

IF you *know how to* regulate your *vocal pitch* in front of your audience, then you should be able to:

A Alter the downward and upward intonation of your voice at regular intervals.

B Display the difference between serious and humorous attitudes.

C Avoid being *monotone* at all times and at all costs.

RHYTHM/TEMPO

IF you *know* your topic well and are seriously practiced and prepared, then you should regularly:

A Begin your speech slowly, then work toward and maintain a comfortable, even pace.

B Regularly speed up or slow down for vocal variety, and to highlight emphasis.

C Take time for pauses and intermittent moments of higher energy.

GESTURES/MOVEMENT

IF you *know* you want to make your words fluent and interesting for your audience, then you should:

A Feel free to use your entire body to express yourself in a natural, unstaged manner.

B Use your hands, arms, and face to illustrate your ideas and main points.

C Avoid using totems, swaying your body, and podium-leaning.

INTERRUPTERS

IF you *know* your speech contents well and have practiced them, then you should:

A Be sure to never rely upon poor grammar, street slang, or "garbage words."

B Remember to *pause* rather than rely upon interrupters in your speech.

C Be skilled: never resort to lazy or careless speech patterns.

Summary

In this chapter we have explored what it means to *deliver* a speech more powerfully and effectively—namely, to communicate a speech well beyond the very words, phrases, and overall *content* of your topic. *Vocal dynamics* are at the heart and soul of keeping your audience not only focused on your topic, but also continuously interested and even entertained by your speaking to them in public. What is essential, in the end, is not only being clear about your facts, figures, and the overall outline of your speech, but also *how* you attire yourself before an audience, and how you use your hands, arms, eyes, and your body itself.

Public speakers must be aware at all times of their voice and its unlimited capabilities to making a speech a powerful, memorable event.

Your speech should always be full of *energy*, have a moderate controlled pacing, and never race or drag in its overall rate. Keeping a smooth and unchoppy presentation, is vital to keeping your audience focused and contented. How you control your pitch and volume makes your speech colorful, energetic, and even teachable and convincing to your audience in the end.

As the presenter of an informative or persuasive speech, you take on the role of a communicator with a unique *vocal timbre*, a role that must command attention and put you in the spotlight not only by *what* you say but also by *how* you go about saying it.

Successful speakers are ever aware of time constraints, and always strive to be heard by everyone present at all times. They avoid poor grammar, garbage words, and interrupters; and are always aware that how they move their hands, arms, and body in general, is a powerful, unspoken tool for communication. Most of all, they are always aware of how important it is to maintain continual *eye contact* throughout their speech.

Discussion Questions

1. What do we mean when we declare that: while giving a speech in public, you must not only speak to your audience about an important topic, but also be sure to make an honest *communicational connection?*

2. Of the eight *vocal dynamics* discussed in this chapter, which three do you feel are the most important, and consequently the most vital, to giving a powerful and effective speech; and why?

3. What are the risks of having a speech riddled with weak grammar, garbage words, and interrupters? How do you think these might be regularly avoided by someone who is not accustomed to speaking in public regularly?

4. What is meant by the more common term *monotone?* Why is it considered by speech experts (and also by audiences in general) to be the most *dreaded* of public speaking shortcomings: one to be *avoided* at all costs?

5. In what ways might a prospective public speaker go about learning how to use hand gestures, body movements, and even facial expressions, in a manner which will enhance the content of their speech, and not be perceived by an audience as staged or robotic?

● ● ● ● ● Quick Quiz

Match the following capsule sentences with the correct letter of the term which best describes the key terms or phrases discussed in this chapter.

1. _____ Making an important visual connection with your audience at all times.

2. _____ The natural and distinctive vocal quality unique to every individual speaker.

3. _____ How you offer your speech apart from your actual words and intended content.

4. _____ When your speech is set in stone and is delivered by mental recall.

5. _____ Speaking from experience, with little research and minimal or no preparation.

6. _____ Use of garbage words and poor grammar, along with "um's" and "ah's."

7. _____ Preferred form of speaking that uses outlines, note cards, and open creativity.

8. _____ A written-out speech (word for word), often like one given by U.S. presidents.

9. _____ Ability to mutually connect with your audience in an honest, public manner.

10. _____ The effective use of your hands, arms, and body to deliver your speech.

A. Gestures   B. Eye contact   C. Extemporaneous

D. Manuscript   E. Impromptu   F. Memorization

G. Delivery   H. Interrupters   I. Communicational relationship

J. Timbre

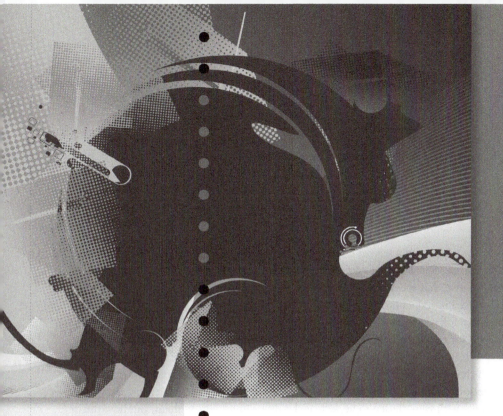

KEY TERMS

"The airplane stays up, because it does not have the time to fall."
—Orville Wright

*"Aviation is proof that, given the will, we have the capacity
. . . to achieve the impossible."*
—Eddie Rickenbacker

Not unlike flying an airplane, a successful speech has three major tasks that need to be skillfully maneuvered. As you may guess, every pilot is obliged to master these tasks: make a triumphant and smooth *takeoff*, maintain a constant *level airspeed* while airborne (as well as making habitual adjustments according to any changing weather patterns), and then build a gradual *descent* that will eventually approach a slower, safe landing. The *descent* must also take place at the pilot's desired destination.

Flying is a commanding, highly skilled technology, as well as an art form. Any pilot will tell you that once you are up there, it takes less dexterity to remain "up there" than it does to smoothly take off, or, even more smoothly, achieve a target-safe landing. *Taking off* and *landing* are everything. After all, they get you up there, where you want to go, and then back down all over again.

As with taking off in a plane, maintaining constant airspeed, and then safely landing, a successful speech has similar parallels. It correspondingly requires a skilled *introduction*, a well-structured *body*, and finally a smooth, steady *conclusion*. As with an airplane, any speech is liable to crash on either takeoff or landing; and if both are indeed safe and smooth, that does not guarantee a constant, level ride while up there high above the clouds. All three are vital to a smooth, safe flight.

In this chapter we will explore how a well-planned *introduction*, *body*, and *conclusion* holds your audience's attention, indicates your purpose and goals, provides a pattern for your speech, and in the end brings you safely to where you intend your speech to land. Each of these, when well executed, will increase the probability that you will arrive at your destination by leaving your audience with a long-lasting, positive impression.

Your Introduction Is Your First Impression

If the truth be told: you never get a second chance to make a first impression. The opening words of your well-rehearsed speech will permit your audience to form early notions about your prepared topic, your speaking style, and the overall *impression* of your live presence. A vague, disorganized, off-the-cuff, or lackluster introduction, will most likely generate a negative impression of yourself, as well as your speech that follows. By contrast, a *crisp, appealing,* and *well-thought-out* introduction will initiate your listeners into a highly favorable impression of you, your delivery skills, your research, and the overall speech itself. This impression is particularly important when the audience you are trying to reach (which includes your public speaking instructor) will be grading your performance.

Your **introduction** communicates a lot of information to your audience. Here, you can help them become familiar with your chosen topic, why it should be important to them, and how you plan to proceed with your public conversation about it.

In most speech presentations, your introduction should contain a proposal that will declare your informational points or the *direction* of your convincing thoughts. It should also, ideally, give your listeners a sense of the kinds of information you will present, or the *approach* to the ideas that which you will offer, as well as the general organization of the body (or main points) of your speech. After experiencing your introduction, your audience should not be expecting any new revelations as they listen to the body of your speech.

> ▶ If at all possible, your introduction should make your audience want to *anticipate* hearing from you. It should welcome their curiosity, making them need to hear the rest of your speech.

Gaining Audience Attention

Your first goal as a speaker is to rouse or *gain* your audience's attention. You need an effective approach to draw them in, something to take them away from the world, themselves, and any conversation or thoughts in their heads prior to the start of your speech. Your **attention-getter (AG)** is your powerful device for gaining, and hopefully keeping, the attention of every listener in the room. Your AG must be the first spoken, unspoken, or visual cues you give to your audience. It is ineffective (not to mention *unexciting*) to directly tell your listeners what you are about to say to them by way of introducing yourself or your topic in a clear-cut, direct manner.

> ▶ N*ever* begin with "Hello, my name is _____ and I am here to speak to you today about _____."

Gaining the attention of your audience can be a challenge, but also an opportunity for personal invention, creativity, and originality. Attention-getting techniques can be fun, inspirational, serious, hilarious, and even sacred. They may include everything from personal stories and quotations to music, video clips, and photos.

The nature of your AG depends upon your general motives for speaking, your topic choice, your audience's demographic, and even the limited amount of time you may have available for your speech. The following are five "help reasons" every speaker should keep in mind when seeking to use an effective attention-getter, or AG.

● ● ● ● ● Five Help Reasons for Using an Effective AG

1. To help focus *awareness on the relevance* of your chosen topic . . .
   Remember: Your AG must directly relate to your audience's demographic.

2. To help entice your audience *to desire to hear more* about your chosen topic . . .
   Remember: You must find an amusing and inventive way to arouse their interest.

3. To help create a *communicational relationship* between you and your audience . . .
   Remember: Both visual and sound resources offer you a chance to *not* use your own words.

4. To help *reduce mutual nervousness* between you and your audience . . .
   Remember: Being entertaining and creative can be a powerful "ice-breaker."

5. To help establish a general *connective premise* for your overall speech . . .
   Remember: Your AG can serve as a guide for your audience throughout your speech.

Keep in mind that, however you may go about gaining your audience's attention, you not only stimulate their curiosity about what you have to say, you also show them how your topic can directly relate to them and their daily lives. But also keep in mind that you must be *ethical* at all times. This means that you must be: truthful, respectful, courteous, and trustworthy by using ideas, creative examples, and public language which are not slanderous, offensive, or discriminatory in your approach to winning their attention.

> ▶ No matter how excellent a speaker you may be, audiences generally enjoy an AG, something to arouse their interest beyond you simply telling them who you are and, what you want to say.

● ● ● ● ● Eight Possible Avenues for an Attention-Getter

There are a number of avenues and approaches to gaining an audience's attention. We will now take a very quick look at roughly eight of them; each will be accompanied by an *example* with an equivalent theme or topic choice. In this case, the example topic is about the endlessly fascinating and controversial notion of UFOs.

1. ANECDOTES AND STORIES

An **anecdote** is a personal story or narrative illustration that may serve as an attention-getter. Story telling is a fun and often powerful way of getting your audience interested in your topic. Anecdotes are most often short accounts or narratives of interesting or amusing incidents; and are intended to help you illustrate or support the main points which will follow in the body of your speech.

In most cases, when used in the form of an AG, an anecdote is an interesting story that is derived from real-life situations. Often it can be quite funny, and it should serve to ultimately entertain your audience. Anecdotes do not necessarily have to be based upon famous people; they could be about anyone you know or have heard about in the past, and even about someone you read about in a popular or scholarly magazine or news article.

Different from myths, fables, legends, and parables, an anecdote does not seek to convey a lesson or any moral teaching. Unlike a short story, which might involve a more complex structure, an anecdote is centered on a single uncomplicated event. You should keep your anecdotes short, simple, and directly related to the main points which will follow in the body of your speech.

> ▶ An anecdote should provide a "lead-in" to the overall message of your speech to follow. For example, the motivating sentence before or after your anecdote could be: "Have you ever experienced an unexplained event that remains with you for months or even years later?"

Example

You may want to tell an anecdote about a friend, relative, or someone you read about in a magazine or article who seriously believes that he or she has experienced an authentic sighting of an unidentified flying object (UFO). You may even wish to speak about a credible source such as a U.S. president or a high-ranking military official at the Pentagon.

2. AMAZING FACTS AND FIGURES

It is always fun to be provocative, even sensational, in a speech. Using amazing facts and figures is a great way not only to gain attention, but also to raise awareness of the significance and timeliness of your speech.

Startling your audience with little-known statistics, alarming facts, and grandiose figures (all of which must be true, of course) sets the stage for listeners who want to hear more, listen further and after your speech is over, might even be willing to ask you a few questions or request some clarifications. It's hard to beat facts and figures. If you are giving a persuasive speech, this is often a great way to gain your audience's attention, and possibly in your favor as well.

> ▶ Always be sure to "fact-check" everything, if you are beginning your speech with amazing facts and figures. Nothing could be worse than an audience member with an iPhone who then later proves you publicly wrong!

Example

You may wish to initiate your speech by announcing how many UFOs go unexplained each year by the U.S. government or even worldwide. Or you may choose to announce how many UFOs have been reported since records started being kept. If you are presenting a persuasive speech, you may even choose to emphasize a few unproven U.S. Air Force cases, or, in turn, you may wish to highlight the statistics and facts gathered on the demystified hoaxes and the thousands of proven charlatans.

3. QUOTATIONS AND EXCERPTS

Quotations are funny, glib, wise, informative, thought-provoking, and even solemn words directly attributed to an individual source. They often express the profound thoughts and experiences of others in a way that many of us many never have the opportunity to experience. They are a form of "fact" and in turn can be verified and fact-checked. Although quotations carry a sense of power and authority, and are widely available on line, you should use them sparingly, and not for the introduction of every single speech assignment you may receive.

If you wish, you may choose to use one large quote, or a series of quotes from several individuals, as an AG in support of your topic to follow. Also, **excerpts,** or "quoting" passages directly from sacred texts, novels, plays, and even poetry collections, can serve as a form of attention-getter. Quotations may be in the form of excerpts from literature, and not just from individuals *per se.*

> ▶ Quotations may be used in persuasive speeches quite manipulatively. A quote taken out of context, can be used to support virtually anything. Be sure to use all your quotes and excerpts with a sense of *ethical* responsibility.

Example

You may wish to quote several reliable sources that are strongly pro *or* con regarding your position on UFOs, if you hope to gain the attention of your audience in a persuasive speech. If you are planning a more *neutral* or informative speech, you may quote sources that are about the phenomena of UFO sightings in general. Or as your form of AG, you can simply read an excerpt from a sci-fi novel, or a reputable magazine article about the scientific prospects of extraterrestrial life.

4. WIT AND HUMOR

When handled appropriately, *humor* can be a powerful and fun way to gain audience attention. It can help relax both you and they, as well as win their positive attitude toward you for the remainder of your speech. Always be sure to be careful and sensitive to all those present. Steer away from ethnic humor and sexual innuendos; and of course always be sensitive to religious affiliations and even sexual orientations as well.

> ▶ Obviously, if your topic is a serious or more somber one, it is best *not* to use humor or wit as your form of an AG.

Example

Search for a funny story or an alien-themed joke as your way of introducing your topic of UFOs to your audience. Google and other search engines have galaxies of true and fictional examples of both alien and flying-saucer humor. A good laugh is a great way to begin a serious talk about this subject, no matter whether your position is that UFOs are very real *or* are simply a crazy, ongoing hoax perpetrated by spotlight-seeking eccentrics.

5. RHETORICAL QUESTIONS

A thoughtful rhetorical question is always a powerful way to get your audience thinking about your topic. A **rhetorical question** is one that is simply philosophical, and requires no expected answer. If a member of your audience wants to comment, however, or if many raise their hands either positively or negatively, you may use this to further the cause in your speech.

If you choose, you may ask more than one rhetorical question. Just be sure to keep each one short and sweet, and to make use of them directly in your speech that is to follow.

> ▶ Always try to be creative with your rhetorical questions. Avoid beginning with "How many of you . . ." *or* "Let's see by a show of hands. . . ." Come up with a clear, focused, original question.

Example

You may begin your speech by asking your audience if anyone present genuinely feels they have personally experienced a UFO sighting, or perhaps knows someone close to them who has experienced what they believe to be a UFO. You may even give a respondent to your question half a minute or so to actually elaborate, and then use their example to your own purpose for the remainder of your speech.

6. ARTIFACTS AND RELICS

A **relic** may be any object *directly related* to your topic that you use to bring attention to your speech. This tangible article or articles should help your audience both *see* and *feel* another dimension of your words, beyond the speech which you are about to present to them. Your relic should be convenient to handle or observe, and simple for your audience to see or touch without much effort.

An **artifact** is considered anything that is *not* directly related to your speech, but that you nonetheless choose to connect to your speech. Artifacts are a very broad category, and may include virtually anything. If you are speaking about UFOs, you may use a camera or binoculars as an artifact. You would need something from the sighting itself, such as wreckage, burnt soil, or a sample of "alien" hair, if you wanted to display a *relic*.

Some speakers choose to exhibit their relics and artifacts after they have entered into the body of their speech, but be wary about this approach. If your relic or artifact is very interesting or in some cases a live animal, your audience may pay more attention to it than to the rest of your message.

Should you need to make use of more than one relic or artifact, exhibit them in succession, and then be sure to remove them from sight also in a timely progression. Relatively speaking, *non-living artifacts work better than live animals*, which cannot always be easily managed or required to perform appropriately when and where you wish them to do so. Remember, animals may also become nervous during a speech and choose, right then and there, to use your introductory time as their chance to gain your audience's attention—they may even go to the bathroom, and make a mess for you in public. Keep in mind that:

> ▶ It is more effective to keep your relic or artifact out of sight when you are not directly referring to it. And live animals are largely to be avoided, unless keep in captivity and well-trained.

Example

You may wish to initiate audience interest in your UFO speech by showing them examples of popular "alien dolls" and buttons, and then by explaining to them why such artifacts are becoming increasingly popular, as both conversation pieces and collectables. Tell them how a fascination with the possibility of extraterrestrials is on the increase.

7. PHOTOS AND SHORT VIDEO CLIPS

Sometimes the use of photographs can be difficult to manage *during* a speech. Unless projected, photographs may be hard for your audience to view beyond the first several rows of your classroom or auditorium. Using photographs (as a form of AG), in most cases, will not be a problem which will cause distraction among audience members, and will most likely *not* pull the focus away from you as the central speaker. Be sure, though, to keep them out of sight during your speech, unless you plan to refer to them again later in your body or conclusion:

> ▶ It is best to project photographs on a screen before all to see as a group, while you *introduce* them as the core focus of your speech to follow.

DVDs and videotapes can provide even more enhanced visual-sound experiences which will boost your AG. Clips from foreign films and Hollywood movies, can be a powerful emotional and narrative resource to help prepare your audience for the body of your speech. Always be certain that you know well in advance the size of room and location of your speech, and whether such a site has the proper tools and equipment to accommodate your prepared electronic materials.

> ▶ Both DVDs and videotapes are a powerful enhancement resource for preparing your audience to hear your speech. They have the imaginative power to carry them to faraway, thrilling, and improbable places.

Example

You may wish to provocatively introduce your UFO speech by showing a comparison between a bogus UFO photo and an authentic one supplied from the U.S. Air Force or Pentagon archives. Or, better yet, perhaps show a quick clip from a sci-fi film in which UFOs invade the Earth! Maybe *Independence Day* or *Close Encounters of the Third Kind,* or a clip from a serious documentary, will be sure to get them interested.

8. SOUND AND PERFORMANCE

Sound, as well as live or recorded performance, can powerfully introduce a topic to your audience by offering the use of resources literally beyond your own words and language. These may involve the use of recordings, such as conversations, interviews, music, sound effects, animal noises, and even clips and bits of speeches by other speakers.

Both *sound* and *live performance* may now be downloaded *via* laptop computer for actual (real-time) use at the beginning of your speech. By augmenting your words and actions, sound and performance resources help make attention-getting more tangible and readily comprehensible for your audience.

Some public speakers also make effective use of sound by temporarily darkening or lowering the lighting level of the room. Always ask yourself: "what can I do, by way of alternative sound resources, to help my audience *desire to hear* my speech beyond the use of my own voice?"

> Sometimes the use of very quick computer-generated slides accompanied by music or poetry, or even narrated by your own voice, may be quite the effective attention-getter your speech may require.

Example

You may gain your audience's attention to UFOs by turning off the lights in the room for thirty seconds; and then play for them a sound clip from the classic 1938 radio broadcast of Orson Welles' *War of the Worlds*.

Be Sure to Practice Your AGs

You should always practice your attention-getters, or AGs, beforehand. Remember that smoothly organizing all technical resources requires both planning and practice. You should practice using your visual and sound resources until they become an instinctive element of your introduction. Always have a backup plan, should all go wrong and fail you.

Your AG above all, should be smooth and effortless. It should help spotlight time and attention upon the body of your overall spoken message.

> Always appear early for your presentation. Arriving in advance and checking on the technical needs for your speech will help you avoid nervousness and stumbling into technical problems.

Always re-check all images for proper focusing, size levels, color sharpness, and any sound volume levels well before your audience arrives. Although visual and sound resources greatly enhance any introduction, you should also be prepared for unplanned technological failures. If you discover that you cannot introduce things as you had planned, you may have to resort to using the chalk or white board as part of your backup plan.

If at all possible, try to bring backup materials such as printed graphs, charts, or photographs which may easily substitute for failed technology.

> You should always be prepared to offer your AG without your visual or sound resources in the event that something does not go as you had planned.

Your Audience Connection

After you have successfully chosen an AG strategy, you need only now attach your attention-getter to a comment that will make your audience directly *connect* to your topic. When speaking to them, always be sure to make use of plural "you" or "we" language. The objective is to encourage your audience to think about how your topic will be connecting directly to them and their daily lives. You need to make *your* interests *theirs*.

Example

After you have succeeded in gaining audience attention by briefly describing and demonstrating a comparison between a bogus UFO photo and an authentic one supplied by the U.S. Air Force or Pentagon archives, you might say to your room of 30 to 40 listeners who are present:

> ▶ "According to U.S. government statistics, it is not unlikely that perhaps three or maybe even four of us here today, in this very room, could find ourselves reporting our own experience of a UFO sighting."

Your *audience connection statement* is equivalent to the decoy found in creative and successful print and TV advertising. The enticement of the AG catches your audience's attention; now they become interested, and desire to continue listening or watching, to experience just how this product or service may be advantageous to their own well-being.

> ▶ Like good advertising, an *audience connection* motivates your listeners to further watch and listen to what you have to say.

Your Thesis Statement Connection

Now that you have connected your topic directly to your audience, you may begin presenting the *thesis statement*, or broad purpose behind your chosen topic—namely, the reason or rationale for your speaking the very words you are about to offer. This should be only one or two sentences that announce the topic, but which also offer your *approach. It is the main plan of your speech.* It is always better to be *simple* than *complex* when it comes to your thesis statement. For our hypothetical UFO example, you may consider saying something such as:

Example

> ▶ "Today I invite you to consider the possibility of intelligent life (within or even beyond our solar system) which may have been visiting planet Earth by way of what both scientists and defense officials around the world popularly refer to as: UFO sightings."

Announcing your thesis statement after you have connected your listeners helps make them interested in further hearing about your topic.

> ▶ If you begin speaking about your topic first, you then seriously run the risk of losing your audience's focus upon both you and your topic to follow.

We have seen how your introduction is your first communication with your audience. In the opening words of your speech you set the agenda for what is to follow, connect your listeners to your chosen topic, and establish your motivation and purpose for wanting to speak to them in the first place. Your introduction is your first impression, and it can be either a positive or a negative one. The following are some "always rules" to keep in mind when you are crafting your introduction.

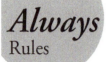

Always A Successful Introduction
Rules

- *Always* be sure that your introduction is muscular and concise. It's supposed to grab everyone's attention and signal the start of your speech. Your audience won't be interested if you simply tell them your name and the title of your speech.

- *Always* be creative and develop different approaches to your introduction, and then select the one which you think is best for your specified audience. Come up with a variety of introductions, and choose the one which you feel will make the greatest initial impact.

- *Always* make the first words before your audience: a quote, an anecdote, a joke, an alarming set of facts or statistics, or a powerful rhetorical question (these are just a few examples!). You must get their attention from the very "get-go."

- *Always* be sure to use "you" or "we" verbal statements. It is the purpose of your introduction to motivate your audience to care about what you are going to talk about later in the body of your speech. Connecting your chosen topic to them and their lives is your main goal.

- *Always* make sure your AG leaves an impact of stimulated curiosity on your audience. Your AG is your first opportunity to get your audience thinking about your speech even before they hear you speak about your topic.

- *Always* be sure *not* to rush through your introduction. Quickly dashing through it will take away from its initial impact, and may even lessen the audience's attention span during the body of your speech.

- *Always* memorize your introduction and practice it a number of times. It should appear and sound effortless, smooth, and inviting. In most cases, a smooth introduction will relax both yourself and your audience.

Your Body Is the Center of Your Speech

Many students struggle with putting together the body of a speech, which is far more meaty and detailed. Often their intended ideas bear little resemblance to their original goals. It is easy for a speech to sound confusing, and drift from jumbled ideas to cluttered ideas. Of course the audience loses interest, and the speech fails to communicate anything in the end.

Keep in mind that the **body** of your speech is its very center, and it includes all of the *main points* and *subpoints* which you hope to convey to your audience. Each of these points must be clear and presented in a logical, connecting sequence. The body of a speech is both the *informational* and *argumentative* core of what every speaker hopes to communicate.

Putting together the body of a speech can sometimes be a challenge, namely because there is the temptation to include *everything*. Not only do you need to narrow down specifically what you want to include in the body, but you have to consider *how* it will be received, and *how* to infuse it with your own conversational tone.

Oftentimes when putting a speech together, you may actually establish the body or *main points* first, so that you can sort out what you really need to present to your audience. In most cases, ideas for the body come more readily and naturally than do the introduction or conclusion; and they should be derived from your *thesis statement.* In a sense, it is helpful to work backwards.

> ▶ Start with your *thesis statement* and work from there in putting together the *main points* or core of your speech. Know *what* you want to say and *when* you want to say it. Afterward, you can develop your introduction and conclusion elements accordingly.

Main Points

If the introduction to your speech may be likened to a plane's takeoff, the *main points* are more akin to the smooth-distanced flight itself. While in the air, the pilot need only make adjustments here and there to weather conditions, but the overall flight is in constant motion and is on its way to its destination.

Your delivery by way of your **main points** is your in-flight travel time. With your *thesis statement* clearly formulated, you now are interested in building a straightforward yet simple structure for the "flight" of your speech. You should begin by writing your main points, or headings, related to the thesis. Remember, these ideas should enhance the thesis, *not* clash with it. Your main points should sustain it, not diverge away from it. It is essential that all of your three to five main points *communicate the essence of your thesis statement* and not meander away from it in different directions, just as a good pilot makes sure his or her aircraft never diverges from its planned route.

You may wish to organize your main points in a progression such as *problem-cause-solution, past-present-future, me-you-they-we,* or in any other fashion which you feel will be clear and logical for your audience to easily follow. There are many progressions and various approaches. Choose the one which makes logical sense for your thesis statement, and the audience for which you hope to offer your speech.

You will discover that it is far easier to consider using a simple fragments as heading points, than detailed phrases or sentences. Details with too much structure will likely cause you to ramble, leading you away from your overall purpose. Details with a simple, concise structure will have stronger organizational impact.

Subpoints

With your main points in place, next write your **subpoints**. These are basically examples, embellishments, and details about each main point. After you have a focused *thesis statement* and useful *main point* headings, adding the *subpoints* should be fairly straightforward, almost like filling in the colorful details. Below each main point heading, you can use different structures, depending upon what you feel may work best for your audience. The following *generic structure* works well for most speeches:

- Present the *premise* of each main point.

- Substantiate or support that premise with concrete examples, (which may include facts, statistics, anecdotes, excerpts, and so on).

- Clearly tie in each main point premise to your *thesis statement.*

- Make a smooth *transition* to the next main point.

- Work your way through each *main point* toward your summary and conclusion.

Example

Premise: Offering the definition of a UFO

Concrete examples: Supply various definitions offered by the U.S., the EU, the airline industry, sci-fi writers, and Hollywood.

Tie-in: Show how these definitions may cause confusion about what a UFO *is* or *is not,* and how this may distort distinguishing authentic sightings from hoaxes.

Transition: "Now that we all understand what defines a UFO, let's take a brief look at the history of UFO sightings, which have their origin in the ancient Near East . . ."

● ● ● ● ● Transitions and Signposts

What are called **transitions** help you shift from one main point to the next, and continuously *signpost* the direction of your speech. A **signpost** is a specific transition that indicates progressive movement in your speech and points toward your conclusion.

Signposts indicate to your audience where you are in your speech, suggest where you hope to go, and also helps bridge thoughts and ideas in a smooth and logical manner. In the main point example offered earlier, which covered the various definitions of UFOs, the *transition* which leads to the next main point about the history of UFOs, was presented as:

> ▶ "Now that we all understand what defines a UFO, let us take a brief look at the history of UFO sightings, which have their origin in the ancient Near East . . ."

For your convenience, here are a few examples of other transitions. The key signposts are marked out for you in italics:

Examples

"*Secondly,* I hope to show that UFOs . . ."

"*Next, we see yet another* example of UFO archival photos which . . ."

"*Finally, we can distinguish* that UFO hoaxes have been . . ."

"*In addition to these*, other startling facts about UFO sightings include . . ."

As you offer information in your main points and subpoints, be sure to draw on your past experiences, research, or a collection of stories, humor, and statistical data to support your overall thesis statement. Remember, a smooth transition between each main point (or subpoint) provides continuity, and in turn helps the flow of your speech.

> Other helpful signposts may include: *besides . . . , and still . . . , likewise . . . , sometimes . . . , speaking of . . . , meanwhile . . . , even so . . . , just as important . . .* , and *on the other hand . . . .*

● ● ● ● ● Your Audience Preview

Your *audience preview* is the summation of your main points and subpoints, condensed in a very concise and conversational manner. In your **audience preview** you sample which main points will be contained in the body of your speech. As you may recall, your speech should have as few as three main points, to perhaps as many as four or five. More than five is not recommended.

As a preview for your audience: briefly and concisely list or discuss your main points for your audience in a conversational manner. This simply assists them in understanding how you hope to proceed. There should be no surprises later in the actual body of the speech. In the preview you are simply offering them your plan or organization before launching into the body of the speech. You audience preview should be inserted between your thesis statement and your main points and subpoints which will follow. Many speech experts consider the *audience preview* to be the last step in the introduction of a speech. Recall that our hypothetical *thesis statement* is:

> "Today I invite you to consider the possibility of intelligent life (within or even beyond our solar system) which may have been visiting planet Earth by way of what both scientists and defense officials around the world popularly refer to as: UFO sightings."

Your *audience preview* for our example speech on UFOs might go something like this:

Example

"In the next few minutes, I hope to discuss both the evidence *for* and *against* the existence of UFO sightings. By first defining UFOs, along with a brief history of them, which spans over four centuries from the ancient Near East to the present, I intend to offer you what both scientists and U.S. Pentagon officials understand about legitimate, unexplained UFO sightings."

"By further supplying you with documented evidence in support of hoaxes and bogus claims, I anticipate inviting you, the curious listener, to come to your own conclusions about UFOs."

"As you will see, today there is supporting evidence for both claims. In everything from alien dolls and T-shirts to blockbuster Hollywood films, our popular culture seems obsessed with the on-going controversy about the possible existence of intelligent life beyond our planet Earth . . ."

Your Conclusion Is Your Last Impression

As with landing a plane *via* a steady, safe descent, any skilled pilot knows that he or she must also reach their targeted destination on schedule. As for the public speaker, so too a skilled descent, along with a targeted destination, is what completes the "flight" of the speech. In order to fully complete a smooth "touchdown," your speech must also leave a memorable impression on your audience—namely, something they can take home with them.

> ► The conclusion of your speech is not only your last opportunity to teach or persuade your audience, but also a last chance for you to leave a positive, lasting *impression of yourself* as a public speaker.

In the **conclusion**, you should: *signal that you are concluding, summarize the main points* of your speech, and then offer your *attention-retainer* (AR); and lastly, provide an *emotional sense of closure* by offering your dismissal to your listeners. While your conclusion should be brief and tight, it also has to be *emphatic, dynamic,* and *confident.* Your final "thank you" to your audience should draw honest, unforced applause (not to mention at times a bit of vocal affirmation as well), thus leaving your audience with a sense of enjoyment and appreciation for your having spoken to them.

Signal That You Are Concluding

Most audiences appreciate it when you clearly signal that you are about to end your speech. Your signal helps them to prepare intellectually and emotionally for your final remarks. As you hint that you are beginning to make your "descent" from the air, some will perk up, while others will even begin to start thinking about questions which they might ask you. Others will stop fidgeting, some may even sit up in their chairs, and, yes, occasionally a few audience members will seem to be glancing at their watches (hopefully in disbelief that the time has gone by so swiftly!).

Example

You may say: *"well, before I end today . . ."* or . . . *"finally, before I conclude I would like to say that . . ."* or something creative which indicates that your speech is beginning its final descent.

Summarize Your Main Points

Your conclusion must include not only a summary of the *thesis statement,* but also a review of the main points (excluding the subpoints) of the speech. In most cases your summary of the main points and thesis statement are bookends which parallel those previously stated in your audience preview, found between the end of your introduction, and the beginning of your main points.

Structurally speaking, your summary and restatements bring your speech back to where you first started, and reinforce to your audience that you have kept your obligation to them as a speaker. Functionally, they help remind the audience that the end of the speech has basically achieved all which they were told it would do in the first place.

Example

"In summary: I hope today that you have come to realize what is meant by the term UFO, and that there is ample evidence both *for* and *against* the existence of authentic UFO sightings. By offering examples from both reputable scientists and military experts worldwide, I hope I have shown that UFOs can be a contentious subject. Along with a brief history from ancient times to the very present, hopefully you now understand that UFO sightings are nothing new, and that both unexplained and hoaxed sightings abound and most likely will continue to do so."

Retaining Audience Attention

Now that you have indicated the end of your speech and have concisely summarized, you need to offer something which will help remind your audience of your speech topic sometime in the future, long after your speech has ended. We call this clincher an **attention-retainer** or **AR.** Retaining the attention of your audience can be a challenge, but also an opportunity for personal invention, creativity, and originality, just as with the AG offered earlier as part of the introduction.

Namely, your goal is to help your audience remember something about your speech topic, long after they have left your presence. But more importantly and perhaps less ambitious, is that an AR should help bring everything you have said to a final, collected experience which provides closure. Like an AG, an AR can be fun, inspirational, serious, hilarious, and even sacred as well.

Your AR may include everything from personal stories and quotations, to music and photos, just as your AG may have done. In some cases if you began with a quote in your AG, you may also end with a quote in your AR. Or if you started with sounds and images, you may also wish to conclude with sounds and images as well.

Keep in mind that the nature of your AR reinforces your general motives for speaking, your topic choice, your audience's demographic, and even the limited amount of time you may have been given for your speech. At best, your AR should remind your audience that your topic exists, and that perhaps they should consider further investigating it on their own time. The following are five "help reasons" every speaker should keep in mind when seeking to use an effective attention-retainer, or AR.

Five Help Reasons for Using an Effective AR

1. To help refocus *awareness on the relevance* of your chosen topic . . .
   Remember: Your AR must directly relate back to and reinforce your main purpose.

2. To help entice your audience *to think about* your chosen topic well beyond your speech . . .
   Remember: You must find a final way to place your speech topic in their memory.

3. To help maintain a *communicational relationship* between your audience and your topic . . .
   Remember: Both visual and sound resources give them a chance to reconnect elsewhere.

4. To help encourage further interest, and even public action surrounding your topic . . .
   Remember: Being entertaining and creative with your AR can be a cause for future action.

5. To help establish a further *connective premise* for your audience beyond your speech . . .
Remember: Your AR can serve as a guide for future investigative research on your topic.

Be Sure to Practice Your ARs

You should always practice your attention-retainers beforehand. Remember that smoothly organizing any technical resources requires both early planning and practice. You should practice using any visual, sound, or video resources until they become an instinctive element of your conclusion. Always have a backup plan should all go wrong and fail you.

Your AR, like your AG, should be smooth and effortless. It should not take any time or attention away from the body of your overall spoken message, but simply enhance it.

> ▶ Always clearly practice your AR. Arriving well in advance and checking on the technical needs for your speech, will help avoid nervousness and stumbling into a weak conclusion.

If you discover that you cannot conclude as you had planned, you may have to resort to a joke, a humorous story, or maybe even using the chalk or white board as part of your bailout plan. If at all possible, try to bring backup materials such as printed graphs, charts, or photographs which may easily substitute for failed technology.

Remember, your conclusion is your last opportunity for your chosen topic to make a lasting impression upon your audience. Because final impressions make a long-lasting mark (and also determine the grade from your instructor!), you want to formulate a conclusion which "descends" and finally "lands" your "speech-airplane" with a smooth touchdown at your planned destination. Your concluding summary and AR should be your last emphatic and possibly even dramatic opportunity, to impart a lasting consciousness about your topic—an impression which will remain long after you have given your speech.

> ▶ No matter how excellent your speech may have been, audiences generally enjoy an AR, something to rekindle their earlier enthusiasm for your speech, something which is stimulating and will continue to succeed long after you are gone from their presence.

Always Rules   A Successful Conclusion

- *Always* be sure that your conclusion is brief and concise. It's supposed to wrap things up and *signal* the end of your speech. Your audience won't be content if your conclusion is lengthy and drawn out.

- *Always* be creative and develop different approaches to your conclusion, and then select the one which you think is best for your given audience. Come up with a variety of conclusions, and *then* choose the one which you feel will make the most impact.

- *Always* use quick summary statements in your conclusion, to briefly abridge what you've said during your speech. A swift overview of your main points is all that is really necessary.

- *Always* be sure to *never* present any new information. Your conclusion should only review what you've offered in the body of your speech, and at best, you should only offer a last personal opinion or final commentary.

- *Always* keep in mind that your AR should leave a memorable impact on your audience. It is your final opportunity to leave your audience thinking about your speech topic after they exit.

- *Always* be sure *not to rush* through your conclusion. Quickly dashing through it will take away from its final effect, and may even lessen the impact you offered in the body of your speech.

- *Always* memorize your conclusion and practice it several times. It should appear and sound effortless, smooth, and convincing.

Your Final Thank You

The very last part of your speech should be your sincere and heartfelt gratitude to your audience. A **thank you** lets them know that you have indeed concluded, and that there are no more ideas, intentions, or surprises to follow. If you make use of projected photographs or video clips, or any other type of electronic media, do not leave your audience hanging. Let them know that you are finished. Not saying "thank you" leaves a sense of uncertainty. Never let your audience have to figure out for themselves that you have concluded. Always make it clear to them that you have finished.

Your **A**, **B**, **C**s for an Effective Introduction, Body, and Conclusion

While **introducing** your speech you should *always be sure to*:

A Approach your entire introduction with creativity, confidence, and practice.
B Realize that your AG is vital to stimulating your audience to listen further.
C Present a clear and concise thesis statement from the very beginning.

While offering your **main points** you should *always be sure to*:

A Never have more than three to five main points (with subpoints) in your speech.
B Offer your audience a clear and well-focused thesis statement.
C Preview all of your main points, and connect them to the thesis statement.

While **concluding** your speech you should *always be sure to*:

A Clearly signal to your audience that you are working your way toward concluding your speech.
B Briefly review or summarize all of your main points (not your subpoints).
C Realize that your AR is vital to your speech topic's living on beyond you.

When **thanking** your audience you should *always be sure to:*

A Clearly offer a word of genuine thanks and appreciation to them.

B Never let your AR end without you personally offering gratitude afterward.

C If a few hands go up, after the applause, acknowledge a comment or two.

Summary

In this chapter we have explored what it means to make effective use of an *introduction, body,* and *conclusion* when offering a speech in public. We have explored how it is necessary to use these three important elements to focus upon the interests and needs of your intended audience; and have stated that creating an organized "flight plan" for your speech is also vital for its successful takeoff, smooth flight, and eventual descent and level landing at your destination.

Making use of an introduction and conclusion leaves a lasting impression not only on your topic choice, but also on you as a public speaker. Having a clear and creative *attention-getter* and *attention-retainer* add interest, fun, and, most importantly, audience focus throughout the beginning, ending, and perhaps even the entire duration of your speech, if done conscientiously.

The *body* of your speech should have no more than perhaps three to five *main points,* and each of these should have no more than perhaps three to five *subpoints.* Your body is the core of your message, and it is the very nature of the speech itself. The body of your speech should be informed by your *thesis statement,* which in turn should continuously fuel and guide your speech to its final conclusion. It is important to never diverge from it, and to continuously build upon it until you reach your concluding remarks.

By utilizing a well-structured introduction, body, and conclusion, along with proper research on your topic, you should be well prepared to make a powerful and long-lasting impression upon your audience, and avoid common pitfalls, like rambling and diverging too far from your planned intentions.

It is important to keep a healthy connection with your audience, and to make everything you say and do directly relevant to them as your patient listeners. Like all aspects of performance, your introduction, body, and conclusion may either detract from or enhance your communicational connection with your audience. If you are willing to take the time and energy to prepare these three major elements of your speech, you will be more than likely to succeed not only in furthering the interests of your chosen topic, but also in making a positive impression of yourself as a public speaker for future speeches to follow.

Discussion Questions

1. Why is it essential for public speakers to establish a sense of credibility by previewing the main points of their speech? Why do you think it is always important to let your audience know everything you hope to cover in advance, and offer no surprises later? Do you believe that is unethical to offer surprise elements in a speech; why or why not?

2. What do we mean by the term *signposts?* How is their ultimate function clearly helpful to both the speaker and the audience?

3. Why is it essential to never begin a speech with "Hello, my name is _____ and I am here to speak to you today about _____"? Why is an AG so important?

4. What is meant by the term *relic?* What do you understand the distinction between a relic and an artifact to be? Do you think that either is ever necessary for a speech to be fully effective; why or why not? Should they ever be avoided at all costs?

5. Why is it vital to have a clear and well-thought-out *thesis statement;* and how does it connect to your eventual three to five main points which must be covered in the body of the speech? What is the danger of not having a clear and focused thesis statement?

● ● ● ● ● Quick Quiz

Match the following capsule sentences with the correct letter of the term which best describes the key terms or phrases discussed in this chapter.

1. _____ A philosophical inquiry which usually requires no expected answer.

2. _____ A personal story or narrative illustration which may serve as an attention-getter.

3. _____ The three to five core ideas which comprise the body of your speech.

4. _____ Your AG combined with your audience preview which supports your thesis.

5. _____ Objects directly from or directly connected to your speech topic, such as samples.

6. _____ Your examples, embellishments, and details about each of your main points.

7. _____ Effective and creative ways of getting your audience's early attention and interest.

8. _____ Completing your thesis obligation with a strong summary and a powerful AR.

9. _____ Words or phrases which connect your main points toward your conclusion.

10. _____ Creative ways of getting your audience to think about your speech after it is over.

A. Conclusion	**B.** AG	**C.** Signposts
D. AR	**E.** Rhetorical question	**F.** Introduction
G. Main points	**H.** Anecdote	**I.** Subpoints
J. Relics		

PART III
Organization, Preparation, and Delivery

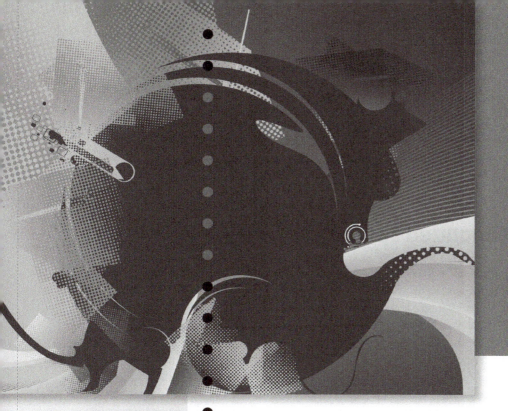

KEY TERMS

organization

path markers

mark of equilibrium

mark of agreement

mark of consistency

mark of major focus

mark of minor focus

conscious choice

outline

transitions

Q & A session

"Organizing is what you do before you do something, so that when you do it, it is not all mixed up and confusing."
—A. A. Milne, creator of *Winnie-the-Pooh*

"I spend eight months outlining and researching the novel before I begin to write a single word of the prose."
—Jeffery Deaver, writer

As was mentioned in Chapter 6, anyone who is preparing to offer a spoken presentation before a live audience may be a bit uneasy about putting together the core, or *body*, of their speech. It goes without saying that the body of a speech requires a central focus, and is the product of timely research, outlining, and attention to details. Unfortunately, there is always the danger that your intended thoughts and ideas will bear little resemblance to your original goals in the end. It is very easy to put together a speech which may sound confusing and waft from *jumbled point* to *jumbled idea*, and then on to even more cluttered information and ideas. An organized outline is the key to success. As A.A. Milne asserts in the above quote: *"Organizing is what you do before you do something, so that when you do it, it is not all mixed up and confusing."* This is a great word to the wise, and is a must for the introduction, body, and conclusion of your speech.

After your introduction and conclusion, the body of your speech is both the *informational* and *argumentative* core of what you hope to communicate to your audience. It is the very GPS of your entire speech. It must be highly organized, or both you and your listeners will end up lost and tossed out of range from your intended destination. Your body is a composite of everything you plan to present, and includes all of the *main points* and *subpoints* that you hope to convey faithfully as your map.

Organization helps you *narrow down* specifically what you want to include in your speech, but you have to consider *how* your speech will be received and *how* to infuse it with your own conversational tone. Each of your points must be clearly organized and then presented in a logical, connecting outline. In this chapter we will explore how a well-organized outline is your key to arriving at your destination.

The Benefits of an Organized Speech

A well-organized speech, as you may imagine, simply does not take shape on its own, just as a well-organized flight plan or a mapped-out guidance sequence on a GPS system will not materialize without any conscious input. It takes a bit of determination and some effort, based upon your participation, to reach your desired location in the end. Of course you need to know where you are at any given moment, and where you hope to arrive in the distant future. Ideally your GPS system will help determine the shortest, quickest, and hopefully the safest route for you. In the end, the secure benefits of safely arriving where you need to go are well worth the price of your time and effort to organize.

In general, **organization** is putting things in a helpful order for both you and your audience. It will be different for each speaker. We all organize differently, yet in delivery our personal approach will hopefully prevail. The key to success is to make good *choices* as to which elements to include (and *where* to include them), and of course which elements to *exclude* entirely. A successful speech must embrace some of the research information available, and at the same time consciously exclude perhaps even a larger percentage of it. Organization includes making choices about which elements to include and which to exclude.

> ▶ Organization involves making choices. Those choices ought to be guided, in general, by a few *path markers.* Marking your path helps you stay on the planned route of your speech.

● ● ● ● ● Path Markers

Path markers provide logical and emotional uniformity to your speech. They are akin to passing landmarks while on a trip which let you know that you are still on your mapped course of travel, and are still heading in the right direction. The most important path markers include *mark of equilibrium, mark of agreement, mark of consistency,* and also marks of *major* and *minor focus.*

Mark of Equilibrium

The **mark of equilibrium** suggests that the three elements of your speech— *introduction, body, and conclusion*—should be largely proportional, and be in a comfortable relationship to each other. There must be a sense of proportion and *equilibrium* among each of them. Your introduction and conclusion are to be of meaningful substance, and should not be simply tacked on for the sake of convenience. They are to be well-thought-out, highly relevant, and by and large have an equal effect on your listeners, as do each of your main points.

Consequently, the main points (as well as your subpoints) of your speech should also be in equilibrium. No one point *or* subpoint should be overemphasized, given too much focus, or overburdened with too much information over the others.

In general, the complete *introduction* to your speech itself should comprise about 15 percent to no more than roughly 20 percent of your speaking time. Ideally the *body* of the speech should take about 70 percent to, say, 85 percent of your concentrated focus. This of course will depend upon how many main points you choose to offer. It is important to note that your *conclusion* (although a bit shorter in length) should take no less than 10 percent to 15 percent of your overall presentation time, in order to leave a lasting impression on your listeners.

> ▶ Keep in mind that the amount of time allotted for each of your *main points* will fluctuate, depending on how many you choose to offer. But as a general marker, each point should be about the same in length, focus, and detail you offer.

Mark of Agreement

Everything you offer in your speech should continuously communicate the same overall intent and purpose. This helps you remain *en route* and not succumb to the temptation of wandering away from your goals. Keeping your goals in mind can often be a difficult chore. Even many experienced and more-mature speakers can get off the topic, lose sight of what they were hoping to say, and go off on a tangent. *Try not to be among them.* Stay on your route.

Staying on your route of course requires that you scratch some of the informational facts and fascinating material which you may enjoy about your topic. If you need to go off your route a bit, you can always save such parallel information for a brief discussion period afterward, or even choose to make such tangential comments during a brief Q & A session.

> ▶ The **mark of agreement,** in a nutshell, states that if something does not communicate *or* contribute directly to your intended speech goals, it should be eliminated from your speech.

Mark of Consistency

> ▶ The **mark of consistency** means that the connections among the various parts of your speech should be understandable and logical to your listeners. It is important to be logical and sequential, just as the results from any good GPS system might be. *Point A* must clearly lead to *points B* and *C* and then to point *D* and so on. Always keep an easy-to-follow sequence. Dissimilar facts and figures or disjointed anecdotes and examples of events, help confuse and lose your audience. Nothing is worse than following confusing directions. Consistency of facts and examples are very important to an audience. Being consistent keeps you and them *en route.*

If you are offering a more persuasive type speech, you should be sure to establish an argument or case, and then consistently pursue that argument with unswerving proposals for solving your case or cases at hand. You should not burden your audience with unrelated stories, facts, or events which may have occurred parallel to or remote from your argumentative goals.

▶ The relationships among the various parts of your speech should be clear to your audience. The mark of consistency helps maintain listener interest and creates speaker credibility.

Mark of Major Focus

As a speaker with just a limited amount of time to present what you need to say, you must always remember that only the most important ideas should be your focus. Try not to spotlight larger amounts of time speaking about minor points, and lesser amounts of time speaking about your major points. You do not want to give your audience a mistaken impression of what is important and what is not. Sometimes even more-skilled speakers will tend to emphasize insignificant facts or figures, or perhaps even highlight minor details or anecdotes which only obscure the message. This eats up time, promotes the trivial, and in the end gives your audience mixed feelings about what is important, and what is not. Keep your major points large and your minor points small.

▶ Always choose which are the major points in your speech, and focus upon them appropriately. The **mark of major focus** means that you clearly emphasize and focus only upon your main points.

Mark of Minor Focus

As an organized speaker, you should try to help your audience recognize the **marks of minor focus,** which are clearly your supporting ideas or subpoints. Of course, every organized speech will have three to five main points, and each of them in turn will have thoughts and ideas which are second or even third or fourth place, to the main points. At times in a longer speech, you may even have subpoints which are even further beyond those in fourth place, and so on. It is important to keep your minor points in minor focus at all times.

Be aware that mixing up major and minor points creates confusion, and consequently gives mixed messages to your audience. At times the danger is that even you, the speaker, may succumb to such confusion as well. You risk losing your focus and may start going off track into unmapped GPS territory. This (surprisingly enough) occurs frequently during college and university lectures. Oftentimes a professor will end up way, way off the lecture from the topic designated on the syllabus. This most often occurs because he or she began losing focus between minor and major points. Losing focus can happen even to the best of speakers.

▶ As an organized speaker, you should try to help your audience recognize the *marks of minor focus*, which are clearly your supporting ideas or subpoints. Keeping them in focus, builds a stronger emphasis of priorities among your listeners.

Six Important Reasons for Path Markers

The following are six important reasons for using path markers. Always keep markers in mind while organizing and then eventually outlining your speech. Like a GPS system, they help mark your way.

1. To help you become an organized public speaker you must make clear choices . . .
   Remember: that those choices ought to be guided, in general, by five *path markers.* They help you stay on the planned route of your speech.

2. To help make your speech well-rounded and not become lopsided for your listeners . . .
   Remember: to keep your *introduction, body,* and *conclusion* in healthy *equilibrium.* Never permit your introduction or conclusion to be weak, in contrast to the main points in your body. All three sections should be well-accounted-for in any well-planned speech.

3. To help add a continual sense of where you are going at all times for your audience . . .
   Remember: if anything you do or say does not agree with *or* does not directly contribute to your intended goals, it should be eliminated from your speech. Do not give in to the temptation of needing to use all of your data, even it if fascinates you.

4. To help remain *consistent* and thus maintain listener interest, and speaker credibility . . .
   Remember: that dissimilar facts and figures or disjointed anecdotes or extraneous events help confuse and lose your audience, while consistency helps maintain listener interest and creates ongoing speaker credibility. Everything should connect at all times—even your visual and sound examples.

5. To help keep your audience riveted on the main focus and goal of your speech . . .
   Remember: to clearly choose which are the *major points* in your speech, and focus upon them appropriately. Your main points are the very core of your message. They are your main focus.

6. To help keep your audience attentive to the minor supporting details of your speech . . .
   Remember: to clearly choose which are the *minor points,* and to focus upon them appropriately in a manner which largely sustains your major points and does not compete with them.

Organizing Your Speech

After you've determined exactly where you want to travel with your speech, by way of your *thesis statement* and overall general goals (informative or persuasive), and after you have generally analyzed your audience and are familiar with *who* they are and *what* they are about in terms of their demographic and their general viewpoints, you must now spend some quality time to organize.

Organization will pay off for both yourself and your listeners. Even if you are not accustomed to translating your thoughts into a logical or progressive order which others may follow, it will be vital to your comfort (and that of your listeners) to take the time to do so.

Every speaker's organizational patterns will be different, even if they are on the very same topic, and even if they have the same supporting materials. Two different speeches on the same topic rarely, if ever, look or sound similar. Each speech is always unique to the presenter.

As you begin work on organizing your ideas and facts, you will have to make choices regarding which ideas to embrace, and when and where to include them. Other ideas, no matter how fascinating, will have to be eliminated. You should always have more information than you can possibly make use of in any one speech presentation.

▶ Making a **conscious choice** means that you personally *choose*, rather than just present your ideas as they come to you, or as you discovered them in your research process. Conscious choices uniquely tailor your speech to you.

• • • • • Tracking Your Ideas

The thought behind organizing your information is to make your speech more successful by helping your listeners easily track your ideas. This is most readily done by creating a clear path and reminding your listeners (on a regular basis) of how established research, and your own ideas logically shape each other. As you progress through your presentation, you must frequently remind your audience of how your ideas smoothly fit together. If you are successful, there is very little likelihood that they will have to do it for themselves. In turn, they are less likely to start thinking in the wrong direction, or to begin making connections and assumptions which will lead them to frustration and confusion.

Tracking your ideas is a powerful informative as well as persuasive tool. For example, if you wish to show how the U.S. Government's unexplained sightings of UFOs contribute to the likelihood of intelligent life beyond Earth, then being clear, logical, and consistent will make your argument far more difficult to refute. If your claims are clear, honest, and on track, you may just find yourself with some new friends who wish to share your enthusiasm in the search for extraterrestrial life.

Organizing Your General Outline

To begin with, as you may suspect, an **outline** is a general plan of what you are going to actually present to your audience. It should include the arrangement and order of your general purpose, audience demographic, actual location, time of day, and any time constraints involved, and so on. Your outline should also include the general approach to both your introduction and your conclusion. In more detail, your outline should also delineate each of your main points (anywhere from three to five) and your subsequent minor points, along with any visual or sound resources you may hope to use. Keep in mind that:

▶ If your speech is to have four main points, then the body of your outline should have four main point sections as well, plus two additional sections for your introduction and conclusion, respectively.

• • • • • Transitions

The general organization of your speech is kept smooth by what are known as transitions. **Transitions** are phrases which help your audience connect to your next main point (or even subpoints). Transitions make it easy for the audience to move easily not only from one point to the next, but also eventually toward the final transition and then to your overall conclusion.

Clear transitions are statements such as: *". . . therefore, as you may clearly see, next we have . . ."*; *". . . this leads us to my next point, which is . . ."*; and even *"Now, let's take a brief look at a powerful photo which illustrates my third point . . . ."* Transitions help your audience follow you and enjoy the presentation, by not having to make connections on their own.

Shaping Your General Outline

Shaping a general outline which encompasses everything from your *thesis statement* and general goals, to your attention-getter (AG), main points, and final summary and conclusion is the master output of your self-designed GPS coordinates. Understanding and having a straightforward outline is the main key to organization, which leads to arrival at your conclusion.

The following is both a general and a partially specific outline template. It is shaped upon our textbook theme of UFOs. Only the general details and the main point headings are provided, since they are included in the thesis statement. As you will see, the supporting subpoints can later be filled in, based upon those informational choices found in the never-ending amount of research data available on UFO sightings, including both the hoaxes and the more credible unexplained ones. Following this outline is a clean template which you may use to shape your own outline based upon your own chosen topic for your speech.

General Topic: UFOs

Audience Profile:

Who: My introductory speech class at my college or university.

When/Where: My 11:00 a.m. class meeting, in a midsized classroom in the School of Communication building, which has roughly twenty-two students in attendance.

Anticipated Time: Roughly a seven-minute speech as clocked by my practice speeches with my best friend

Audience Range: Highly diverse in race, creed, age, and even sexual orientation, *etc.*

Topic Background: No major topic limits or very little, as most of my audience will be, at minimum, moderately familiar with UFO phenomena as presented in the news/TV programs; and will most likely have had general exposure to both hoaxes and the unexplained sightings on special cable programs and in Hollywood films or documentaries.

Speech Type: Informative; I will be careful not to show my personal bias in favor of unexplained UFO sightings; and thus will attempt to offer a balanced approach in my speech.

Thesis Statement/Purpose: To inform my audience of what defines a UFO sighting, the history of sightings, beginning in ancient times and to until the present; and to briefly inform them of both hoaxes and the unexplained facts provided by my research. My overall purpose is to let my listeners decide for themselves about the possibility of intelligent life visiting planet Earth.

Organizational Method or Approach: I plan to take a chronological/historical sequence, from ancient times to the present.

I. **Introduction**

   A. **Attention-Getter (AG):** A quick 30-second TV clip from *Larry King Live* with former President Jimmy Carter speaking about his own UFO sighting experience.

   B. **Thesis Statement:** "I hope today to present both the evidence for and against UFOs, although both unexplained and clearly hoaxed sightings are on record, and no data supports a conclusion in either direction. In the end, only each of us may decide for ourselves if our skies have been visited by intelligent beings from beyond planet Earth."

   C. **Preview of Main Points:** "I would like to begin this morning by defining for you the various meanings of the term UFO, followed by a brief history of UFO sightings from ancient times to the present, along with some amusing UFO hoaxes beginning in the late 19th century. Lastly, I would like to share with you a bit of data supporting the unexplained and credible NASA/Pentagon UFO sightings, in harmony with that which we just witnessed from former President Jimmy Carter."

Transition to the body of your speech

II. **Body**

   A. **Main Point #1:** Defining the various meanings of the term UFO

      1. Subordinate point (e.g., "According to . . .")
         a. Support (e.g., example, statistic, visual, testimonial)
         b. Support

      2. Subordinate point
         a. Support
         b. Support

Transition

   B. **Main Point #2:** Brief history of UFO sightings from ancient times to the present

      1. Subordinate point
         a. Support
         b. Support

      2. Subordinate point
         a. Support
         b. Support

Transition

   C. **Main Point #3:** UFO hoaxes beginning in the late 19th century

      1. Subordinate point
         a. Support
         b. Support

      2. Subordinate point
         a. Support
         b. Support

Transition

    D. Main Point #4: Unexplained and credible NASA/Pentagon UFO sightings

        1. Subordinate point
          a. Support
          b. Support

        2. Subordinate point
          a. Support
          b. Support

Transition

III. Conclusion

    A. Signal Closing

    B. Briefly Restate Thesis/Purpose

    C. Quickly Review Main Points
        1. Main point #1
        2. Main point #2
        3. Main point #3
        4. Main Point #4

    D. Attention-Retainer (AR): A 30-second video clip from the Hollywood film *Close Encounters of the Third Kind* directed by Steven Spielberg

    E. Final Thank You: "I hope this morning that you have had a brief taste of the controversy surrounding UFO sightings; so that the next time you look up into the sky and notice a loud flying object, you will ask yourself whether it is a saucer from Mars, or just simply another jet plane *en route* to O'Hare filled with alien tourists headed for Navy Pier. *Thank you* for your attention."

General Topic: _____

Audience: _____

Who: _____

When/Where: _____

Anticipated Time: _____

Audience Range: _____

Topic Background: No major topic limits or:

_____
_____
_____

Speech Type: _____

Thesis Statement/Purpose: To inform my audience of:

_____
_____
_____
_____

Organizational Method or Approach: I plan to:

_____
_____
_____
_____
_____

I. Introduction

A. Attention-Getter (AG):

_____
_____
_____
_____

B. Thesis Statement:

_____
_____
_____
_____

C. Preview of Main Points:

_____
_____
_____

D. Transition to the Body of Your Speech:

_____
_____
_____

II. Body

A. Main Point #1:

_____
_____
_____

    1. Subordinate point (e.g., "According to . . ."):

_____
_____

        a. Support:

_____

_____

        b. Support:

_____

_____

    2. Subordinate point:

_____

        a. Support:

_____

_____

        b. Support:

_____

_____

Transition

  B. Main Point #2:

_____

_____

_____

    1. Subordinate point:

_____

        a. Support:

_____

_____

        b. Support:

_____

_____

    2. Subordinate point:

_____

        a. Support:

_____

_____

        b. Support:

_____

_____

Transition

C. Main Point #3:

_____
_____
_____

   1. Subordinate point:

   _____
   _____

     a. Support:

     _____
     _____

     b. Support:

     _____
     _____

   2. Subordinate point:

   _____
   _____

     a. Support:

     _____
     _____

     b. Support:

     _____
     _____

Transition

D. Main Point #4:

_____
_____

   1. Subordinate point:

   _____
   _____

     a. Support:

     _____
     _____

     b. Support:

     _____
     _____

   2. Subordinate point:

   _____
   _____

     a. Support:

     _____
     _____

      b. Support:

_____

_____

Transition

III. Conclusion

  A. Signal Closing:

_____

_____

  B. Briefly Restate Thesis/Purpose:

_____

_____

  C. Quickly Review Main Points:

    1. Main point #1: _____

    2. Main point #2: _____

    3. Main point #3: _____

    4. Main Point #4: _____

  D. Attention-Retainer (AR):

_____

_____

_____

_____

  E. Final Thank You:

_____

_____

Beyond Your Outline

Going beyond your outline is permitted, if you wish to allow your audience to ask questions after your presentation. This is, of course, a wonderful way to strengthen your message and continue to help make your topic even further relevant to your listeners. If you are given the opportunity for questions and answers, what is termed **Q & A,** you are more likely to leave your speech without misinterpretations or any misconceptions about the information or ideas you delivered.

There are many benefits of a Q & A session, especially the strengthening and reinforcement of your overall intentions and purpose. Q & A does require you to speak apart from your outline, and does take a bit of courage, particularly if you are new to public speaking. It allows for complete face-to-face conversation, with virtually continual eye contact—no longer any room for frequently glancing at your outline.

▶ It is advisable to create the right conversational energy among your listeners, by telling them early in the presentation that you will have a Q & A period, should they have a need to express themselves, or require any further clarification or questions.

If someone else will be introducing your speech (say, beyond a classroom presentation), be sure to have that individual briefly state your willingness to answer questions at the end of your presentation. Listeners are often more likely to ask questions if you announce at the beginning that they will have an opportunity later to offer their questions and thoughts.

Conducting Your Q & A Session

As you initiate questions, always be sure to directly look at the individual offering the question, and then repeat it simply. If you find that you have a large audience, or if you need a moment to think, or if the question was very involved, ask the asker to loudly repeat it once more for all to hear. By repeating the question, you also ensure that you yourself understood what was being asked. Be sure to answer the question before the entire audience, while being careful not to actually address the questioner directly—as this is now public information which you are going to offer everyone. Keep in mind that you are still under public speaking conditions, and that the entire room should be able to hear your answer. It is also helpful to stand where you are equally distant from all members of your audience. As you conclude your answer, feel free to glance back at the person who asked the question. This helps to confirm that you attempted to answer the question in a satisfactory manner.

▶ Always be sure to keep every response you offer brief and to the point. You risk causing boredom, should you take too long to answer questions. If at all, attempt to answer with a brief "yes" or "no," which keeps the energy moving and will help keep audience interest flowing.

Keep in mind that it is vital during your Q & A session to continually maintain control of the speaking situation. In a sense, you are now giving a second speech when you open your presentation for audience participation, except that this time there are risks of losing control and letting things fall into a state of disorganization. You should always expect the possibility of things getting a bit disorganized at times. Therefore, give the impression of being in control. Never be fearful of saying, "I am not sure" or "I don't know," and then gently move on to the next question. If necessary, you may announce that when you have the opportunity, you will be pleased to get back to any unanswered questions with perhaps an electronic response at a later time.

Lastly, do not be afraid to be gently confront the questioner, if you feel the inquiry is not appropriate or relevant to the situation at hand. Your response might be, *"Thank you, but your question (or comment) doesn't quite relate to, or fit the circumstances of, our discussion here today."* Never lose your cool. If there's a confrontation, simply diffuse it and announce that you will be happy to speak to them privately about their question or comment later.

▶ Keep in mind that many public speeches actually involve two presentations: the official speech you outlined, and the second Q & A session that may follow. For each one, you must remain in control and confident at all times.

Your **A**, **B**, **C**s for Organizing a General Outline with Q & A

While *outlining* your speech you should *always be sure to:*

A Approach your topic by making clear, conscious choices from your research.

B Realize that you must *choose* to exclude certain appealing information.

C Never let your outline wander off-course; stay with your thesis statement.

While choosing no more than five main points, *always be sure to:*

A Take the time to keep your audience in mind as to their previous knowledge of your topic.

B Offer important *supporting* information only in your subpoints.

C Connect all your points by making use of clear transitions between each one.

While making your way toward your conclusion, *always be sure to:*

A Include a statement which signals to your audience that you are beginning to conclude.

B Briefly restate your main purpose and your thesis statement to your listeners.

C Smoothly review each of your main points very briefly in your conclusion.

After you have spoken, and used your AR, which may be visual or aural, *always be sure to:*

A Personally offer a word of thanks to your audience directly as your closing words.

B Save any information which you may have not spoken about for an audience Q & A.

C Diffuse any confrontations, and speak privately to questioners about any problems they have.

Summary

In this chapter we have explored what it means to make good use of organizational skills. Public speakers should be able to make conscious choices about what to present to their listeners, based upon an overabundance of their research findings. Organization is vital because it puts things in helpful order, for both you and your audience. Organization will be different for each speaker. We all organize differently, yet in the end our personal approach hopefully will prevail in a successful speech which an audience will both follow and enjoy.

By making good use of path markers, a speaker provides logical and emotional uniformity to a presentation. Path markers are akin to passing landmarks while on a trip. They let you, as the presenter, know that you are still on your mapped course of travel, and are continuing to head in the right direction. Markers include *equilibrium, agreement, consistency,* and also *major* and *minor focus.*

A general plan in the form of an outline is your GPS guide to what you are going to actually present to your audience, in helping them arrive at your intended destination. A good outline should include the arrangement and order of the general purpose of your speech, the nature of your audience, the location, any time constraints, and any other pertinent information to keep you on course. In addition to both your introduction and your conclusion, your outline should delineate what each of your main points (and subsequent subpoints) are, and how you hope to present them in the body of your speech.

Finally, it is helpful to create the right conversational energy among your listeners, by telling them early in the presentation that you will have a Q & A period at the end, should they need to express themselves by way of questions. Your listeners are often more likely to ask questions if you announce to them at the beginning that they will have this opportunity later.

In the end, being organized by way of an outline means arriving at your summary of the main points, offering a powerful attention-remainder, and finally concluding by genuinely thanking your audience.

Discussion Questions

1. In general, what is meant by the term *organization?* Do you think that being organized is critical to having a fully effective speech; why or why not? Is it ever possible to be effective and not be organized?

2. What do we mean when we say that: everything you offer in your speech, should continuously communicate the same overall intent and purpose? How can this be best achieved through an outline?

3. What do we mean by saying that *consistency of facts* and examples are very important to an audience? How does being consistent keep you and them *en route*? What is the risk of not being consistent, if any?

4. Why is it imperative for an organized speaker to help an audience recognize the marks of difference between a major and a minor focus? If the major focus is rooted in the main points, what is the purpose of the minor points or subpoints? Are they really necessary?

5. What are some of the simple rules to keep in mind when offering a Q & A session? Should such a session ever be avoided, or is it always in order if there is sufficient time available for both speaker and audience?

● ● ● ● ● Quick Quiz

Match the following capsule sentences with the correct letter of the term which best describes the key terms or phrases discussed in this chapter.

1. _____ The best form of organizing your speech in a logical-sequential manner.

2. _____ Essentially, the focus of a speech which will support the main points.

3. _____ Having a well-balanced introduction, body, and conclusion in a speech.

4. _____ A general term for keeping both speaker and audience systematized and *en route*.

5. ____ The opportunity for discussion with an audience after a speech has concluded.

6. ____ Highlighting the subpoints which should support the main points in a speech.

7. ____ The opportunity for discussion with an audience after a speech has concluded.

8. ____ Making sure your introduction, body, and conclusion are in healthy balance.

9. ____ Regularity and reliability in a speech being logical and aimed toward its purpose.

10. ____ GPS indicators to help a speech maintain a sense of logic and uniformity.

A. Conscious choice	**B.** Agreement	**C.** Major focus
D. Equilibrium	**E.** Minor focus	**F.** Path markers
G. Organization	**H.** Q & A session	**I.** Consistency
J. Outline		

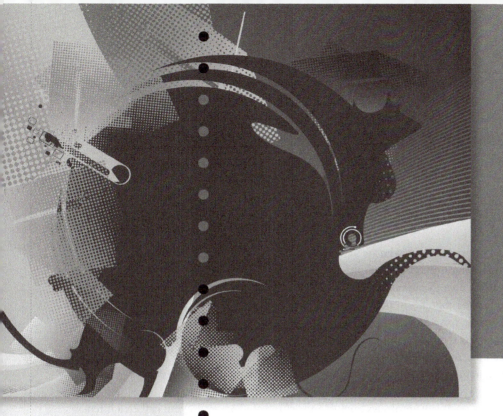

KEY TERMS

word choices

word confidence

vague language

repetitive language

magnified language

jargon

all-purpose words

tangible words

literal words

figurative words

hyperbole

ethical word choices

position of partiality

global plagiarism

patchwork
  plagiarism

incremental
  plagiarism

"One day I will find the right words, and they will be simple."
—Jack Kerouac, "Dharma Bums"

*"The difference between the right word and almost the right word
is the difference between lightning and a lightning bug."*
—Mark Twain

Beyond choosing the right topic and approach for your audience, comes choosing the right words. By being well organized and highly knowledgeable, a public speaker can motivate an audience with his or her choice of words. *How, when,* and *where* to use your words can make all the difference between an ordinary speech and a very powerful one. The best public presenters make use of an extensive vocabulary, good-quality grammar, and accurate pronunciation; and are skilled at making use of various shapes and styles of sentence usage and length. By their word choices they create imagination in an audience.

The competent use of words in public speaking, is a skill which you can continue to learn as you progress with each new speech you offer. Learning a few trouble-free skills, slightly increasing your vocabulary, and acquiring a taste for better phrasing, can greatly improve your use of words in a style which can elevate you from an ordinary to a great public speaker.

It is important as a performer of words in public, that you clearly know how to express an idea in a way which keeps your audience interested not only in your chosen topic, but in your very word choices themselves. A skilled public speaker can inspire people by making use of the appropriate language tailored to his or her own audience. In this chapter, hopefully you will become more aware of how to choose words and phrases that best express your views with clarity and precision. As a public speaker, you should be able to command your words, not merely your research and your ideas. The words you choose say a lot about you as an individual, and also help maintain

133

credibility for you as an ethical speaker. The intentions, attitudes, and assumptions which inform your word choices also can greatly impact your speech.

Appropriate Language Choices

It may come as a surprise to those who are new to public speaking, but a successful speech is really not all about delivering humorous examples, being able to offer a few convincing or alarming quotations, or being able to present a clever anecdote to your audience. Nor is it having all of your main points and subpoints in perfect working order. Those are important, but they are not the complete formula for a powerful presentation. Rather, the approach to creating a powerful speech lies in choosing the *right words,* as Mark Twain aptly announces in the quote offered below our chapter heading. Your entire speech, in essence, is about your words—the *right* words; and, according to Twain, such could be *". . . the difference between lightning and a lightning bug."*

> ▶ If you are always careful in the *choice* of your words, your gathered listeners will most likely have no trouble grasping your ideas, and responding to them in harmony with your goals.

It is important that you be careful enough to choose language that expresses your views with clarity and precision. As a public speaker you should be able to yield command over your words, phrases, and examples. **Word choices** tell us a lot about a speaker, for they are the means by which we express our thoughts and beliefs, and then communicate them to others. They should be carefully chosen. They are the nouns, verbs, adverbs, and adjectives you choose to present within the context of your main points. When we casually talk to a friend face-to-face or even to a small group, we subscribe to a separate set of language choices to communicate with each of them. We change how we communicate on a regular basis. There is a basic difference between a casual conversation with friends, and a formal speech before an audience.

In contrast to face-to-face conversation, when speaking before an audience there is always a definite goal involved. Examples of a goal are: to persuade them to believe that UFOs do indeed exist, and that global governments are collectively covering up the evidence to avert wide spread panic; or to inform them of the evidence which supports many authentic or unexplained UFOs along with myriad data buttressing the thousands of false claims and hoaxes, which have occurred over time. Either way, remember:

> ▶ The words of your speech should complement your thoughts. The words chosen are the channel through which your own ideas are transported to the audience.

Thus, *word choices* give command to your speech. The right choices help you to organize your thoughts in a significant pattern and, in the end, help authenticate your credibility as a competent public speaker. We will now take a look at language in general, to see how it governs the ways in which an audience receives information and how it perceives the speaker offering it to them.

General Language Choices

There are a few general directives to keep in mind, when hoping to make the right choice of words in a speech before gathered listeners. Always remember that as a public speaker, your first aim is to create an impact—*to make a difference.* You want to influence the ideas, thoughts, and even opinions of your audience. Thus, choosing which words to use and meaning exactly what you imply to say are imperative. Your language should contain those words which will create maximum influence on your audience. The precise word choices not only present your ideas in the most credible manner, they also add a bit of uniqueness to your presentation. They can quickly transform a humdrum speaker into a powerful, dynamic one.

● ● ● ● ● Confident Language

At minimum, all public speaking is about convincing an audience to think in your direction and to appreciate your ideas and thoughts, *irrespective* of their own viewpoints. To achieve this, you must be *confident* with all of your word choices, remembering that:

Having **word confidence** means that you make it clear to your audience that you intend to use the very words they are hearing. Being confident implies that you know and understand the words that you are using, and are always in command of them. Never stumble over words or use any word or phrase with a sense of trepidation or uncertainty. Never say, *"I'm not quite sure . . ."* or *"I think that maybe . . ."* Always know about, be well informed about, and be sure of what you say, otherwise *do not say it.* Never sound apologetic, appear unsure, or, worse yet, sound as if the words are not yours or that you are using them for the very first time. If a word is daunting and confusing to you, it will be the same for your audience and will make you appear insecure as a speaker.

● ● ● ● ● Vague Language

Oftentimes speakers will make use of words and phrases that sound indistinct, at times fuzzy, or at best simply vague. **Vague language** is unclear and neutral language which does not indicate apparent ideas, thoughts, or intentions. Vague words and phrases will make your message weakened and stale. It is important to *say exactly what you mean,* and in turn to *mean exactly what you say,* at every point in your speech. Although vague language is not clear language, is not incorrect language either—thus we are tempted to make regular use of it. Public speakers will resort to vague language when they are unable or unwilling to give accurate information, or when they think it is unnecessary or socially out of place to be exact about things. Vague language is very common when using numbers or when expressing quantities, as in: *"a couple of . . ."* or *"only a few of . . . ."* or *"a great percentage of."* These are not clear commodities, and they do not help the listener. Also, when referring to time, exactness is often substituted by inexact phrases such as *"roughly,"* *"about,"* *"around,"* or *"at nighttime."*

> ▶ Using phrases such as *"it's about . . . ,"* *"well, roughly around . . . ,"* *"almost . . . ,"* or *"it's almost . . ."* are all phrases which will leave your audience with an imprecise and vaguely believable sentiment about your overall speech.

Only if you are clearly offering your opinion (and then only on rare occasions) is it permissible to use more-vague language, such as *"I think . . ."* or *"in my estimation . . ."* and the like.

● ● ● ● ● Repetitive Language

If you are prone to using one particular word or phrase repetitively, you run the risk of your presentation sounding monotonous. **Repetitive language** is an excessive use of the same or very similar words and phrases. Repetition is far more than boring; it creates an opportunity for your audience to turn off your speech entirely. Repetition highlights a speaker's failure to understand all the information they are presenting and to see all the angles of an argument. It says to your listeners that you may have not really thought about your topic and looked at it from different perspectives, nor have you understood the depth and breadth of your research—since it appears to lack variety and range.

Various aspects of your speech should require an assortment of expressions, that is, *different* words reflecting a *different* perspective on your topic as it relates to new or changed conditions. Each new main point of your speech requires *its own* new word-choices and phrases. Always be colorful and rearrange your wording in differing ways.

Remember, too, that by not repeating words or phrases over and over, you show your listeners how well you've prepared yourself to speak to them. By utilizing a diverse and subtle variety of expressions, you show how you have thought about your topic and how it relates to your audience. Namely, the depth and range of your word choices indicates the carefulness of organization and preparation you have put into your speech.

> ▶ When your speech is richly textured with a wide variety of word choices, it's easier to believe what you are telling or attempting to convince your audience of; and they are now more likely to become convinced.

● ● ● ● ● Magnified Language

It is important not to give in to the temptation of using an overly inflated vocabulary and, in turn, attempting to sound like a stereotypical public speaker. Never try to impress your listeners by consciously speaking above their heads. When you are speaking, always make sure that you are choosing authoritative words which will make an impact with your audience. **Magnified language** means that a speaker is making word choices that are inflated or which have the intention of making an impression. An inflated vocabulary makes you look and sound inauthentic, and will cause your audience to view you as not being genuine. It is important *to be* a speaker, and not try *to appear* like one.

> ▶ Never seek to impress your listeners. By choosing an honest vocabulary level, you can invite your audience to follow your speech from one main point to the next, while preserving your credibility and not appearing as a show-off.

• • • • • Specialized Language

You should always be careful to choose your language according to the level of your audience (male/female proportions, age groups, religious affiliations, professions, and so on) and what they need and desire to hear from you. Also, take into serious consideration the reason for your speech, so that your language is able to set the right mood. Adapt to the jargon level of your audience. **Jargon** is the technical vocabulary which professionals, such as scientists, lawyers, and various artists, rely upon to communicate with each other. This language is essential within their fields. Jargon may refer to specific ideas, specialized processes, and even tools or instruments. For specialized audiences, jargon is clear-cut and obviously registers with professionals in a given discipline. Unless you define each piece of jargon for your listeners, you will sound and appear intimidating, and cause them to stop listening to you. Use professional jargon when communicating with professional audiences. Eliminate the use of jargon when speaking to a general or diverse audience, for it will always make your speech appear ostentatious and turn listeners off.

On the other hand, do be careful of overly simplistic language as well. If your audience is well-informed or a group of more professionally minded listeners, and you sound overly plain and uncomplicated, they may think less of you and question your credibility and knowledge of the topic. If, for example, you are speaking to the drama or photography club at your school, then photo and stage jargon will most likely be welcomed, even expected.

In short, if your audience is a collection of well-informed and intelligent professionals, use a more formal tone, and fill your speech with logical arguments to appeal to their commonality. On the other hand, if you are addressing an audience who has limited language facility or you are speaking to them in what is their second language, be careful not to make too many language choices based upon cultural phrases, specific idioms, or words and references that may be uncommon to them.

> ▶ Avoid technical language and technical terminology if you are speaking to those outside of your chosen topic. Audiences will quickly tune out if they are presented with jargon or terms they are unfamiliar with.

Always Rules · Using Language Appropriately

- *Always* let your audience come away from your speech feeling as if you just had a public conversation with them and not a lecture, by *choosing your words carefully,* just as you have carefully chosen your topic and what main points to include.

- *Always* remember that *vague words* and phrases will make your message weakened and stale. Always *say exactly what you mean,* and *mean exactly what you say* at every point of your speech.

- *Always* be sure to avoid *repetition.* It creates boredom as well as an opportunity for your audience to turn off your speech entirely. Repetition exposes a speaker's failure to understand all the information, and to see all the various angles of an argument.

- *Always* try not to make use of an overinflated vocabulary, as it will fly high above the heads of your audience, turn them off, and most likely make you look self-important.

- *Always* be sure to choose words according to the make-up of your audience (male/female ratio, age group, religion, professional background, etc.) and what they expect to hear from you. Your word choices should be able to set the right language level and mood for your listeners. No one should be left out.

- *Always* keep in mind that when your speech is richly textured with a *wide variety of word choices*, it's easier to believe what you are telling or attempting to convince your audience. Be colorful and offer an assortment of colorful word and language choices.

Specific and Effective Word Choices

When you are speaking, your time will be limited, and so will be the attention span of your audience. Therefore, you want to make every word and phrase count by making your main points and supporting subpoints with the fewest possible words. Being specific about what you think, feel, and believe, is essential to fully communicating with your audience. When you are not specific, you become ineffective in what you have to say. The following are a few guidelines to help you be more *specific* and *effective* with your word choices.

All-Purpose Words

All-purpose words are words which are of a general nature, and offer the listener no real concrete sense of any meaning. All-purpose words will always weaken the power of your speech because they are *ineffective* in telling your audience exactly what you feel, think, or believe as a speaker. They are very formless, are of a general nature, and in the end really have nothing at all to say about anything. Words such as *good, bad, wonderful,* or *nice* do not help an audience see, feel, or understand anything in a specific manner.

> ▶ Announcing that something is *good, bad, wonderful,* or *nice* is far less effective than saying it is *helpful, discouraging, refreshing,* or *enjoyable*. Using *all-purpose words* always weakens the power of your speech.

Tangible Words

It is also important to regularly use words which are tangible. **Tangible words** are words that are very specific or concrete to the listener. As was said earlier, using words like *good, bad, nice,* and *wonderful* are not in any way *effective* words. The more tangible the word, the better for your listeners. Even colors, sizes, and dimensions can be made more tangible and vivid by choosing to be more detailed. Making use of *bright turquoise* for *blue,* a *1968 Lincoln Continental* in place of *an old car,* and *his high-rise Chicago apartment* in place of *his urban home* are powerful and tangible word choices which create an honest sense of what you hope to describe to your audience. Being tangible creates a sense of imagination in the minds of your listeners.

> ▶ Remember, it is not the number of words, you use but the tangibility of the words which then demonstrate that you are a competent speaker. Audiences appreciate details. The more detailed you are, the better!

• • • • • Literal Words

When you make use of **literal words**, you express precisely what something means. You are centered on the facts and want, foremost, to inform your audience. Literal words are most often the first meaning offered in a dictionary. So the word *bomb* would be classified as a detonation or perhaps as an explosion of some kind. When speaking about terrorism, World War II, or nuclear disarmament, the literal use of *bomb* must be clear and well-intended to mean "the ignition of a blast or some kind of explosion." Literal use of words is essential when giving speeches about historical events, scientific phenomena, medical-related topics, and engineering or legal subjects.

> ▶ Literal words tell your listeners factual meanings. They are accurate clarifications or statements; they help with truthful communication of information. They are also very important when you are speaking on a topic or making points about something which is of a more solemn nature.

• • • • • Figurative Words

Figurative words are the exact opposite of *literal words*. We use what are called "figures of speech" in our daily conversations; they add color and depth to what we have to say. *In many ways, figurative words awaken the imagination.* Figurative language is everywhere, from Shakespeare and various translations of the Bible, to Harry Potter and unconventional TV commercials. They force listeners to use their mind's eye and understand much more than concrete, simple, or precise words. Figurative words are the reverse of literal words, and are not all intended to be factual. When you make use of literal words, you express exactly what something means, whereas **figurative words** mean something more dramatic and dynamic than the literal meaning of words.

Figurative words are more poetic in nature. They are used by artists, musicians, playwrights, poets, and preachers. As stated earlier, the word *bomb* of course *literally* indicates an *explosion* or a *blast*. But figuratively speaking, it can mean to *fail seriously* or denote something *sensational*, as in: *"that new horror film bombed in both Chicago and L.A. last week"* or *"Wow, Dave's new girlfriend is a bombshell!"* And of course, most college students love to have a *blast* at any party.

It is important to recognize the distinction between *literal* and *figurative* word usage. There are many figures of speech which are commonly used on a daily basis. Keep in mind that if your audience does not recognize your words as *figurative*, and thinks that they are *literal* (or vice versa), they will then find it difficult to understand what you actually intend, and even at times could take offense at it.

> ▶ Literal words tell your listeners the factual meaning of a word. Figurative words tell them something that is more poetic or comparative. Literal words force imagination and create depth to your speech.

• • • • • Exaggerated Words

Oftentimes great speakers, politicians, and even preachers, will use figures of speech which clearly make use of *exaggerated* or *inflated statements* to create an alarming emotional response from an audience. We call this hyperbole. **Hyperbole** is a figure of speech that uses an exaggerated or extravagant statement to generate a strong emotional response. As a figure of speech is definitely not intended to be taken literally. Sometimes hyperbole is used to create humor in a speech. It is often used by late-night comedians when commenting on current news events, or by politicians when engaged in a tight political race. Phrases such as *"He has more money than all of Europe combined," "She is by far more beautiful than any goddess of ancient Greece,"* and *"He is faraway older than Moses"* are classic examples.

Hyperbole can be fun and create a sense of bonding with an audience. Using exaggerated language is, of course, not appropriate in every speech or for every audience. Again, be cautious when and where you choose to use exaggeration and hyperbole. While they may not usually be perceived as outright lies, a speaker who continually exaggerates cannot be completely trusted by an audience.

Although most comedians rely on exaggeration to make their stories funnier, and some cultures use exaggeration as part of their communicative style, it is best to use it for perhaps an attention-getter or at the conclusion of your presentation. If you choose to exaggerate too much, you run the risk of your presentation becoming too entertaining by diluting the facts, and will then diminish the ultimate purpose of your speech.

> ▶ Hyperbolic statements are not literally true, but speakers make use of them to command attention, emphasize a main point, create humor, or cause a shocking reaction.

Your A, B, Cs for Specific and Effective Word Choices

ALL-PURPOSE WORDS

Keep in mind that *all-purpose words* are of a generic nature and offer the listener no real concrete sense of meaning.

A You should use them only sparingly, and when you wish to offer no details or focus.

B They are *unproductive* in telling what you actually know about your topic.

C They are *inefficient* in telling exactly what you feel as a speaker.

TANGIBLE WORDS

Keep in mind that *tangible words* offer specific or concrete meanings to your listeners.

A They create an honest picture of what you hope to describe concerning your topic.

B They demonstrate that you are a precise and detailed communicator.

C They help create an honest picture of what you hope to describe according to your own specifications

LITERAL WORDS

Keep in mind that **literal words** offer exact meanings, as stated in the dictionary.

A They are essential when giving speeches about historical events, scientific phenomena, medical-related topics, and engineering or legal subjects.

B They create a sense of information and exactness for your listeners.

C They are important to wisely use in more solemn topics, such as Hiroshima/Nagasaki, the Holocaust, natural disasters, or the U.S. 9-11 tragedy.

FIGURATIVE WORDS

Keep in mind that **figurative words** promote a sense of imagination in an audience.

A They are always more dramatic and dynamic than the literal meaning of a word.

B They add color and depth to otherwise simple or plain language.

C If your audience interprets your words as *figurative* and thinks that they are *literal* (or vice versa), you will cause confusion.

EXAGGERATED WORDS

Keep in mind that **exaggerated words** create arousing responses in listeners.

A A figure of speech is never intended to be taken literally, ever.

B *Hyperbole* is an extravagant statement made to generate a strong emotional response from an audience.

C *Hyperbole* should be used to command attention toward a main point, create an emotion, or cause extreme humor.

Using Language and Words Ethically

Being a powerful speaker involves more than just the exchange of consistently well-placed words and phrases throughout a presentation. No matter how good your word choices may be, whether they be *tangible, literal, figurative,* or *very hyperbolic,* many factors influence how and why we make the word choices that we do. One of the most important aspects of public speaking involves the *intentionality* and the *attitude* behind how we approach our word choices. Every word chosen is accountable before the public, and in some instances can even be subject to legal action. As speakers making word choices, we are all called upon to be *ethical* and to seriously consider how our words will have an effect on others.

● ● ● ● ● Reflection: Seven Basic Ethical Considerations

The following is a reflection based upon *seven considerations* which ethical speakers should take into account when making word choices. In order to think about attitudes, intentions, and appropriate use of borrowed materials, you should ask yourself these questions before each speech you hope to offer.

1. Are my word choices offering the full truth or only the partial truth?

2. Are they honestly fair to all, or slightly biased in one direction over another?

3. Do my word choices overly reflect my own biases and opinions?

4. Will my words foster a sense of goodwill and improved relations among all my listeners?

5. Are my words offered out of a need to please my audience, or are they completely honest?

6. Will my word choices be beneficial to all my listeners (and to myself) in the end?

7. Are all of my words my own, or am I giving credit to those whom I am borrowing from?

By reflecting upon these seven considerations, hopefully you will become more ethically responsible in your word choices and phrasing when presenting your information to your gathered listeners.

Ethical Considerations Behind Your Word Choices

Making **ethical word choices** means being aware of how words reflect rightness and wrongness in public speaking presentations. To choose words with a sense of ethics in mind, means far more than being sensitive to religious values, sexual orientation, gender, or political sensibilities. Such awareness does not guarantee that we will be ethical in our attitudes or approach toward our audience.

To be ethical does not mean simply following a definition, code, or set of rules, whereupon we have suddenly become an ethical speaker because of our sensitive word choices. When we speak of ethics we are, in essence, speaking about the ability to be *honest, straightforward, fair,* and *openly accountable,* whether speaking before a small group or in a large auditorium filled with hundreds of listeners.

Public speaking always involves being honest and not engaging in distortion, lying, or deceit. The goals of your speech should be aimed at the betterment of your audience. This begins with you being fully prepared for each speech you present. Every audience you speak to, whether in your classroom or beyond, deserves to hear a well-designed and well-rehearsed speech. It is important not to waste your listeners' time or mislead them through lazy research, unclear word choices, or inconsistent facts. It is vital to be fair and honest in everything that you say or show, and to never distort the truth for emotional, personal, or material gain.

Ethical speaking always avoids pointing the finger at others, name-calling, and other forms of abusive language. Name-calling is essentially using language or word choices to defame or degrade other individuals, nations, religions, or political groups. Name calling demeans the dignity of those being targeted.

> Keep in mind that we actually take on definite ethical responsibilities by our language and word choices. *How* they convey information or ideas to others in a public setting, is far more important than *what* they actually say in the end.

Words of Partiality

Public speakers know there are a number of ethical notions which apply to how fairly information is presented. Whenever an individual or group deliberately presents information which unevenly favors or discredits one side of a topic, the speaker is presenting what is called a **position of partiality**.

Although it is more or less impossible to be completely objective, there must at minimum, be consideration toward being as objective and impartial as possible. Often we hear of a media bias, which may be quite difficult to avoid. Fox News, CNN, TBS, PBS, and MSNBC, for example, must attempt to reduce often-convoluted, controversial topics into a news story which lasts only a few broadcast minutes. Because of this challenge:

> ▶ News programs and public speakers alike, are obligated to take careful consideration of partiality when researching, collecting data, selecting information, and presenting their word choices to audiences.

Words Not Your Own

As a student, it is important for you to understand the severity of *plagiarism* and the importance of making responsible, honest choices in words and language. Of all the ethical choices a public speaker can make, few are more problematic than choosing to plagiarize. The worst choice a speaker can make is to be involved in **global plagiarism**; this is, quite simply, extracting a speech entirely from a single source and passing it off as your own personal presentation. This is more frequently done than most people are aware of, and will most assuredly result in a failed grade, if not expulsion from your school. Less audacious but equally unethical is **patchwork plagiarism**, which is essentially patching a speech together by copying, more or less word-for-word, material from a number of separate sources. Whenever you present a speech, you must be sure it represents your work entirely. This entails your own thinking, your own language, your own words, and your own examples and visual resources. Also keep in mind what is termed **incremental plagiarism**, which occurs when a speaker fails to give recognition for explicit quotations and paraphrases which are "borrowed" from other individuals, pieces of literature, or any resources not their own.

> ▶ Lastly, keep in mind that, in addition to your ethical responsibilities as a public speaker, you have ethical duties as a member of a classroom audience. Always listen courteously and attentively to others who will also be presenting speeches.

Never send texts or look at any other form of literature (including your own note cards, if you are also scheduled to speak that day) while others in your class are presenting their speeches. *Always offer the same attention to others which you yourself hope to receive.* Be sure to avoid prejudging other speakers in your class. Be open to the free and honest expression of ideas and new ways of thinking. On those occasions when you disagree, be sure to be considerate and respectful. All speakers should support each other, no matter what the topic or argument. In every way possible, be sure to let your speech class become an emotionally safe place for all to learn how to speak in public. As a member of the class audience, you also have an opportunity to watch and learn from others.

• • • • • Ethical Learning and Listening

It is essential that college and university students recognize, and be able to identify different modes of ethical awareness as listeners. Since ethical standards are not noticeably defined, codified, or in many ways completely objective, it is easy for information to be vague, imprecise, or distorted, even from the lectures offered by your professors.

By reflecting upon the *seven basic ethical considerations* mentioned earlier, we are better able to identify when we ourselves may be misled, misdirected, or in turn have been offered a prejudicial bias or *position of partiality.*

> ▶ Therefore, ethics is particularly important to consider from the vantage point of being a listener and audience member, within a university setting.

Hopefully, your speech instructor will provide a safe, comfortable classroom atmosphere, by permitting student speakers to appraise the ethics of each speech, as well as help student speakers to develop critical listening and evaluation skills of their peers.

Evaluation of the lessons and teaching concepts which instructors are utilizing, should also be subject to ethical reflection. As with all public presentations, including those of the news media, college instructors are accountable for shaping and influencing what students are receiving and learning, as well.

TWIN RULES

Twin Rules for Making Ethical Word Choices

Words of partiality

A. **Remember:** There are a number of ethical notions which apply to how fairly information is presented in public.

B. **Always be sure** to understand that it is totally impossible to be completely objective, but it is imperative to attempt to be as objective and impartial as possible.

Words not your own

A. **Remember:** Plagiarism is always a temptation, done to save time, and is a serious breach of ethics. It destroys credibility and could cost you the loss of your education.

B. **Also** be sure to properly cite and give credit to your sources by way of information, quotes, and even phrasing and ideas which are not fully your own.

Words as a listener and learner

A. **Remember:** It is essential to recognize and be able to identify different modes of ethical awareness as a listener of other students' speeches, speeches and as a student in general.

B. **Always be sure** to reflect upon the *seven basic ethical considerations,* to be better able to identify when you yourself may be misled, misdirected, or offered a continual *position of partiality.*

Summary

In this chapter we have explored what it means to make word choices in order to deliver your speech more powerfully and effectively. *Word choices* are the creative center of your topic. They not only help keep your audience focused on your information and ideas, but they also help keep them continuously interested and even possibly entertained.

It is essential not only to be clear about your facts, figures, and the overall organization of your speech, but also to make careful word choices. *All-purpose words* will always weaken your speech because they are *inefficient* in telling your audience exactly what you feel, think, or believe. By not being vague, and by having *word confidence,* you can make plain to your audience that you clearly *intend* to use the words they are hearing. Being confident implies that you know and understand the words that you are using and are in command of them.

When you make use of *literal words,* you express exactly what something means, you are centered on the facts, and you want foremost to inform your audience. Literal words are most often the first meaning offered in a dictionary. On the other hand, figurative words are not literal and offer a sense of color and imagination. Using *magnified words* or *language* means that a speaker is making word choices which are inflated or have the intention of making an impression. An inflated vocabulary makes you look and sound inauthentic, and will cause your audience to view you as not being genuine.

In short, when you are speaking, your time is limited and so is the attention span of your audience. Therefore, you want to make every word and phrase count by making your main points and supporting subpoints packed with the fewest possible words. Being specific about what you think, feel, and believe is essential to fully communicating with your audience.

Finally, when we speak of *ethics,* we are in essence speaking about the ability to be *honest, straightforward, fair,* and *openly accountable,* whether talking to a small group or a large auditorium filled with hundreds of listeners. Ethical awareness also includes being a listener. By reflecting upon the *seven basic ethical considerations,* we are better able to identify when we ourselves are being misled, being misdirected, or being offered an informational bias or *position of partiality.*

Discussion Questions

1. What do we mean when we say that while giving a speech in public, you must not only speak to your audience about an important topic, but also must be sure to make an honest approach toward being ethical? Is it possible to use fair, considerate, and honest word choices and language, yet still be unethical? If so, *how?* Please offer some examples.

2. Of the *seven basic ethical considerations,* which do you think may be the most challenging for a public speaker to pay close attention to? Are each of them equally important, or are only a few of them truly necessary?

3. What are the risks of having a speech riddled with weak words, or peppered with all-purpose phrases, and the repetition of information? Under what conditions, if any, do you feel hyperbole should be avoided?

4. What is meant by using *magnified words* or *language*? Why is this not considered to be authentic public speaking, in spite of the fact that it pays close attention to grammar, word choices, vocabulary, and even careful phrasing?

5. Why is *plagiarism* in public speaking considered dangerous territory? Of the various varieties of plagiarism, which is the most easy or tempting to partake of, and how can it be best avoided? How would you feel if someone informed you that another student offered a speech in his or her class which was stolen from you the previous semester; and would you address the situation?

● ● ● ● ● Quick Quiz

Match the following capsule sentences below with the correct letter which best describes the key terms or phrases found in this chapter.

1. ____ Excessive use of the same or similar words and phrases which creates boredom.

2. ____ Word choices that are inflated or with the intention of making an impression.

3. ____ Being certain of the things you say; and saying them with a sense of assurance.

4. ____ The more poetic or comparative use of a word in a speech.

5. ____ Technical or specialized language characteristic of a specific group or profession.

6. ____ Words which are broad and have interchangeable meanings for the listener.

7. ____ The exact meaning of a word in a speech or its factual usage.

8. ____ The precise language options we make use of to convey our ideas.

9. ____ An exaggerated or extravagant statement to generate a strong emotional response.

10. ____ Words which are not formless, but are clear and specific to the listener.

A. Repetitive language	**B.** Jargon	**C.** Word confidence
D. Figurative words	**E.** Tangible words	**F.** Word choices
G. Literal words	**H.** Hyperbole	**I.** Magnified words
J. All-purpose words		

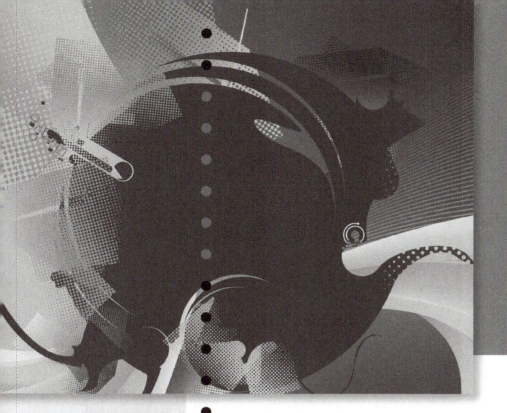

CHAPTER 9

Visual and Sound Resources

KEY TERMS
• • • • • • • • •

visual resources

sound resources

audiovisual resources

eye contact

blackboard/
  whiteboard

artifact

photograph

handouts

poster

graphics

sketch

charts

map

DVD

videotape

audiotape

MP3

computer-assisted
  resources

speaker-centeredness

*"Humanity is acquiring all the right technology;
and for all the wrong reasons . . ."*
—R. Buckminster Fuller

"Technology is so much fun, *but we can drown in our technology.
The fog of information can drive out . . . knowledge."*
—Daniel J. Boorstin

The 21st century has been dubbed "The Age of Communication," and public speaking, once largely considered to be an art, is now quickly evolving into a savvy technology, as well. These days technology puts forward a considerable array of visual and sound resources that can boost the effectiveness and influence of any well-prepared speech. The advent of computer technologies and other resources which include both material and technical ones combined, can illuminate and supplement any oral presentation. In this chapter we will analyze the traditional and the more cutting-edge resources available to you, as well as help you identify the ways in which they may be best used to your advantage as a public speaker.

Everything from simple human artifacts, charts, and printed handouts to digital maps, DVDs, and innovative software such as PowerPoint offer today's public speaker a virtually infinite number of options. Of course, understanding *how* and *when* to make appropriate use of these resources is of vital importance. Oftentimes those of us new to public speaking *underuse*, *overuse*, and at times even *improperly use* the resources available to us. For instance PowerPoint, the very icon of contemporary presentation media itself, can enormously enhance any speech, or very much overwhelm your listeners, or, in many instances, completely turn off a listening audience.

Exploring Your Five Senses

Always keep in mind that all of the five senses may be utilized, when it comes to involving your prepared words as you speak to your gathered audience. *Taste, touch, smell, seeing,* and of course *hearing* can all be enhanced by the creative incentive of a well-organized public speaker. All you need is a bit of enthusiasm, coupled with your own imagination. But first, always ask yourself these two quick questions:

1. Which of the five senses can I utilize to help my audience experience my speech more truth-fully in a way which will enhance my words?

2. What careful measures should I take to help them better receive my speech, and still not overwhelm them, when I explore the senses?

In this chapter you'll later be introduced to the most common visual and sound resource options available today, including basic considerations for appropriate usage, design options, and finally more effective presentation of the *human person* as the central and most natural resource for a successful visual and sound experience. Hopefully, you will learn that when integrated appropriately into a speech, even traditional and low-technology resources can significantly enhance the look, feel, and overall energy of your speech.

According to *Public Speaking: An Audience-Centered Approach,* by Steven A. Beebe and Susan J. Beebe, both visual and sound resources "enhance understanding, enhance memory, help listeners organize ideas, help gain and maintain attention, and help illustrate a sequence of events or procedures." These are all things that words alone cannot achieve so readily in our visually and digitally centered 21st century. As was mentioned earlier, *all of the five senses* may be utilized when it comes to fully involving your words as you speak to your gathered audience. You may invite them to both smell and taste food items that you bring along as part of your informational experience for them. You may ask them to directly feel objects, both inanimate and live—including various small or larger pets. All you need is a bit of imagination, and of course preparation, to be a winner with your approach. But first we will take a brief look at two of the primary senses used in every speech, *seeing* and *hearing,* by way of visual and sound resources.

Visual Resources

Visual resources help you present your speech in a manner well beyond your own words and language. They are enhancements which your audience will see, in addition to or beyond you, the speaker in front of them. These visual resources may include objects or artifacts, such as: clothing, rocks, coins, flags, personal relics, and even food items. When most people think about artifacts, they sometimes imagine fascinating objects found by archeologists in the ground, dug up from ancient civilizations. But in a broader sense, an *artifact* may be any object (inanimate or even alive) that you bring to your presentation to help your audience both *see* as well as *feel,* another dimension of your words beyond the language you use. Other visual resources may include: common household items, photographs, design models, diagrams, sketches, charts, and actual artwork. By enhancing your words, visual resources help you put together a more tangible and comprehensible presentation for your audience. When used properly, visual resources help an audience to more fully appreciate every word of your speech outline you offer to them. Always keep in mind that, on the whole, audiences enjoy some level of visual stimulation beyond you, the central speaker.

> ▶ No matter how excellent an orator you may be, audiences generally enjoy something *beyond* your words to help them *visualize* your words.

Sound Resources

Sound resources help you focus on the use of sound, literally beyond your own words and language, and will often involve the use of recordings, such as conversations, interviews, music, sound effects, animal noises, even perhaps clips and bits of speeches by other speakers. Both *sound* and *visual* resources may now be downloaded *via* laptop computer for actual (real-time) use during your speech. By augmenting your words and actions, sound and visual resources help make your ideas and your approach to your speech more tangible and readily more comprehensible for your audience. Some public speakers also make effective use of sound by temporarily darkening or lowering the lighting level of the room. Always ask yourself: "what can I do, by way of alternative sound resources, to help my audience *hear* my speech beyond the use of my own voice?"

Sometimes the use of computer-generated slides accompanied by music, poetry, or a more detailed narrative, may be quite effective as well. At other times, presentations may be best served by the use of videotapes (DVDs and VCRs) which may include excerpts from: movies, TV programs, or cable commercials, or even home-made videos. We refer to all of these technologies as **audiovisual resources.**

• • • • • General Reasons for the Use of Visual and Sound Resources

We discussed that both visual and sound resources help amplify the natural limitations of using only spoken language as a sole means of communication. As powerful as your spoken language may be, it can often be abstract and loaded with concepts, ideas, and intangible impressions. Thus, making use of spoken language alone can produce a sense of incomplete communication. As such, additional visual and sound resources give your audience a more instinctive connection with your overall message. They can strengthen speeches in many different ways which words alone cannot do. But a great speech must never solely depend upon these resources alone, because:

> ▶ There is *no* substitute for a powerfully prepared and inspired speaker. If used improperly (or even for that matter too extensively), visual and sound resources can become a liability to any good public speaker.

Six HELP Reasons for Using Resources

The following are six general reasons every speaker should keep in mind when seeking to use visual and audio resources:

1. To help make your descriptions more tangible and immediate for your audience . . .
   Remember: A *visual example* may be worth a thousand *words*.

2. To help add a sense of variety and diversity to your overall spoken message . . .
   Remember: Sound resources can help eliminate monotony and possible boredom.

3. To help reduce fatigue and anxiety on the part of you, the central communicator . . .
   Remember: Both visual and sound resources give you a short break from speaking.

4. To help increase the audience's memory of your more important material . . .
   Remember: When things are presented with additional resources, it promotes retention.

5. To help increase a sense of power toward the credibility of your topic . . .
   Remember: Visual and sound resources help reinforce a sense of authority and persuasion.

6. To help address a multiplicity of learning methods and other possible approaches . . .
   Remember: All people learn differently—the more resources you employ, the better you can speak.

Always Control Your Visual and Sound Resources

As you consider the six HELP reasons for utilizing visual and sound resources which we have listed, you should be aware there may be some inherent disadvantages involved when deciding to make use of them. There is always the risk that any resource, no matter how effectively it may be perceived, could at times pull away audience interest from you, or, worse yet, from your actual message. Your audience may become so involved in your visual and sound resources that they may disregard your live, spoken message altogether. If a photograph is too alarming or a handout is too engaging, your listeners may focus on those items and no longer on *you,* their live speaker. Should you offer a chart or graph which is too detailed or even puzzling, they may begin to overly analyze it or may simply disengage from your presentation entirely.

On some occasions your presentation resources may even reduce eye contact between you and your audience. *You should control your resources; they should never control you.* Finally, keep in mind that **eye contact** is always essential for any good speech. If you focus too much upon your charts, maps, graphs, projected photos, or the chalk board, rather than on your audience, you will lose both credibility and effectiveness.

Further, it is important to keep in mind that when using electronic equipment you are held to the functional destiny of technology, and it may fail you. If the location where you are giving your speech is not equipped for computerized technology enhancement, then you must rely upon other possible resources. If you do not supply your own equipment, you should be well aware of what is or is not available to you. And if your technology will not operate for whatever reason, don't waste time sulking and fretting. *Keep your cool, and be prepared to move on without it.* Remember: You are at the center of your speech, *not* your technical enhancements or resources.

Now we will take a quick survey of the most commonly used *visual* and *sound* resources. By no means is this listing an exhaustive one, but, at least, it includes the most recommended ones for your possible consideration.

● ● ● ● ● Common Visual and Sound Resources

The variety of visual and audio resources available takes on many forms in the 21st century. Particularly with the advent of digital computer technology, ranging from continually updated iPads and iPhones to PowerPoint and Twitter, public speakers have a variety of options at their disposal. In most cases the choices are virtually limitless, and require only a sense of imagination and inventiveness on your part.

What follows is a brief discussion of the more common and frequently used forms of visual resources: blackboards, artifacts, photos, handouts, graphs, sketches, and maps. As for those speakers who wish to combine visual and audio resources, we will take a brief look at a few, including DVDs, MP3 files, and the ever-popular PowerPoint application.

Blackboards and Whiteboards

"Visual storytelling of one kind or another has been around since cavemen were drawing on the walls."

—Frank Darabont

The blackboard was invented by James Pillans in Edinburgh, Scotland. He was the headmaster of the Royal High School there and introduced it into the United States in the mid-19th century. Ever since, the blackboard (or chalkboard) has remained the standard for visual illustration and demonstration the world over. Blackboards were originally made of smooth, thin sheets of black or dark gray slate. Today most boards are green because the color registers easier on the eyes. Nonetheless, blackboards are always a great way to draw or write anything on the spot, with, of course, the great convenience of visual removal at any split second.

Many classrooms today are also equipped with what are now termed whiteboards. These have a glossy, usually white surface for nonpermanent color markings. Whiteboards are comparable to blackboards, allowing the public speaker the luxury of marking and erasing information at any quick moment. They have become a fixture in many offices, meeting rooms, university classrooms, and other work environments. Ideally, **blackboards** and **whiteboards** should be utilized when brainstorming with your audience about proposals, plans, and design ideas and *not* for presenting visual materials *per se*. You will most likely be more effective and further be recognized by your audience as more prepared, if you resort to other means of visual resources in a university or college speech setting. Chalkboards and blackboards work best for teachers and business professionals, and are not standard fare among public speakers in general.

Artifacts and Photographs

As we mentioned earlier, an **artifact** may be any object you bring to your presentation which helps your audience both *see* and *feel* another dimension of your words beyond the language of your speech. Your artifact should be conveniently handled or observed, and simple for your audience to see or touch without much effort. Always keep in mind that:

> ▶ It is more effective to keep your artifacts out of sight when you are not directly referring to them.

Some speakers chose to exhibit their artifact throughout their speech, but be careful about this approach. If your artifact is very interesting (or in some cases a live animal), your audience may pay more attention to it than to your message.

Should you need to make use of more than one artifact, exhibit each in succession, and then be sure to remove each from sight in the same way. Relatively speaking, nonliving artifacts work better than live animals, which cannot always be easily managed or required to perform appropriately when and where you may wish. Remember, animals may also become nervous during a speech and choose, right then and there, during your presentation, to use your speech time as their restroom break!

Sometimes the use of **photographs** can be difficult to manage during a speech. Unless projected, photographs may be difficult for your audience to view beyond the first several rows of your classroom or auditorium. Passing photographs around (as a form of artifact) during a speech is always sure to cause distraction among audience members, and is likely to pull the focus away from you as the central speaker. Therefore:

> ▶ It is best to project photographs on a screen before all to see as a group, while you explain them as the core focus.

Color copiers these days can create low-priced enlargements from snapshots and camera photos. Enlarged photos beyond 8.5 by 11 inches are a suitable size for use in most classroom settings. It can be even more effective, if you choose to mount your photos or pictures on cardboard or poster board, for more efficient and formal simplicity of presentation. Also please keep in mind that digital photos can be utilized in PowerPoint slide presentations, or even made into projections for use on most laptop computers, and then be made into enlarged photographs.

All photos or pictures (such as paintings or sketches) should be chosen for their particular significance to your speech. Keep in mind that they ought to be displayed only as you discuss an important point, and then be taken out of view from your audience. Remember: You the speaker are at the center of the message, not your photographs or pictures. They should visually amplify your words and not the other way around.

Finally, it is important to note that artifacts or photographs, designed to shock or alarm your audience as a form of attention-getter, can oftentimes cause problems and even create trouble with university authorities, perhaps even violate state laws.

Artifacts that are illegal, possibly dangerous, or potentially offensive should be completely avoided. *Any weapons, alcohol, drug products, pornography, grossly violent photos, or ethnically offensive images, should not be used in a college or university classroom setting.*

Handouts and Posters

Making use of printed **handouts** may be quite useful when your topic is complicated, or difficult to fully communicate by the use of words alone. If your speech requires a lot of statistical information or scientific inquiry, oftentimes handouts may serve you well. If at all possible, always be sure to pass out handouts *after* you have concluded your speech. This helps avoid distractions, and also serves as a great keepsake of your speech long after your audience has departed. Handouts, in most cases, will increase the overall impression of your speech, while at the same time endorsing the information you have personally provided. If you choose to distribute a handout prior to your speech, be sure to request that your audience keep it turned over until you request that they look at it in combination with you, as you instruct them on how to utilize it—otherwise the handout will compete with you as speaker.

> ▶ Have your audience read your handouts with you, so as to avoid losing their attention.

Quite simply, you should distribute handouts only when it is required for your audience to refer to them during your presentation. Also, keep handouts to only one or two pages for a standard classroom speech. Longer speeches such as medical or business presentations may require extensive handouts, but for your classroom needs, multipage handouts are longer than is necessary. It is important to note also that you may decide to use a handout in combination with other forms of media, such as video clips or a PowerPoint presentation, and then distribute a handout which provides a listing of other references, websites, phone numbers, or any additional information about your topic.

The use of **posters** (an old-fashioned visual aid) can still be used quite effectively to exhibit pictures, photos, and textual graphics. For the average classroom speech, an effective poster size should be roughly 14 by 17 inches in width and height. Posters are great since they are quite easy to handle and manipulate. Posters have been used for decades by public speakers in medical and governmental meetings, as well as in the business world. Posters are notable in that you can even paste note cards on the reverse. That way you can remind yourself about what you need to emphasize and point out about the given image(s) at hand.

> Always keep poster designs simple, clear, and neat. Posters should never be overly detailed or complicated.

Remember that the whole purpose of a visual resource, is to simplify or make things obvious. Should you use a long series of posters, always be sure to number them, as you do with your note cards, so as to keep them in chronological arrangement. Always use bold, clear lettering and strong, bright colors if you need to have any written text on your posters. Your posters should amplify, and in a visual manner, sum up what you are trying to *say* to your audience. *The more simple the poster, the better it usually is.*

Graphics: Sketches, Charts, and Maps

We term resources which visually represent information in a speech as **graphics**.

These may include such sources as: *sketches, charts,* and *maps.* Graphics should always be displayed for only short amounts of time during your speech, and then (as if on a blackboard) they should be quickly removed. Each graphic should focus upon one concept or idea. Keep in mind that a visual resource is only effective if it can be readily viewed by your audience. All images and colors should be intense, all lettering should be bold, and the whole thing should be in razor-sharp contrast to the background.

Sketches are freehand or simplified illustrations of what you are speaking about. If you or a friend is designing a sketch, draft it first on white paper and then enlarge it for your desired use later. Oftentimes children's books and language books can become a great resource for you. Using simple and bold sketches of common objects and ideas can make a clear, profound impression on your audience. Should you find what you're looking for, you may then conveniently trace it as presented, or use it as a template to elaborate upon for your own desired imagination. *Sketches are always simple and direct.* They should lack, detail and be used for the straightforward illustration of a basic concept or idea. For instance, the stick figure is the classic model when illustrating the human person.

Charts are quite helpful to public speakers, since they offer visual reviews of connections and associations which are not readily visible themselves. Oftentimes charts can be detailed and quite complex in nature. A problem arises when charts are utilized, because they frequently provide far too much information for your audience to take in at one glance.

> ▶ Remember that disorderly and complicated visual resources sidetrack an audience. They will always compete with you as a speaker for focus and attention.

It is best to use a series of simplified charts which you present in an ordered sequence, rather than one highly detailed or visually busy chart. It is far better to present numerous clear charts, one at a time, and then (perhaps at the end) present one chart which attempts to "tell it all" to your audience, as a visual summary.

Remember that your audience should be able to understand and decipher all charts easily, with the help of you as their speaker and guide. Oftentimes you may ask your audience to focus upon certain elements of a chart, and to ignore any other material as not being critical to your discussion at hand. No matter how simple or complex your charts may be, it is you, the speaker, who is in charge and not vice versa.

Maps have been around since ancient times (even long before chalkboards). Today, commercially prepared maps include far too much information and detail for effective use in public speaking. The most successful maps are those that focus specifically upon your speech. They should be simple, appropriate to your point at hand, and never cluttered or overbearing. Maps ideally should be used to put questions or problems into perspective, and simply illustrate for your audience geographically where events of interest included in your speech, were historically or currently happening. Once again, as with charts, the simpler a map, the more helpful it usually becomes.

Keep in mind that you can always design a map to your own specifications. A simple, undetailed map, can be marked up and drawn upon to focus on those details which serve your speech best. You may even draw your own map ahead of time, and then add to it even further during the course of your speech. Maps should always assist and never distract.

DVDs and Videotapes

DVDs and **videotapes** can provide a great added visual-sound experience which will enhance your speech. As with foreign films and Hollywood movies, DVDs and videos can be a powerful emotional and narrative resource to help underscore any presentation. As was mentioned earlier in this chapter, always be certain that you know well in advance the size and location of where your speech will take place, and whether such a site has all the proper tools and equipment to accommodate your prepared electronic materials.

Both DVDs and videotapes are a powerful enhancement resource. They have the imaginative power to carry your audience to faraway and dangerous places, ones which otherwise they may never have a chance to visit. Such technology may help them see the inside of a smoldering volcano, or virtually travel deep within the human body. Although you may successfully attempt to describe sharks scavenging at the bottom of the Atlantic Ocean, or the interior walking quarters of the Great Wall of China, your verbal efforts will better achieve visual reality if you offer actual scenes by way of video clips, or projected scenes from documentaries.

Of course, making use of DVDs and videotapes can offer some special problems for the public speaker. You always run the risk of bright moving images attracting more curiosity and notice, than the very words you have to offer your audience. You then, of course, also need to be sure that you edit your clips specifically to your needs at hand, and never give your audience too much to see and hear.

> ▶ In a five-to-eight-minute speech, your clips should not exceed thirty seconds or so.

Most likely you will need to do some editing of your visual resources. Keep in mind that good editing takes know-how as well as a sense of what is needed and when, and should not detract from you yourself, the main event of the speech.

Since editing often takes great skill, along with the appropriate equipment, it is best to simply transfer all of your clips onto a special media resource CD. This DVD can be especially designed for your speech, and it can be easily created on most PCs by utilizing your DVD/CD burner capability. Creating a special media resource CD will give you the smooth transitions your speech requires, without you ever having to attempt to cue the scenes or segments each time you wish to show them.

Oftentimes you may simply wish to film your own video, and provide your audience with personal, home-made video clips. Using a handheld device or even your iPhone capabilities, personal clips can be a snap. One student at Northeastern Illinois University offered a speech on how to make great spinach lasagna. She showed her audience several clips of she and her sister in their suburban kitchen preparing a few of the preoperational main items. She then later ended her speech on-location in a high-end restaurant where she zoomed in on the same dish being served to them in smaller portions, and at a very high menu price! She ended her speech on camera by asking, "Why eat out at a high price, when you can dine-in at home for well over half the cost?" By customizing her own video to fit her needs, this young woman was able to help us visit both her own kitchen, and an upscale Italian restaurant. Utilizing this approach, she was able to make her speech more meaningful and fun for her listening and viewing audience. Today there is no limit to being creative with your own digital resources.

> ▶ You must never lose sight that you are at the center of the speech, *not* your "technological guests."

Audiotapes and MP3s

Audiotapes, sound effects and music on CDs, or **MP3** files may also be quite useful as purely sound-enhancement resources. Insect sounds, animal calls, rare whale and exotic bird songs, and even bits and pieces from the speeches of famous individuals at historic moments, can all be offered as sound enhancements to your speech. You may choose to make use of commentary from friends and relatives, because not every voice needs to be that of a well-known individual.

Oftentimes, recorded music to accompany your speech, can be quite powerful and enjoyable. One student at Roosevelt University used soft flute music to underscore his informative speech about Native American tribes in Arizona, Utah, and New Mexico. Another student gave a persuasive protest speech on the war in Iraq, and regularly resorted to the sounds of gunfire between each of the main points of her speech. There are a number of creative ways in which sound alone may be used as an enhancement resource for your spoken words, not unlike how music may be used to underscore a Hollywood film.

Keep in mind that sounds may also be used to complement visual displays, ranging from charts and maps to graphs and even artifacts, that you may pass around to your listeners. As with video, you can either create your own sound elements, or of course can make use of prerecorded material. This also permits a number of options for storage, replay, and even entrance and exit music, as your audience may enter or leave the place where your speech will take place. You may choose to play music yourself, or have someone else play live music on your behalf.

> ▶ Music and sound are an excellent way to make a point, *or* to focus in on a section of your speech which is vital to your overall message.

Used conservatively, sound can also be more directly handled to accompany visual displays, to establish mood, or even to emotionally support your main points. Another student at Roosevelt University offered a speech on her life in Cuba, by showing PowerPoint photos while highlighting Cuban geography and the arts. She used recorded salsa music to underscore her entire presentation, to quite a successful outcome. You may even use recorded commentary and interview excerpts during your speech. Another student at Northeastern Illinois University offered a speech on the extremely poor in America. During his speech, and at critical moments at which he wished to emphasize a given point, he played anonymous live commentary which he personally recorded from lower-income people living in Chicago.

As with the use of video recordings, always be sure to first practice your speech with any technology you hope to interject into it. Also remember to never permit your sound enhancement elements to overwhelm either your listening audience or, for that matter, yourself as the main speaker.

Computer-Assisted Resources

In the early 1980s, developments in the world of computers changed the way all public presentations were produced. Reasonably priced, specialized applications then made it possible for any motivated public speaker with a PC or a Macintosh, to create professional-looking presentation graphics to enhance their speech before any audience. These computer-assisted resources (also called presentation graphics programs) are computer software packages used to display information, normally in the form of an attractive slideshow. Such resources normally include three major functions: an editing capability that permits you to insert and format your content, a method for inserting and manipulating graphic images, and a slideshow system to display the entire content before your waiting audience. Originally these programs were used to generate 35 mm slides, to be presented using a slide projector and a screen. Today slide projectors have become virtually obsolete.

Always keep in mind that a computer-assisted program is supposed to help the speaker more easily access his or her ideas, and to assist any other participants with visual and sound information which should always complement the spoken presentation at hand. There are many different types of presentations, including professional (work-related), education, entertainment, and general communication (as in your speech class assignments). These programs can either supplement or replace the use of blackboards/whiteboards, handouts, charts, posters, slides, or handheld artifacts. Computer-assisted resources can also accommodate film and movie clips, and other objects which can be positioned on individual pages or "slides" or "foils" that combine several elements, all navigated under the personal command of the presenter. When utilizing a computer for developing a presentation, be cautious not to become caught up in the glamour and visual spectacle of the technology, and by doing so lose the awareness that you and your speech should always be the main focus.

> ▶ Using highly developed technology as part of your speech presentation, does not pardon you from using the traditional delivery skills required of you as the main speaker.

Remember, it is better to always feature yourself, than any extravagant technology. As for computer-assisted options for college students in a public speaker course, the most popular choice is, of course, PowerPoint. This technology is replete with both power and weakness for any public speaker.

The Power and Weakness of PowerPoint

"There are many true statements about complex topics that are too long to fit on a PowerPoint slide."

—Edward Tufte

PowerPoint is a computer-assisted presentation program developed by Microsoft Corporation. It is part of the Microsoft Office system, and runs on both Microsoft Windows and the Mac OS computer operating systems. Its use in North America has grown considerably since Microsoft first patented it to help accommodate the business world way back in 1990. Needless to say, PowerPoint has become quite a popular visual and sound resource, for a number of good reasons. Often it is prepackaged for many computer sales outlets, and is endorsed as a "required" component for most business and educational institutions. It is friendly to use, and it includes a step-by-step module to help tutor even the most perplexed user.

PowerPoint is a powerful visual as well as sound resource, and when used properly it can make any public presentation look and sound smart, organized, and well-planned. On the other hand, the ease with which PowerPoint can be utilized also subjects it to improper and ineffective use as well. Putting together a weak PowerPoint presentation is not all that difficult for university students these days, since the software contains pattern-templates and includes user-friendly instructions. It also boasts the luxury of permitting the user to insert up-to-the-minute material (on the spot) while speaking.

Over the last few years PowerPoint has begun to receive a lot of negative feedback and criticism by public speaking professionals and communication scholars. According to Peter Norvig in "PowerPoint: Shot with its own bullets" (Lancet, 2003), the problem essentially lies with poorly trained users of this innovative technology, not, of course, with the resource itself. We have included a few "Always Rules" for you to follow when availing yourself of PowerPoint. In most cases, however, unless you are a more advanced public speaker, we recommend *not* using PowerPoint in your classroom speeches unless it is welcomed by your instructor.

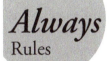

Always Rules — The Effective Use of PowerPoint

- *Always* be prepared to use PowerPoint as a *guide* for your audience; and remember it is never a substitute for you, the central speaker. Your audience has gathered to hear and see you, not any fancy technology!

- *Always* convey a conversational sensibility while using PowerPoint, and never directly read from your slides. You are a public speaker, *not* a public reader. No one likes to be read to except perhaps primary school children at bedtime!

- *Always* be sure that your projected text is large, clear, and bold. Using words too small to be read causes disorder and stress for your audience. The whole purpose of any visual resource in the end, is to be clearly observable.

- *Always* be sure to think about the use of color contrast in your PowerPoint slides. Making clever color contrasts can be confusing, while overly inventive designs can cause some items to appear unclear. Simplicity in the use of color should always be your rule.

- *Always* be sure *not* to include harebrained sound effects or overly intrusive music accompanying your visuals. Sound can be an invasive element, and can cause your audience to be jarred into losing their focus upon your spoken presentation.

- *Always* be sure *not* to use too many "flying" images, texts, or pictorial designs. Too much movement trivializes your presentation, and gives your audience the feeling of a sideshow or perhaps that of a corporate advertisement or TV commercial.

Practice Makes Perfect

You should always practice your speech beforehand when using any visual or sound equipment, and should always have a backup plan in case things go wrong and fail you. Practice is important, so that you may learn to efficiently incorporate the effects into your speech. Oftentimes speakers will overlook the fact that they have presentation resources, and will not consider them until they begin their speeches. Always include bold reminders on your note cards, indicating when you should stop to incorporate your visual or sound elements. Some speakers prefer to highlight their visual and sound cues with various colored markings, as a bright reminder to stop and offer a new visual or sound resource.

> ▶ Always appear early for your speech. Arriving well in advance and checking on the technical needs for your speech will help avoid nervousness and stumbling into technical problems.

Check all images for proper focusing, size levels, color sharpness, and any sound volume levels well before your audience arrives.

Although visual and sound resources greatly enhance any public speaking event, you should also be prepared for unplanned technological failures. Oftentimes, on-the-spot repairs are possible, while at other times you may simply be required to continue your speech without the desired technology you so enthusiastically planned to use. Under these circumstances you will have to rely on your own imagination, and the power and preparation of your own voice as the sole center of your message. Oftentimes you may have to resort to using the chalkboard or whiteboard as part of your backup plan. If at all possible, try to bring backup materials such as printed graphs, charts, or photographs that may easily substitute for failed technology. You should always be prepared to offer your speech without your presentation resources, in the event that something does not go in your favor.

Remember that smoothly organizing technical resources requires both planning and practice. Practice using your visual and sound resources until they become an instinctive element of your presentation. They should be smooth, seem effortless, and not take any time or attention away from the core of your overall spoken message.

Your **A**, **B**, **C**s for Better Use of Visual and Sound Resources

While conducting your speech you should *always be sure to:*

A Approach your topic with confidence and preparation.

B Realize that sound/visual resources should never substitute for you as the main speaker.

C Never permit your resources to upstage you—you are the core speaker.

While handing out artifacts or printed materials you should *always be sure to:*

A Take the time to pass things around, and offer guidance about what you are doing.

B Offer important information while things are being passed around.

C Repeat the importance of what your audience is receiving and why.

While making use of electronic resources you should *always be sure to:*

A Check and recheck the workability of the technology well ahead of presentation time.

B Have a backup if what you want to do electronically turns out be absolutely impossible.

C Be prepared to smoothly give your speech without resources if need be.

Before actually making use of your resources, you should *always be sure to:*

A Practice using any electronic sound or visual resources prior to facing a live audience.

B Test any equipment immediately before beginning your speech.

C Find out if any technical staff or safety personnel are available to you.

You the Speaker as Primary Visual and Sound Resource

As we have discovered in a previous chapter, public speaking has formally been around for many centuries. Humans have been effectively communicating in public since the dawn of human emergence—no one knows for sure just who, when, and where human people began to present information in a formal, gathered fashion. It is safe to assume, though, that no visual or sound technology was around to help make a speech more visually or acoustically effective, way back in ancient times—and with no recorded sound or PowerPoint at hand! We refer to this emphasis in public speaking as **speaker-centeredness**. Speaker-centeredness is at the heart of every good speech.

> ▶ Mastering the art of public speaking begins with you: *your* body, *your* voice, and *your* knowledge and passion for *your* subject at hand.

When presenting information on subjects and themes (whether informative or persuasive) of which you have significant knowledge and personal experience, you in essence are the best possible visual and sound resource. Like the ancient peoples and tribes before us, human voices and human presence are the most basic media. Oftentimes your unique voice, culture, religion, and personal life story, can be far more effective than any organized technology or map.

When giving a speech, consider how you may dress for the occasion. If you are presenting a speech about a given culture or a subject within a given cultural context, how you dress may serve half of your speech as a live visual resource. You may dress in traditional attire, and bring several artifacts along with you. You may offer to speak some words in your native tongue of origin, and even sing or dance in your traditional folk sound-and-movement customs. Live people inspired and sharing themselves, are often far more effective than electronically induced charts, photos, and inventive PowerPoint presentations. Consider putting some spice into your presentation by performing for your audience, reciting literature, or even acting out (alone or with a friend or two) something directly related to your speech. Remember, for millennia humans have communicated effectively in public with none other than their own bodies and voices. Great philosophers and prophets used only their own human resources, coupled with imagination and inspiration. You, the public speaker, are always the primary visual and sound resource.

TWIN RULES

Centering Your Speech Around You, and Not Technology

Be pleased with your own unique voice.

A. Remember: Be loud, be clear, and never pretend to be a "public speaker." If you speak with a foreign accent, that is just fine! Your audience most likely will enjoy a different way of speaking in public.

B. Your goal: Be heard clearly and emphatically. Be sure to speak more loudly and perhaps a bit more slowly if you have an accent—hearing everything is vital for your "foreign" audience.

Be mindful of the way you dress for your speech.

A. Remember: When giving a speech, whether you dress in a way that suggests your native culture, or simply in a neat and presentational way, you are already a visual resource for your audience. Look and feel "smart" before them.

B. Your goal: Engage everyone; to help your audience focus on the way you appear before them in a live setting. You are all they have firsthand to look at, so be well-dressed and prepared for success. How you look is half your presentation!

Be open to performing for your audience.

A. Remember: Audiences love a live performance. If you can sing a song, play a musical instrument, or recite a poem or significant text, this most likely will be far more appreciated than videos, DVDs, or sound recordings.

B. Your goal: Offer practical, engaging, live visual and sound resources. The more you give of yourself, your culture, and your talents, the better for all involved. *You are a living artifact.*

Be willing to have friends help you present your speech.

A. **Remember:** Having a friend perform with you is always a powerful visual or sound resource. Using a dance partner, a scene companion for a drama piece, or a live musician playing as a sound resource is a powerful tool indeed.

B. **Your goal:** Bring yourself and others into an immediate connection with your audience, one that transcends any dependence upon outside technology, or the use of merely recorded and prepared resources.

Summary

In this chapter we have explored what it means to make effective use of both visual and sound resources. Public speakers should use these resources to draw focus upon, and offer emotional attention to enhance their spoken topic at hand. Visual and sound resources should be used only to illuminate a point, support an argument, or help your audience experience something which they may not otherwise encounter, due to limited geographic considerations or social experience. All visual and sound resources should be kept simple, clear, and always to the point. They should never be extensive, and must never overwhelm your audience or dominate or upstage you as the central speaker.

Long-established resources, such blackboards/whiteboards and handheld artifacts, along with more elaborate electronic technologies, permit you to vastly enhance your speech, while at the same time hold your audience's attention. Although there is always the risk of too much dependence upon visual and sound resources, the usefulness of software programs such as PowerPoint and computer-generated slides offers virtually unlimited options in creating vibrant speeches that will help you to become a success with your audience.

By utilizing your visual and sound resources, which involve careful preparation and live usage, you can make a powerful impression upon your audience and avoid common pitfalls. It is important to keep a healthy equilibrium between you as the central speaker and your "visiting guests," your visual and sound resources. With all of the resources currently available in the early 21st century, still the most important resource is *you*—the human one. Remember: You, the live public speaker, will always be the most important visual and sound resource before any gathered audience.

Discussion Questions

1. What is meant by the term *artifact?* When are the best and worst times to make use of an artifact during a public speaking event? Do you think artifacts are necessary for a speech to be fully effective? Why or why not? Should they ever be avoided?

2. What do we mean by the term *graphics,* when speaking about visual resources? Which graphic resources may be best utilized by which types of speeches, or are all graphics equally applicable to any kind of speech style or topic?

3. What do we mean by the term *speaker-centeredness?* Why do you think it is important for the public speaker to be at the center of any speech? Do you think there are ever times when the speaker himself or herself should *not* be at the core of speech? If so, when and where may this ever be deemed appropriate?

4. What is the best way to make use of DVDs and videotapes, in your estimation? Is it ever appropriate to make your own DVD or videotape to accompany your speech? If so, how does this more fully help to contribute to speaker-centeredness?

5. What are the strengths involved in making use of *PowerPoint* when presenting a speech? Why do you think PowerPoint is being reevaluated with skepticism by public speaking experts and communication scholars these days? What is the solution to their skepticism?

● ● ● ● ● Quick Quiz

Match the following capsule sentences with the correct letter which seems to best describe the key terms or phrases discussed in this chapter.

1. ____ Freehand or simplified illustrations of what you are speaking about.

2. ____ Helps makes visual connections and associations not visible to an audience.

3. ____ A visual and sound application invented by Microsoft for public speakers.

4. ____ Printed materials that you supply for your audience to use during your speech.

5. ____ Those resources that help an audience better "see" what you are saying.

6. ____ Your efficient use of MP3 files, recordings, and live music during a speech.

7. ____ Effective use of organized charts, maps, and sketches during a speech.

8. ____ Old-fashioned erasable panels mostly used by teachers and businesspeople.

9. ____ Any animate or inanimate objects you use during your speech presentation.

10. ____ A speech focused primarily upon the live speaker, and not upon technology.

A. Speaker-centeredness	**B.** Sketches	**C.** Charts
D. Handouts	**E.** Sound resources	**F.** Visual resources
G. Blackboards/whiteboards	**H.** PowerPoint	**I.** Graphics
J. Artifacts		

PART IV
Styles of Speeches and Varieties of Approaches

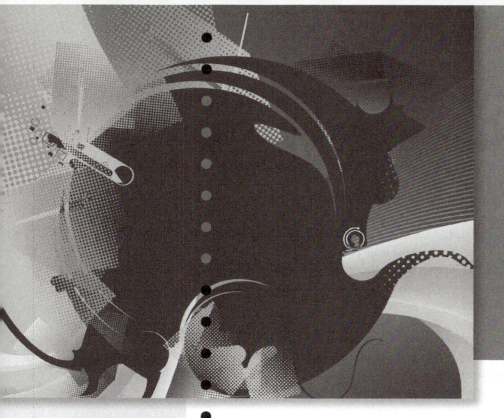

CHAPTER 10

Informative Speaking: You Become the *Teacher*

KEY TERMS

level of unawareness

educational significance

narration speech

exhibition speech

speech of clarification

speech print

room blueprint

order blueprint

time blueprint

group blueprint

contrast blueprint

factual contrast

symbolic contrast

actual contrast

room blueprint

order blueprint

time blueprint

group blueprint

contrasting blueprint

grounds blueprint

"There are certain things in which mediocrity is not to be endured, such as poetry, music, painting, and public speaking . . ."
—Jean de la Bruyere (1645–1696)

"Information is a source of learning. But unless it is organized, processed, and available to the right people in a format for decision making it is a burden, not a benefit."
—William Pollard

When we gather as a community for a speech, a slide presentation, or a public lecture, the truth is that we often attend these events with many preconceived ideas and notions about what the actual intention is. Whether a noted guest speaker at our university, a presidential State of the Union address, or even to a lesser degree a fiery sermon by a member of the clergy, the final expected result is usually to be *informed* in some way, shape, or form. We could say that, in a broader sense, all types of speeches inform or *teach* an audience about an idea, a concept, or some topic of relevance to those who care to pay attention in the first place. Every speech includes some level of information, whether it be in facts, figures, percentages, or both visual and sound data. After all, a good speech should provide information about someone, something, someplace, or some idea in the end.

In this chapter we will learn what it means to present information formally within a public setting; and will explore how an *informative speech* shares information with the public, in order to boost their knowledge or comprehension of the facts, ideas, and views that you, the organized speaker, hope to present before them. We will take a look at different *styles* of informative speeches, and suggest approaches and techniques for achieving well-prepared, stimulating, and highly educational presentations. When you speak to inform, you hope your audience will seriously learn from what you have to tell them, so in a sense you become a *teacher* in the truest sense of the word.

The Informative Speech

A successful informative speech should provide your audience with valuable information, and even perhaps answer many of the questions which were in the back of their minds *before, during,* and sometimes even *after* the delivery of the speech itself. In short, an informative speech *informs.* It is essentially interested in *teaching* an audience about a given topic of interest. When we ourselves give such a speech, where the main purpose is to inform, in essence we become a teacher within a public setting for the actual duration of our speech. Perhaps we are not an actual professional teacher, but we are a teacher nonetheless, so it is our job to be concise, clear, confident, and above all: well-informed about our topic.

By sharing facts, figures, statistics, and ideas along with helpful and instructive analysis, an informative speech reduces a **level of unawareness** for those watching and listening to you speak. It is your job not simply to repeat information the audience already is aware of, but rather to add **educational significance** to that which they may have brought with them before they even decided to attend your speech.

> ▶ Keep in mind that the educational significance of a speech is measured by how much innovative and supportive information and level of awareness you provide for your audience.

As you begin to prepare yourself for your graded informative speech, reflect upon the very nature and purpose of what you may uniquely offer your listeners, an approach which they may not acquire from anyone else. Consider reflecting on the following six questions before you begin any actual preparation.

• • • • • Reflective Questions for the Informative Speaker

1. At what level may my audience already be knowledgeable about my topic, by living in our contemporary information-accessible society of instant information and messaging??

2. Will my approach to my topic be significant and interesting enough to deserve speaking before a live audience in the first place?

3. What more may I offer my listeners which they cannot simply look up for themselves on the instant-information networks already available to them?

4. Do I comprehend and appreciate my topic well enough to help others learn and understand more about it, in a new and creative manner?

5. What qualifies me personally, and motivates me specifically, to need to speak about my chosen topic?

6. In what ways can I be inspirational and passionate in a manner which will permit my speech to be something more than simply teaching or offering information to the public?

Your personal answers to these six reflective questions should help you begin to think and plan your speech in a manner which will provide your listeners with a higher level of awareness about your topic. Remember, there is a level of accountability for you as a public speaker, namely to be ethically responsible about the information you provide to your audience. A successful speech which has honesty and integrity, should cover as many angles on a topic as is possible; and offer all vital information. This should also include information which you yourself may not agree with, or perhaps at times have any personal interest in at all. Remember, your listeners will most likely come from various lifestyles and diverse ethnic or religious backgrounds. It is *unethical* to consciously delete or even distort information which may not be of interest to you but may be of value to others in your audience.

▶ As you prepare your speech, be sure to seek out a variety of materials from sources which present different perspectives and approaches to your topic.

Styles of Informative Speeches

As was mentioned earlier in Chapter 1, we live in an information-driven society—a world often governed by cell phones with high-resolution cameras, iPods, twitters, instant e-mails, and those omnipresent laptops. Because of this, the importance of effective informative speaking can hardly be overemphasized. The nature of informative speaking is rooted in our very nature as members of the human species. As such, three general *styles of informative speaking* have endured over many centuries, ones which are used regularly and in various approaches by speakers the world over, and often in very creative ways as well. These three main styles are *narration speeches, exhibition speeches,* and *clarification speeches.* Each of these will be discussed in detail in the sections which follow. Keep in mind that in some instances, you may be asked to speak on a specific topic where the nature of the speaking event will dictate the length and manner of your speech. Understanding the different informative styles will help you to decide how to organize your speech, and to choose an approach which may be most beneficial to you for use beyond your classroom assignments.

Narration Speeches

Narration speeches focus on description. They *tell* about something. Daily we hear narrations on the radio, see them on television, and read them on the Internet. They may describe or *narrate* to an audience information about activities, persons, places, objects, and ideas. In a sense, think of the definition of the "noun" we all learned way back in elementary school; and then briefly discussed in Chapter 4. A *noun* is always a person, place, thing, or idea—as you may recall.

▶ A narrative speech should provide your listeners with a clear concrete and colorful description of a person, place, thing, or idea which is of importance to you, your audience, or better yet both.

Most radio programs include a narrator, and every football or baseball broadcast has a commentator who is vital to understanding every detail of the game. As narrator of your speech you must be concise, colorful, and as descriptive as is possible. Most forms of literature, such as novels, short stories, and poems, are highly descriptive and narrate all events to the person who reads them. Good narration provides information in such a vivid manner, that characters and settings come to actual life in the minds of every booklover. For instance, consider the following verses by the author of your textbook. The poem is entitled "Here; They Meet Jointly."

Here; They Meet Jointly

i.

HERE; they meet jointly peering out, amid
    Morning's red-farm-house-window . . .
    He will park hay with her, as high, high

Up above, two blue jays fondle a worm through
    A secret view from their far-off limb . . .
    And a nearby pond listens . . . and listens

ii.

SHE embraces him, and once more two brazen
    Yellow-Burnt-orange monarchs will shudder,
    And both will watch and witness.

As they behold, they quiver, stare and shiver
    From their firm-limbed, cocoon . . .
    As the sun further, mounts its morning rays.

iii.

A YOUNG couple with frail feet; and now a ring,
    Hail this spring dawn of four wheels
    As proposal of their union echoes;

Now, with crowded nature watching:
    One season gone; death and then . . . new bells

iv.

BIRTH of all life—still never fully severed.
    She and he will go on, and once more . . .

Complete each other's limbs as
    Was ever destined to be, they will say: "I do."

—John Ross, Jr. (2010)

Although the language of poetry may be uncommon to listeners who may read or, better yet, hear this poem read aloud, the power of descriptive language is still at the forefront. Colorful narration, including illustrative details, paints a picture for the reader or listener. One which, upon reflection, describes a young wheelchair-bound couple and their pledge of marriage to one another. A red farm house engagement takes place before a simple morning sunrise, and in the midst of witnessing birds, butterflies, and a listening pond. This poem narrates a simple yet traditional event most often accompanied by a public display normally within the hustle and bustle of an elegant restaurant, and perhaps before or after dinner and some champagne.

But in this poem we are brought into a private countryside setting, while only nature watches and bears witness to this wedding engagement. Here the narration of the poem seems to suggest that even among those we may perceive to be disabled (e.g., "frail feet"), love, procreation, marriage proposals, and the cycle of nature both are inclusive and will ever endure.

Unlike the poem "Here; They Meet Jointly," narrative speeches should attempt even more clearly to generate a clear description of events to your audience.

> ▶ It is important not only to offer information, but also to colorfully narrate your topic at hand. A narration should always paint a clear picture for listeners.

If for instance you were to speak about the phenomena of UFO sightings around the world, you might first define what UFOs are, and then attempt to illustrate their history over time up to the early 21st century, and then briefly share with your audience descriptions of how there have been both fraudulent, hoaxed sightings as well as authentic unexplained ones. Describing such sightings can be a thrilling and engaging narration for your audience. Thus, you should leave all decisions about UFOs to your audience, and only supply them with a general knowledge, understanding, and overall description of the topic. As with the poem "Here; They Meet Jointly," only the colorful, narrative facts are offered, and no judgment or assessment of the events governed by the poet's or the speaker's opinion.

Exhibition Speeches

Oftentimes it is necessary when giving a speech to not only *tell* but also *show* your audience how to carry out a task or procedure, or simply demonstrate to them how to do something. In a sense, your speech becomes an exhibit. We refer to this style of presentation before a public audience as an **exhibition speech**. Cooking instructors show us how to prepare a fine French meal at home for our friends. Others may tell us how to make effective use of a new computer software program, or perhaps how to begin the fine art of watercolor painting. The important element in the exhibition speech is to exhibit or visually *display* before your listeners the very essence of what you wish to tell them.

> ▶ What is at the center of exhibition speeches, is that they demonstrate a procedure, a specific process, or a proper manner of doing something.

Successful exhibition speeches empower listeners to easily carry out procedures and processes for themselves at work, at home, and in situations of their choosing. One student at Roosevelt University in downtown Chicago recently demonstrated to her listeners how to manage time more efficiently, using her favorite self-help book on saving time and saving money, by a best-selling author. She guided them through seven basic principles designed to save both time and considerable money for those living on a typical student budget. She used an approach which we call a *sequential method*.

Another student at Northeastern Illinois University, located in the vicinity of Albany Park in northwest Chicago, exhibited to his listeners how to take an exclusive tour of the major sights and attractions of "Chicagoland": namely, downtown Chicago and the neighboring tourist areas. He made use of what we refer to as a *spatial method* of approach. Both of these speech approaches will be delineated later in this chapter.

The hallmark of exhibition speeches is that they often make use of presentation aids, concrete visual resources, and even at times musical or sound enhancement. This topic is covered more thoroughly in Chapter 9. Exhibition speeches may include commonly found objects or artifacts, special tools, photographs, sound recordings, videos, even live animals or special guest assistants. In short, the speaker *exhibits* and discusses objects which listeners must see or use to achieve some goal or task. What is effective about an exhibition speech, is that it is literally an old-fashioned type of presentation which we at one time glibly identified way back in grammar school as: "show 'n' tell."

Clarification Speeches

When we attempt to present a speech which provides information about a specific subject, a complex situation, or an abstract idea, we refer to this style of presentation as a **speech of clarification**. Since the purpose of this speech is comprehension and explanation, a speech of clarification should offer clear definitions of ideas and terms, along with plentiful examples and illustrations. In his speech clarifying the myths and misunderstandings surrounding the current HIV/AIDS epidemic in the United States and Canada, another Roosevelt University student last year presented the significant characteristics of the epidemic in the following seven-step sequence:

1. The student began by simply classifying the HIV/AIDS syndrome as defined by the World Health Organization (WHO), and by the U.S. Surgeon's office in Washington, D.C.

2. He described to his audience the actual course and progression of the syndrome, thus giving his audience clarity about how professionals view the disease.

3. He concisely identified the risk factors associated with the syndrome worldwide, thus giving a global perspective on the phenomenon.

4. He explained the medical and emotional consequences of the virus for those dealing with it, their immediate families, and their significant others.

5. He clearly illuminated how average individuals can minimize receptiveness to the syndrome, and avoid it in their own lives.

6. He then made known the financial burdens and costs of the virus for both the United States and Canada.

7. Finally, he concluded his speech by describing and directly quoting well-known individuals currently living with HIV/AIDS, and then invited his audience to have a greater awareness and understanding of the syndrome among all men, women, and children as well as among those who label themselves as gay or lesbian.

> ▶ Be sure to remember that, when you decide to give a speech of clarification, you present the essential features of your subject in a logical and precise arrangement for your audience to follow easily.

Be sure always to define your subject, explaining its importance to the lives of your audience, and then of course describing any manner by which it develops. Always make sure your speech is replete with examples and perhaps case studies. And be sure of course to include a variety of testimonials and personal commentary from authorities far more knowledgeable than yourself or your friends.

TWIN RULES

Informative Speeches

Narration Speeches

A. **Remember:** This speech is about *telling* and describing. Be sure to always be a storyteller or reporter.

B. **Always be sure** to make your speech come alive with powerful, colorful words, and phrases.

Exhibition Speeches

A. **Remember:** Make wise use of visual aids, including photos, diagrams, charts, and even perhaps PowerPoint slides!

B. **Always be sure** to offer to your listeners a clear and orderly succession of steps to follow.

Clarification Speeches

A. **Remember:** Clearly define your subject, and always explain all technical or special terms to your listeners.

B. **Always be sure** to have good examples and to quote well-known individuals and experts.

Blueprints for Speeches

After you've selected an interesting topic (as discussed in Chapter 4 of this text) which should provide some helpful new information for your listeners, and have completed some basic research, gathered some excellent examples and quotes, and then have formed an overall strong comprehension of your materials at hand: then it is time for you to create a *blueprint* for your speech. A **speech print** is, in general, a structure which will help frame your speech in an effective pattern which will best enable your listeners to receive it. A blueprint, not unlike the rendering that architects utilize in constructing a new building, is what gives an informative speech its foundation. After you have your blueprint "drawn," you need only concern yourself with presenting your speech. There are several categories of blueprints available to the public speaker. In this particular text, we will concern ourselves with six of the basic useful blueprint patterns: Room, Order, Time, Group, Contrast, and Ground blueprints.

Room Blueprints

A **room blueprint** is appropriate for speeches which most often develop their topics within a geographical setting, not unlike the arrangement of a room in a house or office building. The arrangement of your speech is based upon the geographical relationship of things arranged in space.

> Room blueprints are quite useful for speeches of narration, which they assist your listeners in visualizing the physical relationship of objects to one another.

Room blueprints operate just as furniture in a room may be arranged in accordance with established entrances, exits, windows, closets, and the like. In short, room blueprints create a pattern for an informative speech which arranges the main points as they occur in tangible *time* and *space*.

The following is a quick general overall structure using a room blueprint for taking a self-guided tour of Yellowstone National Park. The presentation for such a speech should also include information about how Yellowstone National Park is America's first national park. Located in Wyoming, Montana, and Idaho, Yellowstone is home to a large variety of wildlife including grizzly bears, wolves, bison, and elk.

Preserved within Yellowstone are *Old Faithful* and a collection of the world's most extraordinary geysers and hot springs, as well as the *Grand Canyon of the Yellowstone*. In the box below is a possible general outline which I would consider if I were giving the speech based upon my own experience there:

A Self-guided Tour of Yellowstone National Park

I. **Everyone's primary stop should be the South Entrance Visitor's Center. This is the central place to visit for a knowledgeable and well-informed early introduction to this vast national park, encompassing territory in three states.**

    A. Be sure to speak first with a park ranger to help plan your trip according to your own personal interests and time constraints.

    B. If you plan to see the park over a few days' time, inform the ranger so he or she may help arrange a more comprehensive schedule for you, including places to lodge and dine.

    C. Be sure to make yourself present at one of the many lectures or film presentations to enhance your experience, as well as to familiarize yourself with the park's geographic density and sheer size.

    D. Gather any cogent information, books, and specialized maps available in the bookstore, to make your visit less stressful and more significant within your time frame for visiting.

II. **Second, either drive or hike in a northwesterly direction through what is known as *Geyser Valley* to make an unsurpassable visit to the world-famous natural wonder we have all come to know as: *Old Faithful*.**

    A. Afterward, consider hiking on the boardwalks in the *Upper Geyser Basin*, a must-see, must-do event. Many visitors pass up this wonderful experience as they rush to do too much by taking only a quick overview of the park.

    B. Take the time to join the anticipating crowds who await *Old Faithful's* exploding on schedule. This is for most people an once-in-a-lifetime occurrence, and is a thrilling natural event experienced by visitors from all over the world.

C. Be sure to take time to join the crowd for a meal and some dessert, at the well-known Old Faithful Inn. There, a great tradition continues of visitors meeting many people from all over the world, and other parts of the United States.

III. Third, continue north to *Mammoth Hot Springs*. Here is another essential must-see attraction. If at all possible, plan to use up the evening to spend a night in the Gatehouse Lodge, or one of the many cabins available to the public.

    A. Be sure to be present at many of the evening lectures or featured films about the fascinating and evolving history of the park, as a natural wonder.

    B. Be sure to have your binoculars handy to spot various birds, mammals, and other wild animals. *Mammoth Hot Springs* gathers many critters nearby its surroundings.

IV. Lastly, hike or drive southeasterly to the *Grand Canyon of the Yellowstone*, another must-see nature event. It is not as large as the *Grand Canyon* in Arizona, but is equally extraordinary. It is another great photo spot.

    A. Be sure to take some phone pictures as you view the splendor around you from the vantage spot found at: *Inspiration Point.*

    B. Don't forget to hike down the marked path for a more improved observation of the waterfalls. Again, there is often animal life to take notice of and even photograph.

● ● ● ● ● Order Blueprints

An **order blueprint** moves your audience through *order* or time. Informative speeches designed around an order blueprint characteristically present steps for your listeners to follow in a clear and defined succession. This type of blueprint is most effective for exhibition speeches which attempt to display or demonstrate a concept or a "how-to" progression of steps. You simply initiate things by identifying the needed steps, and then carry on in the required order in which they must be taken. Actually, it is these steps themselves which should become the actual main points of your speech. In short, simply keep in mind that:

> ▶ An order blueprint is a general pattern for informative speeches which presents the necessary order involved in the procedure you hope to display or exhibit before your audience.

Further, your blueprint should have no more than four or five ordered steps for a short five- to eight-minute speech presentation. In the box on the next page is an abbreviated outline, which provides an order blueprint for how the uninitiated reader might approach reading poetry in order to gain a more complete appreciation and comprehension, of what many people see as a perplexing and sometimes very difficult task.

How to Read a Poem

I. Begin at first by scanning the overall shape and length of the poem.

    A. Read the poem at least three times (nonstop) without caring about any comprehension or understanding of its meaning.

    B. Then ask yourself: What is the general theme of this poem? Attempt to encapsulate its theme, by a few words, or at best by a simple sentence.

    C. Look up any words, foreign phrases, or terms contained in the poem that are unfamiliar to you.

    D. Consult any footnotes or commentary if offered by the poet or publisher.

II. Second, reread the poem, only this time *out load*, and without stopping.

    A. Attempt to pay close attention to the sounds and rhythms of the language.

    B. Make notes in the margins of the poem about any questions you may have.

    C. Ask yourself: how many characters, if any, do I hear in the poem?

    D. Ask yourself: from whose point of view is the poem being written?

III. Third, seriously consider the title of the poem.

    A. Attempt to discover the relationship between the title itself and the poem.

    B. Ask yourself if the title of the poem provides any insights into its meaning? If so, what are they? If not, why do you believe the poem has been titled as such by the poet?

    C. From your understanding of the poem *thus* far, do you approve of the title, or would you change it if you could? If so, what better title would you assign to the poem?

IV. Finally, after putting the poem away for at least three days:

    A. Go back and review your notes in the margins. What are your impressions of them now, after some time has passed?

    B. Reread the poem once more (out loud), this time as if to a child or younger individual than yourself.

    C. Now attempt to tell that individual, in your own words, what this poem is all about as if you had written it yourself!

    D. Imagine that you have clearly discovered the poem's meaning. And that the original meaning you were searching for is incorrect, and that you, the reader, actually do help complete the poet's meaning and purpose!

● ● ● ● ● Time Blueprint

Our next speech blueprint, which is closely related to the *order blueprint,* follows the organization of noteworthy events in the history of a person, place, or distinctive occasion. In short, a **time blueprint** is a pattern of speech organization which follows the succession of important events in a historical pattern. Using this blueprint for your speech, you may begin with the earliest history of your subject, and trace it up to the very present moment, or simply vice versa. In order to keep your speech interesting and easy to follow, you must be selective in the order and particular number of points you choose to present to your listeners. Of course, you should choose momentous events as the core of your main points, and then assemble them in a genuine, easy-to-follow order. Consider the following general time blueprint about the history of T-shirts as a good example:

The General History of T-shirts

I. **T-shirts began solely as an undergarment in the early part of the 20th century, beginning sometime around 1905–1910.**

   A. The first T-shirts with sleeves were intended for American sailors, to help conceal their exposed chests and armpits in the presence of nonmilitary communities; and so as to not cause any offense in public places off ship where sailors may gather. They served as an early form of garment for public modesty; and never intended to be worn in public.

   B. T-shirts began to be sold commercially to the public beginning in the late 1930s and well into the next decade. Gradually their popularity grew and grew differently, decade-by-decade. T-shirts continue to evolve to this very decade well into the 21st century.

   C. T-shirts were never used as a sole form of outerwear until the advent of World War II, and have now become a common form of casual and popular dress. They have even become a form of acceptable wear at what were considered more formal events, such as: symphony concerts, cinemas, attending the opera and at Broadway shows.

   D. T-shirts were easy to wear, easy to care for, and porous in hot weather, which added to their popularity in summer and warmer fall seasons. They became even a focus for designers of new spring and summer collections for both men and women.

   E. T-shirts became all the rage in Hollywood films such as *Rebel without a Cause* and in popular Broadway musicals such as *Show Boat* and *South Pacific.*

II. **T-shirts later became embellished with pictures and personal messages in the late 1950s and '60s and even into the early '70s.**

   A. Children's T-shirts began to offer pictures of storybook characters, nursery rhymes, popular TV cartoon figures, large-scale Disney characters, and big-city themes surrounding well-known tourist sites in New York, London, Paris, and Chicago.

B. Later in the 1970s more mature-theme T-shirts became very popular with sports figures and emblazoned with sports teams among adults and adolescent sports fans. Even T-shirts with the actual names and numbers of basketball, football, and baseball players became quite popular. Even bold names of blues, jazz and rock bands became features.

C. Beginning in the 1980s T-shirts became popular among political candidates and featured grand political comments and political statements about human rights, war, disease, famine and even global warming.

III. Now people everywhere are authors of their own T-shirt fashions or revolutions.

A. Anyone anywhere may fashion and customize their own image or message on their own T-shirt. Many people make T-shirts at home, and then sell them online from a visual catalog which they have also made available online.

B. Anyone anywhere may fashion and customize their own borrowed or self-taken photographs and place them on their own T-shirt. One made to their own specifications. T-shirts with photos of deceased parents, children, and grandparents have become immensely popular; even ones advertising home-made products or services.

C. You can purchase T-shirts previously owned by celebrities or politicians, and even ones used in Hollywood films or at rock concerts and by Olympic medalists.

Group Blueprints

You may consider using the **group blueprint** when you are discussing with your audience the use of inherent or routine divisions within a topic. Divisions and categories help us mentally classify information so that we may have a better understanding in the end. Most individuals find order and comprehension of the world around them, by seeking ordered divisions within it or by finding effective ways to partition it.

In a group speech, each division in the blueprint becomes a main point for growth and development. Keep in mind that you should expand each of these points with supporting data which details, validates, and demonstrates what you are speaking about to your listeners.

> ▶ In a group blueprint you should provide information about items, and show how they are commonly thought to constitute a group or category for some useful motive or end.

An example might be an informative speech about retroviruses. The term "retrovirus" is used to classify a group of viruses like Chronic Fatigue Syndrome (CFS) which are fundamentally different from other viruses, a term chosen for important societal reasons. Here are a few tips on how you may approach how to design a *group blueprint* for such a speech. The following is not a detailed outline *per se*, but simple tips on how to approach designing your own blueprint:

Tip #1: You should begin with groups or categories that your audience may already be familiar with. You may approach your outline by clearly telling your audience that they may already be aware of viruses (which you should nevertheless define for them), but more importantly scientists have isolated a unique group of viruses which behave in a further and acutely different manner than ever known previously.

Tip #2: Attempt to explain why each particular category of viruses makes a crucial difference, and why this is important both to your audience and to society at large.

Tip #3: You should then consider explaining just *how* each particular group makes a difference, and *why* your audience should care.

Tip #4: You should make clear to your audience that this is not just high-brow science for elite minds, but that it has implications for each category which may affect each of them on a daily basis.

Contrast Blueprint

You may find a more *contrasting* approach to giving your speech if your chosen area of focus is one which is abstract, or often difficult to understand by the general public. This blueprint is also helpful when you wish to discuss changes or advances in a subject, such as the perfection of a given technology, or the advances in a medical procedure, or say in an industrial process. One of my favorite speeches in class was by a Northeastern student who explained the latest advancements and improvements in vision care. She gave a highly informative and lucid presentation on the state-of-the-art optical technology in laser surgery and contact lenses. A **contrast blueprint** is simply a plan for an informative speech that correlates an unfamiliar subject to something your listeners are already acquainted with, or for the most part have a basic knowledge or understanding about.

Oftentimes when we make such comparisons, they are usually *factual, symbolic,* or what I like to term as *actual* contrasts. Offered below are bullet points to help you take a look at the three varieties and approaches to utilizing contrast blueprints.

Utilizing Contrast Blueprints

- *You should utilize:* a **factual contrast** when the subjects *or* ideas you wish to match up fall within the same realm of knowledge or familiarity.

  Such as: contrasting the political philosophy of socialism with that of communism as practiced in the world today.

- *You should utilize:* a **symbolic contrast** when the subjects *or* ideas you wish to match up fall within different realms of knowledge or familiarity.

  Such as: contrasting the human body's immune system with that of, say, two opposing sports teams or an armed forces operation during a war confrontation.

- *You should utilize:* an **actual contrast** when the subjects or ideas you wish to match up may be conveniently contrasted by actually pointing out both similarities *and* differences between them point-by-point.

  Such as: contrasting the similarities and differences between the two Houses of Congress in the United States with the two Houses of Parliament in the United Kingdom.

It is often fun and interesting to make use of factual and symbolic contrasts. They may be quite revealing in how they convey and highlight information to your audience. Oftentimes an analogy is just what makes things click for an audience. In 1959 Watson and Crick explained their famous discovery of the DNA molecule in great detail to their fellow scientists (and the world) as a twisting and ascending double-helix ladder. Namely, they presented it as a ladder whose overall steps had been twisted around a central pole. It was not unlike the compact spiral stairs found leading to the top of the Statue of Liberty, or perhaps those found leading down into a submarine. Further, the notion of a ladder helped reinforce the idea of "stepping higher-up to go somewhere," thus being a reference to the function of DNA as a central component to evolutionary growth of animal and plant life, over millions of years.

Be careful when you make contrasts this way. If you attempt to force *or* even stretch the comparison, your whole speech will collapse and you will only confuse and frustrate your audience. In the end you will lose both credibility, and possibly your confidence for any further public speaking.

> ▶ In your contrast blueprint, you simply want to take a familiar noun—an event, a place, or a thing—and compare it to one which is most likely familiar to your audience.

To make your speech nonbiased, you should compare your two parallel topics one to the other, while not arguing which one is better than the other. Here are a few general tips on how you may approach a *contrast* outline when comparing a war for independence between two different cultures—the United States and Mexico:

Tip #1: Most Americans are familiar with their own war for independence, but not so with perhaps that of our neighbor to the south, Mexico. Make your audience aware of a noble war of independence which took place just below us on our very own North American continent.

Tip #2: In your contrast outline, you should attempt to parallel (point-by-point) the contrast between the American war for independence from the kingdom of Great Britain, with that of Mexico, fought against the kingdom of Spain.

Tip #3: You should help your audience be able to make connections based on the information which they are already comfortable, and are largely aware of by general knowledge; if you cannot do this, then you should be prepared to help re-educate them along the way.

Tip #4: Never assume anything, unless perhaps your listeners are history club members, history majors, or history buffs. Always spell things out clearly.

● ● ● ● ● Grounds Blueprint

A **grounds blueprint** for an informative speech shows how one circumstance creates, or is possibly created, on the grounds of another. This blueprint is often utilized in speeches of *clarification*, where you may express a topic either as a result of certain grounds, or on the grounds of a certain outcome.

▶ Usually the speaker initiates a grounds blueprint by recounting the topic and its significance, and then either questions how it came about, or what its end result might be.

It is important in this style of speech not to draw hasty conclusions, or to make things out to be easier than they actually are in reality. Most situations are, of course, far more complicated or involved than they may appear to be at first inspection. What is important, is to have your grounds built upon strong factual resources, and if possible upon experimentation and tests. The following is an abbreviated outline of a Northeastern Illinois University student's approach to the benefits of taking daily multiple-vitamin capsules.

Basic Premise: Receiving your daily recommended dose of vitamins can provide you with energy; can help prevent colds, flu, and other common communicable infections; and can help you better perform daily functions which are not supported by any other available nutrient.

I. A. A daily small dose of 200 percent of the daily requirement can benefit your heart.

   B. It may then lower the chances of a second heart attack by nearly 30 percent.

   C. It may reduce the risk of death during heart attack by as much 23 percent.

II. Daily vitamin doses can also prevent certain common cancers.

   A. Vitamins have been known to lower the risk of colon cancer.

   B. They have been known to reduce the risk of esophageal cancer by 80–90 percent.

   C. They have been known to lower ovarian cancer by 25 percent.

III. Daily doses of vitamins offer other enormous possible benefits.

   A. They may reduce risk of stroke by 25 percent.

   B. They may help counter dementia and Alzheimer's by increasing blood flow in the brain.

IV. Daily doses of vitamins may also have a few irritating drawbacks.

   A. They may cause gastrointestinal bleeding.

   B. They may delay blood clotting and be weak in stopping bleeding.

   C. They may encourage other varieties of strokes.

   D. Be sure to always ask your doctor's advice about the role of vitamins in your life.

Informative Speeches: Which Blueprint and When?

1. You should consider the **room blueprint**:
   When: your topic could be presented by how it is positioned in a geographical layout or a natural setting.
   It will permit you: to take your listeners on an orderly and logical adventure.

2. You should consider the **order blueprint**:
   When: your topic could be arranged by time, or by a chronology of events.
   It will permit you: to present your topic as a clear, ordered process.

3. You should consider the **time blueprint**:
   When: your topic can be presented as a significant historical event.
   It will permit you: to present an important progression of noteworthy instances.

4. You should consider the **group blueprint**:
   When: your topic consists of inherent or traditional divisions.
   It will permit you: to effectively classify large amounts of information.

5. You should consider the **contrasting blueprint**:
   When: your topic is theoretical, highly technical, or not readily understood by the public.
   It will help you: present a complex topic in a more digestible manner by known contrasts.

6. You should consider the **grounds blueprint**:
   When: Your topic may be explained best in terms of fundamental causes and effects.
   It will help you: account for existing circumstances or even forecast potential options.

Making Yourself Lucid

Presenting your topic clearly and efficiently is the hallmark of any successful speaker. We learned so far in this chapter that an informative speaker, is essentially *teaching* his or her audience about a topic which is of interest to both. Enhancing understanding and appreciation of your topic is the chief task of an informative speaker.

> ▶ Always keep in mind that being lucid, moment-by-moment, is the hallmark of teaching or informing anyone about anything. So be clear at all times.

As a speaker in general, you may think you are being obvious and apparent about all you say and do. The truth is, only your individual audience members can really tell if they have actually received your message clearly. Therefore you must watch and feel for their reactions to you words. If they seem lost or confused, though your presentation may be crystal clear to you, it may not be to them.

Pamela J. Hines (*Journal of Experimental Psychology:* Applied 5, 1999) conducted an intriguing study in which she discovered that it is a simple assumption by most public speakers that if all of their information is *lucid* to them as speaker, then it will also be crystal clear to their audience as well. The popular delusion seems to be, that if you are familiar with the subject or topic at hand, you are likely to think it is equally clear to everyone else as well.

When speaking in public, it is essential that you give personal consideration to how you may help your listeners understand your particular message. To become a successful and powerful speaker, you must help them by consciously developing and presenting ideas with them always in mind. It is important to realize that teaching is not about tossing information before an audience, and trusting that it will then sink in. Informing an audience is an acquired art. It requires passion, insight, and an ardent desire to be heard and understood. Here are some simple tenets for you to keep in mind while you are giving a speech. Hopefully these will help you enhance your message, and imbue it with clarity and understanding. I like to refer to them as the: *always rules for teaching your audience.*

Always Rules — Teaching Your Audience

- *Always* tell your listeners how one previous point does *or* will relate to your next point, thus creating a more-total approach.

- *Always* be sure to summarize your important ideas frequently, thus reinforcing them in the minds of your listeners on a regular basis.

- *Always* distribute any handouts or printed matter *prior* to your speech, so as to avoid having your audience become distracted while you speak.

- *Always* be sure to remain focused on your central topic, thus avoiding the temptation to go off on a related or interesting digression.

- *Always* be sure to remain confident and assured that you are in control of your speech. If you make an obvious mistake, or need to correct yourself, remain self-assured.

- *Always* pay close attention to the faces and general *awareness level* of your audience. If they appear confused or puzzled, take time to ask them if you are understood.

A Successful Teacher Creates Inspiration, Intension, and Preservation

One of the main obstacles which every teacher has to face during his or her presentation is the question: "will it actually enter the minds (and, to a further degree, the hearts) of my listening audience?" "What if my words simply fall only upon plugged ears and blocked hearts?" "What if my audience simply pretends to pay attention, but is mentally elsewhere during my lecture or presentation?" In short, "what if my work becomes largely ineffective in the end?" The truth is, you are less likely to fail if you strive to make a conscious effort to help your audience understand; and pay close attention to every word you have to say.

To make it easier for your audience to learn and remember your message, you must *inspire* them by establishing the significance of your words in their own lives. Holding their attention moment-by-moment throughout your speech is essential. You must also be sure to have a clear and easy-to-follow *blueprint* to help each of them preserve (or remember) your words long after they have left their seats.

Remember: you must speak with *inspiration, intension,* and *preservation.* You must actually *desire* to be heard, which is key to actually *being* heard. A popular 1970s and '80s talk show host by the name of Dick Cavett (of the popular *The Dick Cavett Show*) is famously quoted to have regularly announced:

*"It's a rare person indeed who wants to hear what he (or she)
themselves doesn't want to hear."*

Cavett's words are a wonderful rule of thumb to keep in mind at all times. *If you are interested in what you have to say, it is highly probable your audience will be, too!* You should always bear in mind how much your audience may already know about your topic at hand. You should be certain to pay close attention to their possible level of interest. Also, be sure to consider what preconceived notions (or prior ideas about what you have to say) your audience may already be bringing with them to your speech. These questions will help you devise the right approach and energy level of your speech.

Your **A**, **B**, **C**s for Better Audience Understanding

If you *know* your audience will be basically **uninformed**, then you should:

A Provide the fundamentals of your topic.
B Avoid being assumptive and using insider jargon.
C Use plenty of examples and metaphors to help them relate.

If you *know* your audience will be basically **informed**, then you should:

A Reinforce your authority and familiarity of the topic throughout your speech.
B Go into further detail and feel free to expand upon your topic.
C Recognize and offer alternative perspectives upon your topic.

If you *know* your audience will be basically **unconcerned**, then you should:

A Establish an effective way to make it relevant to their lives.

B Use plenty of visual or audio aids and practical, helpful examples.

C Try to keep your presentation simple, short, and always direct.

If you *know* your audience will be basically **unempathetic**:

A Be sure to admit your recognition and respect for their dissimilar views.

B Remember to make your overall approach warm and favorable.

C Use known sources your audience will value and respect.

Summary

In this chapter we have explored what it means to be *informative* when giving a speech in public—namely, to communicate information to your listening audience about something they know nothing, or very little about. What is important in the end is to be clear about your facts, figures, any examples you may provide, and your overall approach to your topic.

Your speech should always be relevant to your audience, immediately useful, and accurate in a digital age where anything may be fact-checked at the press of a handheld device.

As the presenter of an informative speech you take on the role of a teacher. As a teacher you must be credible and motivated, and must offer your listeners something far and above what they may acquire via electronic technology. You must make your speech easy to remember, limited in scope, and focused.

Good teachers are aware of time constraints and never attempt to cover too much information in one sitting. In the end you must be inspiring by all you say and do. And if you endeavor to be understood, you are most likely to communicate a successful speech which achieves all your goals in the end.

Discussion Questions

1. What do we mean when we say that the purpose of an informative speech is to decrease the *level of unawareness* in your audience?

2. What do you think constitutes an effective and lucid teacher? In light of this definition, what basic skills borrowed from teaching do you think help make a lucid public speaker?

3. Of the three *styles of informative speeches*, which do you think requires the most research, preparation, and challenging skills overall? Why or why not?

4. Of the six *speech blueprints* we learned about in this chapter, which of these do you find the most engaging? Which of them are you more readily interested in using yourself? Which of the six do you find the least appealing to utilize, and why?

5. What ways might you go about making an audience listen better to your speech if you suspect they may be distrustful of you, or feel you are not a credible source?

Quick Quiz

Match the following capsule sentences below with the correct letter which best describes the key terms or phrases found in this chapter.

1. ____ Speeches which *tell* something and tend to focus on description.

2. ____ A blueprint which correlates something new to something your listeners know.

3. ____ A blueprint which follows a series of important events in a historical pattern.

4. ____ Speeches that *teach* others by reducing their lack of knowledge.

5. ____ Speeches which show a procedure, or demonstrate how to do something.

6. ____ A speech on "How to Read a Poem" would utilize this type of blueprint.

7. ____ The importance or value which an informative speech bestows upon listeners.

8. ____ A speech blueprint which develops its topics around a geographical locale or setting.

9. ____ A successful informative speech should reduce what among your listeners?

10. ____ A speech whose purpose is explanation and comprehension.

    A. Clarification   **B.** Informative   **C.** Exhibition

    D. Narration   **E.** Time blueprint   **F.** Educational significance

    G. Room blueprint   **H.** Level of unawareness   **I.** Order blueprint

    J. Contrast blueprint

Persuasive Speaking: You Become the *Preacher*

"The most important persuasion tool you have in your entire arsenal is . . . integrity."
—Zig Ziglar (motivational speaker)

"A reasoned argument is meant to reveal the truth, not to create it."
—Edward de Bono

When most people think about persuasive speeches, perhaps one of the first things that enters into their thoughts is "I suppose we are expected to be swayed by someone's opinion here, right?" Or possibly: "We are supposed to be converted by this individual's testimony; that his or her religion is the only way to personal peace? Really?" Or maybe even: "They're trying to influence me to purchase beyond my interest in their products here . . . this is all about money, and convincing me to spend, correct?" The truth is we often listen to persuasive words while having many ideas and notions about what the actual rationale behind them is supposed to be. Whether it be TV or radio commercials, special-election radio campaigns, online pop-ups, around-the-clock infomercials on cable channels, or a fiery religious message by a storefront preacher, the final expected result is usually to be *persuaded* by some method, technique, or approach.

The art of persuasion, and other forms of reasoned argumentation, have been around for millennia. Because persuasion is such an ever-present phenomenon in contemporary life, it is vital for you to understand how and when it works best before a live audience. In this chapter we will attempt to help you both understand and present a persuasive speech. We hope to assist you in sharpening your argumentative and persuasive skills. Since the very nature of a persuasive speech is to change or reinforce attitudes, values, beliefs, and even at times specific actions or behaviors, then speaking to persuade must be grounded in solid reasoning and argumentation. In a persuasive speech the speaker actually invites the audience to make a choice for an option of some kind, rather than simply presenting an array of possible options.

As a persuasive speaker you will not only teach your audience; you will have the task of *preaching* to them as well. To encourage a particular point of view successfully, you as the preacher must be compassionate toward and also clearly understand, your audience's own attitudes, values, beliefs, and past behavioral patterns.

The Persuasive Speech

As was pointed out in Chapter 10, all types of speeches inform or *teach* an audience about an idea, a concept, or some topic of relevance to those who may care to listen. In many ways we could say that a **persuasive speech** convinces by simply attempting to change our current attitude or manner of thinking about a topic. Even more significantly, persuasive words often are interested in attempting to change our behaviors too. A successful persuasive speech will hopefully provide an audience with challenging arguments, and perhaps even answer many of the thorny disagreements which were in the back of their minds before and during the delivery of the speech.

> ▶ In short, a persuasive speech argues or convinces. It is essentially interested in influencing an audience's thoughts about a given topic or awareness.

When we give a persuasive speech whose main purpose is to influence, in essence we become a preacher (within a public setting) for the actual duration of the speech. We may not be a professional or ordained member of the clergy, but we function as a preacher nonetheless. As such, it is our job to be concise, well-informed, and quite confident about the nature of our topic, as we would with any informative speech.

It is important to note that persuasion always involves a free choice in the end. If not, then we are engaging in coercion. **Coercion** is forcing a person to think or behave in a certain manner by which they are made to feel obligated to believe, or act under pressure or threat. *Brainwashing or intimidating people to obtain a desired outcome is not persuasion!* Democratic societies such as ours, are founded on the rights of individuals to choose their own thoughts and behaviors. Therefore, all good, persuasive words should inspire. So, as persuasive speakers, we should help stir our listeners into wanting to pay close attention to what we have to say, think, and hopefully even do.

By sharing facts, figures, statistics, and ideas, and by offering argumentative analysis, a persuasive speech reduces its listeners to a level of contentment. It does not simply repeat persuasive information the audience already is aware of, but should also adds new information based upon an alternative point of view. One which they brought with them previously, even before they decided to come a listen to our speech. The convincing significance of your speech is measured by how much innovative and challenging information, or greater awareness you can provide for your listeners.

As you begin to prepare yourself for your persuasive speech, reflect upon the very nature and purpose of what you may distinctively offer to your audience, an approach which they may not acquire otherwise. As you do, consider reflecting on the following five questions before you begin any written preparation or investigation into your persuasive approach. Many of these questions are very similar to those discussed when we were exploring informative speeches.

Reflective Questions for the Persuasive Speaker

1. At what level may my audience already have been influenced about my topic, by being recurrently showered by digital information, TV, radio, and the Internet?

2. Will my approach to the topic be significant and interesting enough to warrant challenging, attempting to sway, or even changing the behavior of a gathered audience?

3. What convincing arguments may I offer my listeners which they cannot already simply look up for themselves on the digital and information highways already available to them?

4. Do I understand and honestly believe in my topic; well enough to help others learn and understand more about it by offering a fresh or opposing mind-set?

5. What qualifies me personally and truly motivates me to speak about my chosen persuasive topic?

● ● ● ● ● The Ethics of Persuasion

Answering these five reflective questions should help you begin to think about and plan your speech in a manner which will provide your audience with a high level of awareness toward your persuasive arguments. Remember, as with any kind of speech, there is a level of accountability for you as a public speaker, namely to be *ethical* about the information you provide to your audience. A successful persuasive speech which has integrity should cover as many angles on a topic as possible; and offer all vital information. This must also include information which you yourself may not fully agree with, or perhaps even find challenging to speak about. Remember, your listeners will most likely come from various lifestyles, including various political, economic, ethnic, and religious backgrounds. Keep in mind that:

> ▶ It is unethical to consciously delete or even distort information which may not be of interest to you, but may be of value to others in your audience.

As you prepare your speech, be sure to seek out a variety of materials from sources that present different perspectives, yet are still in agreement with your arguments. It is important to offer a well-balanced, well-rounded speech in favor of your perspective on the topic. Whether in the classroom or in a more realistic public setting, you will also have to be aware of time constraints. What you include in a five- to eight-minute classroom speech, is far different from that of a twenty-minute speech which you may prepare as a candidate running for a student government position, or for your own religious talk or testimony which you may offer at your house of worship.

As was mentioned in Chapter 10, we live in an information-driven society—a digital age often governed by cell phones with high-resolution cameras, tweets, instant e-mails, and of course those omnipresent handheld personal communication devices called: BlackBerries, smart phones, and the like. Because of this, the importance of ethics can hardly be overemphasized. Anything you may say or do can be quickly fact-checked from a variety of countering resources—and virtually at any moment! Having your speech rooted in accuracy and integrity, is easily verifiable by audience members who may swiftly consult their digital resources at the conclusion of your speech. So you must be honest at all times, and always be prepared to be confronted or challenged at any time.

Your **A**, **B**, **C**s for Better Ethics in Persuasive Arguments

You should *always* make your audience **comfortable** by:

A Approaching your topic with sensitivity and caution.
B Avoiding brashness or an approach that may be considered "offensive."
C Using plenty of comfortable metaphors to help them relate.

You should *always* make yourself **credible** by:

A Reinforcing your authority and trustworthiness by avoiding any known fallacies.
B Going into details with sound reasoning supported by clear examples.
C Exposing possible fallacies that may counter your argument.

You should *always* be aware of your persuasive **integrity** by:

A Establishing your argument for the good of others, not solely your own good.
B Bolstering your argument so others may continue beyond your speech.
C Establishing your present reputation in future speeches.

You should *always* evaluate your speech's **reasonableness** by:

A Not being too "preachy" or pushy in your attitude or approach.
B Making your overall approach warmhearted and constructive.
C Inviting your audience to evaluate and analyze your arguments.

The Power of Persuasive Speaking

The power and nature of persuasive speaking, is rooted in our very souls as members of the human species. We all need and want something, somewhere, somehow, and at various times in our lives; and more readily at various moments as well. As such, it is important to take a moment to explore just what gives persuasive speaking its force or power in ways which contrast with that of informative speaking, which we have explored in Chapter 10. Informative speaking has its power rooted in teaching an audience. Persuasive speaking has endured for many centuries; it has been and continues to be at the foundation of all political and civic growth; and has been present in all societies since the very birth of civilization itself. Speaking to persuade means that your primary goal as a speaker is to influence both the *attitudes* and the *actions* of your listening audience.

Persuasive speaking often entails reinforcing the beliefs and feelings which your listeners may already hold, and are quite comfortable holding on to in the first place. It may also mean that you need to challenge those very beliefs and attitudes, *or* at best, weaken them so as to permit your audience to be open for viewing things from a different perspective, namely yours. As a result, the general power you hold as an agent of persuasion, can take on various distinctive goals, depending on the given circumstances of your listeners.

The Goals of Persuasive Speaking

Persuasive speaking characteristically is interested in spotlighting three broad goals: *intensifying loyalty*, *reducing resistance*, and *inspiring action*. The first two goals are interested primarily in changing mind-sets or established attitudes, while the third goal is committed to transforming audience thoughts, feelings, and attitudes into actions. We will now take a brief look at each of them.

Intensifying Loyalty

The majority of persuasive speeches given on a regular basis involve themselves with intensifying a sympathetic or unbiased audience loyalties, thus making those loyalties or allegiances more solid than before, by strengthening their already prevailing attitudes and feelings about a topic. Political and civic speeches often attempt to strengthen audience loyalty by heightening their concern about a particular issue. Most well-crafted informative speeches can be made into persuasive speeches, by focusing your general approach from offering solid information and simple awareness of a topic, into enforcing a loyalty or specific attitude about that topic. The persuasive speech differs in that you are going beyond raising awareness, by offering knowledge which influences your audience's feelings and attitudes in addition to that awareness. For example, if you are speaking about the general definition and classification of UFOs, and the possibility of life on other planets, you may transform your informative speech into a persuasive one by persuading your audience to not favor the various hoaxes, or the plethora of inconsistent reports and doubts offered by scientists and military personnel. You could choose to focus on those scientists and military personnel who have allegedly witnessed UFOs themselves; and who are in turn advocating the lesser amount of data which seems to support this aerial phenomenon, and which in turn seems to have no rational explanation. As such, you have now become an advocate for visitations to Earth from realms beyond our own.

Strengthening audience loyalty often necessitates that you engage them on both the loyalty, and the values level. What we mean by **values**, are those relatively firm loyalties which individuals or groups may hold about the worth or advantage of material items, actions, or ultimate aspirations. This may incorporate religious values and moral values, including such notions as: equality, fairness, and justice, or even loftier values concerning the appropriate religious attitude to a topic such as traditional marriage, as opposed to gay or lesbian marriage. Compared to beliefs, values are surprisingly more difficult to influence or change in an audience. They are developed over a long span of time, are often rooted in experience, and begin at a very early age. We are socialized into our values by our parents, teachers, and clergy, and at times by our playmates or those adult friendships we may foster.

Reducing Resistance

A persuasive speech becomes more challenging when your audience does not favor your position on a topic. Your power as a persuasive speaker now resides in your ability to reduce their level of resistance. For instance, imagine that you are speaking to the biology club at your university and the vast majority of your audience finds the existence of UFOs to be oddball, unsophisticated, and at best, unscientific. If you are going to address them with any success at all, you must first find out the very core of their resistance. Namely, you must seek out the popular reasons that highly skeptical, scientific-minded individuals have against the possibility of UFOs. If you can calmly and intelligently address some of their opposing reasons and therefore reduce their resistance, you have found the key to making them more open to your point of view.

Reducing opposition or resistance is at the foundation of civic, religious, and political loyalty and is also at the heart of dialogue and the exchange of ideas. We fortunately live in a democratic society in which we are free to respectfully engage one another with opposing perspectives, and continuously challenging viewpoints. Although you may not convince your scientific-minded classmates that UFOs are visiting planet Earth on a regular basis, you may indeed successfully convince them that the full evidence against UFOs is not scientifically conclusive. Further, you may show them that many credible scientists are sympathetic to the possibility of intelligent life from beyond Earth, and that although the evidence is quite meager, it is not beyond the realm of possibility. We must keep in mind that *reducing resistance*, then, is not about getting your opponents to entirely alter their steadfast viewpoints, but rather about encouraging them to honestly see your position within a more favorable and compassionate framework.

Inspiring Action

The third major goal of persuasion is *inspiring action*. Persuading your audience to vote for a given class senatorial candidate, encouraging your university president to change a particular academic policy, or simply motivating your classmates during your speech to begin saving now for their distant retirement, are all examples of how a persuasive speech can help *promote* action. The main goal here is not only to change attitudes or reduce resistance, but also to actually *inspire* your audience to identify practical steps in order to *take* action.

Inspiration is the key to successful political campaigns and effective advertising, and of course for any religious leader who hopes to inspire his or her congregation to help the poor, avoid workplace dishonesty, or better yet, increase their monthly financial contributions!

> ▶ The successful persuasive speaker is not called to bully, compel, or intimidate, but ultimately to *inspire*.

The success of great persuasive speakers lies in their ability to arouse. Martin Luther King, Jr., John F. Kennedy, and Mother Theresa were all effective in their ability to persuade, and each is identified with being inspirational. **Inspiration** may be defined as an ability to emotionally enable your audience to connect with your point of view. In such a way as to cause them, by their own promptings, to desire and truly feel they need to take action in manners which you may suggest to them. Persuasive speeches which more directly incorporate inspiration, are ones which occur at places of worship, sporting events, political rallies, national events, leave-takings, and graduation speeches.

Inspiring action may take a variety of forms. In terms of civic responsibility, the challenge might be to get volunteers to help at your school's annual bake sale to raise money for the local homeless shelter. In terms of politics, it might be to help get a new candidate on his or her feet to help oppose your current and ineffective student body president. In terms of marketing or advertising, it might be getting people to purchase a product by means of actual testimonies. And by religion, it may be by helping those recently out of prison to remain so, by advocating specific religious and ethical principles which they may begin to place into action. In each of these situations, the persuasive speech is designed to influence and direct the action of others by sincere inspiration.

TWIN RULES — Persuasive Goals

Intensifying Loyalty

A. **Remember:** This speech is given to an audience who for the most part is already in harmony with your point of view or is, at best, neutral about it.

B. **Your goal:** Intensify and encourage them in their loyalty; and help bring them to a deeper level of commitment or, even better, to a more extensive or even new level of understanding in a particular direction.

Reducing Resistance

A. **Remember:** This speech is given to an audience who for the most part is in disagreement with your point of view, or at times may be hostile toward it.

B. **Your goal:** Focus on the core reasons or central basis for their resistance. Show genuine compassion for their viewpoint, and attempt to make clear to them how your position may be reasonable when placed in context with their own.

Inspiring Action

A. **Remember:** Never be too forceful, demanding, or bullying. Let them see that you are in solidarity with them, and are inspired and willing to take action with them.

B. **Your goal:** Offer a practical and safe set of actions for all to take. Encourage them with your solidarity; and be sure to make clear how taking action has been effective in similar past instances; and how they may be involved in shaping the future.

Matching Your Topic with Your Goals

After you have selected a convincing topic which may provide some helpful new information for your listeners, and have completed some basic research, gathered some excellent examples and quotes, and then have identified some overall persuasive goal for your materials at hand, it will then be time for you to create an argument for your speech. An **argument** is the degree to which you as a persuasive speaker, furnish logical reasons for claiming your point of view. These normally include: facts, figures, statistics, testimonies, and your capacity to challenge counter-arguments held by your opposition. It is important to frame your speech with an effective design which will best enable your listeners to receive it. An argument not unlike the rendering which an architect may utilize in constructing his or her new building, is what gives a persuasive speech its power. Remember that:

▶ Any strong argument must be based on sound, logical evidence.

After you have built an argument upon evidence, you need only concern yourself with delivering your speech with inspiration, confidence, and integrity. There are several avenues of evidence that may be used when crafting an argument, but we will concern ourselves with three of the most basic varieties, along with their corresponding terms from classical rhetoric (as discussed in Chapter 2); these are rational evidence (or *logos*), emotive evidence (or *pathos*), and credible evidence (or *ethos*).

Rational Evidence–*Logos*

When your speech is essentially rooted in facts, figures, statistics, and documented information, you are working from a more *logos* or rational standpoint, logically attempting to convince your audience. Of course, such data is subject to how you choose to use it. Facts and figures alone do not guarantee the persuasion of an audience. You must have conviction combined with order and strategy, in your approach to presenting your data. Nonetheless, good sound facts are quite hard to take issue with, when they are passionately presented to an audience.

Emotive Evidence–*Pathos*

An audience, whether in front of a flat-screen television, a large silver screen at the local cinema, or an assembly gathered in a large auditorium, continually receives information by way of feelings and emotions. We are all living, breathing communicators who feel our way, as well as think our way, through life.

When public speakers tell humorous or serious stories, laugh along with an audience, or unexpectedly cry during their speeches, they merge the power of *pathos* evidence with that of their credibility. The emotional tone you set during your speech will help to effectively connect you to your audience. Emotional connection is particularly important when needing to call an audience to immediately respond on some level. Emotional evidence works well when it gently taps into an audience's present beliefs and genuine needs. It is quite powerful since it can strengthen or even seriously alter an audience's point of view. More importantly, emotional evidence can inspire and stir an audience into taking direct action.

It is important to note that evidence should always be used with restraint and at times even with a bit of caution. If an appeal to feelings is too transparent or seems manipulative, it can recoil on the speaker, causing your audience to discredit both you and the persuasive message you are trying to offer. When you attempt to make use of emotions, feelings, or passions, you must be sure to align them with firm evidence. A simple rule is to let your overall energy, voice, and body movements play down rather than overemphasize your emotional content. Always be emotionally honest and never be melodramatic.

Credible Evidence–*Ethos*

Every time you give a speech, your audience must immediately feel that you are not only a person of conviction and seem to know and understand your topic, but also that you are honest and sincere by your very presence. In short, it is essential that you create an impression of trust in yourself, as well as the information which you are presenting. It is important that you create for your audience the *ethos* that you are not someone who is subject to distorting the truth or over accentuating the facts. The moment you begin to speak, you are judged by your audience. From the early first minutes of your speech, you are quickly evaluated as to your credibility (McCrosky, 2006). Such credibility may increase or decrease, depending upon your ability to appear and sound credible throughout the duration of your presentation.

A great percentage of your credibility is also rooted in your delivery, as discussed in Chapter 5. If you sound confused, stumble over technical terms and phrases, or slip-up when saying foreign words or names, your credibility decreases. It is important also, to keep a confident and measured pace during your speech. Racing your words or dragging them while grappling for your thoughts affects your evidence and your presentation of facts, no matter how profound they may be. Keeping eye contact is also vital. If you are immersed in your note cards, your audience feels disconnected, so you must continually make eye contact with your listeners, regularly. Always attempt to be conversational and not "preachy" or condescending in attitude or tone.

Demonstrating Persuasive Evidence

- *You should demonstrate:* **rational evidence** by being well-acquainted with your topic, aware of countering rational viewpoints, and familiar with principles of logic and clear, consistent thinking.
  Do this by: utilizing verifiable facts, figures, documented examples, and personal testimonies by experts in the area of your topic.

- *You should demonstrate:* **emotive evidence** by being moderate in your pacing, by restraining your gestures and tonal quality, and by choosing to understate all your emotional content and high-lighted examples.
  Do this by: gently tapping into your audience's present beliefs and perceived genuine needs, and by never manipulating their emotions.

- *You should demonstrate:* **credible evidence** by showing that you are trustworthy, not by your words alone, but by your honest and sincere presence before your audience.
  Do this by: never appearing confused, never stumbling over technical language or foreign words, maintaining good eye contact, and never becoming "preachy" in your approach.

● ● ● ● ● American *Mythos*: Sermons, Consumers, and Politics

When you are giving a persuasive speech, it is often quite powerful and appealing to make direct use of religious values, religious faith, societal identity, and good old traditional American beliefs. These approaches, among many, can be communicated in time-honored stories, customary sayings, and the use of established songs, symbols, and even consumer products and services. Such appeals arouse religious, political, and customer loyalty by their very own nature. They often are quite effective at unifying an audience and can strike a chord with them. Effective use of what is termed ***mythos*** (or mythology) is a form of proof that bonds a persuasive topic to a given cultural, societal, or traditional set of narratives (or stories) to a given audience. Such narratives may remind them of their forgotten heroes and of just who their enemies might or should be, and they may prompt them as to who their adversaries were all along.

Political speeches can be quite effective at invoking and quoting from grand patriots such as: Abraham Lincoln or George Washington. Invoking the significance of the American bald eagle or the importance of the colors "red, white and blue," can be equally effective during campaign speeches for any office and at any level. Such mythic phrases as: "land of the brave" or "home of the free" during any speech, can be quite valuable at unifying your audience, as well as building your credibility as a loyal American who can be trusted and admired.

> Appeals to *mythos* may even be grounded in traditional principles of capitalism, such as success stories built upon the principles of hard work or our struggling immigrants.

Appeals to national character may also draw upon religious narratives such as the Judeo-Christian heritage or the Bible. These may provide a rich, credible element to persuasive speeches, not only in sermons and political speeches, but also in the successful marketing of products and services.

Like every other approach to persuasion, the use of *mythos* can be used or misused. At its very best, the effective use of *mythos* can intensify our positive reception of who we are as a nation of diverse peoples and, can help endorse stability between cultural values, religious beliefs, and the appropriate course of public action. On the other hand, the misuse of *mythos* can create an atmosphere which invokes the sentiment that there is only one, true, genuine culture. It can forcibly imply that there is only a single approach to a problem or way of being, seeing, or even purchasing. Abuse of *mythos* can lead to certain appeals to cultural identity which may abuse those who cannot (or choose not to) conform to the majority values, or those who belong to secondary cultural or religious groups such as: Asians, Latinos, Muslims, or even agnostics or atheists. Such appeals can result in splitting apart the social fabric of our society, and can cause serious separation and resentment. We must be cautious about how use the "American myth."

Making Yourself a Lucid Preacher

Presently, your topic clearly and efficiently is the hallmark of any successful "preacher." We learned so far in this chapter that a persuasive speaker is essentially *urging* his or her listeners about a topic of interest to both the speaker and the listeners. Enhancing further understanding and argument of your topic is the dominant task of a persuasive speaker. And being *lucid* moment by moment is the feature of imploring anyone about anything. You must be clear at all times. As a speaker in general, you may think that in presenting your own argument, you are being obvious and apparent about all you say and do. The truth is, only your individual audience members can really tell if they have actually received your line of reasoning clearly. Therefore you must watch and feel for their reactions to your passionate words. You must be connected to them, and be aware of their reactions and cues as to the reception of your speech, point by point. If they seem lost or confused, you must attempt to slow down and be more sensitive. Remember, your presentation may seem crystal clear to you, but not to them.

As with an informative speech, it is essential that you give personal consideration to how you may more easily help your listeners understand your particular approach to your line of reasoning when making your argument. To become a successful and convincing speaker, you must help them by consciously developing and presenting ideas with them always in mind.

▶ It is important to realize that "preaching" is not about tossing argumentative facts before an audience and trusting that the facts will connect with one another and then sink in, it's about being honest, inspirational and lucid.

Convincing an audience is an acquired art. It requires passion, insight, and an ardent desire to be clearly heard and understood. Below are some *Always* Rules for you to keep in mind while you are giving a persuasive speech. Hopefully these will help you enhance your message and imbue it with clarity and understanding. I like to refer to them as the *always rules for "preaching" to your audience.*

"Preaching" to Your Audience

- *Always* tell your listeners how one previous point does *or* will relate to your next point, thus creating a more complete argument.

- *Always* be sure to summarize your important arguments frequently, thus reinforcing them in the hearts and minds of your listeners.

- *Always* distribute any handouts or printed matter *prior* to your speech, so as to avoid having your audience become distracted during your speech.

- *Always* be sure to remain focused on your central topic, thus avoiding the temptation to go off on an interesting digression.

- *Always* be sure to remain confident and assured that you are in control of your speech. If you make an obvious mistake, or need to correct yourself, remain self-assured.

- *Always* pay close attention to the faces and general *awareness level* of your audience. Should they appear offended or bewildered, take time to ask them if you are making yourself clear or even if they are upset.

To Be Convincing: You Must Be *Honest* and *Avoid Fallacies*

"Logical errors are, I think, of greater practical importance than many people believe; they enable their perpetrators to hold the comfortable opinion on every subject in turn."

—Bertrand Russell, *A History of Western Philosophy*

One of the main obstacles which every speaker must face when attempting to convince an audience, is the possibility of error in their logical reasoning. Errors in reasoning will immediately weaken your argument. This is what we term a **fallacy.** Fallacies may come in many sizes, shapes, and forms. The test for effective persuasive speakers and their audience rests in properly recognizing fallacies. On the surface, fallacies often seem legitimate and, at best, quite sensible. Upon closer inspection fallacies are clearly erroneous, and in the end are evident upon reflection. Fallacies in a speech, even if they are not willful, are unacceptable and will cause the speaker to be no longer credible; and in some cases never trusted again by anyone in public. Including fallacies in a persuasive speech—no matter how unintentional they may be—mirrors distortion upon the speaker and in the end amounts to unethical conduct. The following is a list of common fallacies which every speaker must strive to avoid:

Biased-Pigeonholing Fallacy

We were all youngsters once, and most likely when we fought with our friends and siblings we engaged in pigeonholing. For the most part, this biased approach categorizes people or groups by placing an unfair marker on them. Bullying terms like "sissy," "chicken," or "dummy" still abound among children in their name-calling endeavors. Such labels as "religious fanatic," "raging liberal" or even "fascist" are often bantered around among political supporters during various local and national campaign seasons. It is important in your speech to avoid such unfair labels at all costs. Oftentimes, name-calling and pigeonholing individuals or groups, may result in hurting your own credibility in the end. It is important to refer instead to an individual's proven record, and to stick only to the facts. Always let your audience decide on their own about how to mark a person or group, since it is not the job of the public speaker to label or pigeonhole anyone.

It's-So-Simple Fallacy

The method behind the it's-so-simple fallacy is to welcome words and phrases that embrace some highly accepted positive norm or virtue. This invites an audience to approve of an idea without examining any thought-out plan or forms of evidence. Politicians during election season and on heated televised debates, make every government problem seem easily solvable. For example, "All this current president needs to do to quickly end this prolonged war is to X." Or "Our country needs to stop doing Y, and then unemployment will drop suddenly within the next quarter or so." These statements misuse our very positive desire to see political development and change, without acknowledging or analyzing the complexities involved. Only the generalized answers are offered in a sweet, no-nonsense approach, and in the end we learn that it's not so simple after all.

Get-with-the-Program Fallacy

With the get-with-the-program fallacy, the persuasive speaker encourages the audience to believe or even do something, because that's what "everyone else" is doing these days. This fallacy is about encouraging listeners to "get with the program" and be trendy. Advertisers adore this approach to selling their products and services. Persuasion here is simply based upon being stylish, being hip, and being fashionable. For example, "If you are sexy and intelligent and know how to be a successful woman who knows what she likes, then you should buy and use X regularly." And during election season: "Morally responsible people of faith, and those who are true Americans, like our country's founders once were, are all voting for Y for president."

Thinking-in-a-Circle Fallacy

The thinking-in-a-circle fallacy utilizes two unproven propositions to provide evidence for each other. When you think and argue in a circle, you repeat the same "tune" over and over and essentially attempt to argue one thing by defining it by another. An example would be: "Marijuana should be outlawed because it is a harmful drug. Harmful drugs are never legal; they are controlled, or are deemed as crime by those who use or sell them, and therefore marijuana should not be legalized."

This-or-That Fallacy

The this-or-that fallacy assumes that all issues are binary or polar opposites, and that every issue has two clear and opposite positions. It erroneously proposes that everyone must be on one side or the other. Politicians and advertisers alike love to suggest: "You are either on our side or not," or, my favorite: "It's either America—*love* it, or America—*leave* it." Such a fallacy here, of course, denies any possibilities for growth or change in the nation. The heart of this fallacy lies in the fact that it does not recognize that most issues, of course, are complicated and are subject to numerous points of view.

This-Because-of-That Fallacy

There is a famous Latin phrase often used by lawyers which states: *"post hoc ergo prop hoc."* Simply translated, this means: "after this; therefore, because of this." This popular fallacy attaches adversity and disaster to a given event or circumstances which occurred before such misfortunes themselves, even though there is no evidence of any connection. Fundamentalist preachers of all religions often attribute storms and natural calamity to a specific group of public or private actions which they may find to be undesirable or immoral. A classic example is Christian evangelist and TV host Pat Robertson, of *The 700 Club,* who vehemently stated: "The flooding of New Orleans is a sign that God is tired of seeing His creation mocked by the Mardi Gras and its perverted display of debauchery and exposed breasts." The lesson here is that just because two things appear to be occurring closely together does not mean that one caused the other to take place. It is important for students of persuasion to realize that often events occur closely in time by chance or coincidence, and not because one triggered the other.

Summary

In this chapter we have explored what it means to be persuasive when giving a speech in public—namely, it means to offer a convincing argument to your listening audience about something in favor of a position with which you yourself either agree or are against. What is important in the end is to be clear about your facts, figures, any examples you may provide, and your overall approach to your topic. Your speech should be relevant to your audience, immediately useful, and always accurate in a digital age where anything may be fact-checked at the press of a handheld device. As the presenter of a persuasive speech, you take on the role of a "preacher." As such you must be credible, honest, and inspiring. You must offer your listeners something far and above what they may acquire *via* electronic technology. You must make your speech easy to remember, limited in scope, and focused in the same manner as if it were an informative speech. Good preachers are aware of time constraints, and never attempt to offer too much information in one long setting. In the end, you must be inspiring by all you say and do; and if you strive to be understood, you are most likely to communicate a successful speech. One which achieves all your convincing arguments and goals in the end.

Discussion Questions

1. What do we mean when we say that the purpose of a persuasive speech is to convince an audience to be for *or* against a given set of principles or arguments?

2. What do you think constitutes a helpful and reasoned persuader? In light of your textbook's formal definition, what basic skills from preaching do you think help make a trustworthy and convincing speaker?

3. Among the three types of argumentative evidence (*logos, pathos,* and *ethos*), which do you think requires the most research, preparation, and challenging skills overall; and why? Is each form of evidence of equal importance? If so, why or why not?

4. What is meant by the term "ethics" in persuasive speaking? Why is ethics such an important code of conduct in the digital age? What does it mean to be constantly aware of your persuasive integrity throughout the duration of your speech?

5. In what ways might you go about making sure you do not subscribe to any fallacies in your attempt to convince an audience? Which of the five fallacies we discussed, do you feel is the most risky, and why so?

● ● ● ● ● Quick Quiz

Match the following capsule sentences that follow with the correct letter which seems to best describe the key terms or phrases found in this chapter.

1. ____ Speeches that *convince* others of something, and tend to focus on sound arguments.

2. ____ A fallacy which correlates with labeling someone (or a group) unfairly.

3. ____ A fallacy which attempts to prove by using two or more unproven arguments.

4. ____ Not being too "pushy" or "preachy" in your attitude toward your audience.

5. ____ When you subscribe to religious values or good old-fashioned beliefs.

6. ____ Evidence which shows that you are trustworthy beyond your spoken words.

7. ____ Evidence which is logical, clear, and sound throughout your speech.

8. ____ The degree to which you furnish logical reasons to support your view.

9. ____ Bringing your listeners to a deeper level of commitment and obligation.

10. ____ Unethically forcing an audience to believe in a given manner or approach.

A. Rational	**B.** Loyalty	**C.** Credible
D. Coercion	**E.** Argument	**F.** Reasonableness
G. Persuasive	**H.** Thinking-in-a-circle	**I.** Pigeonholing
J. Mythos		

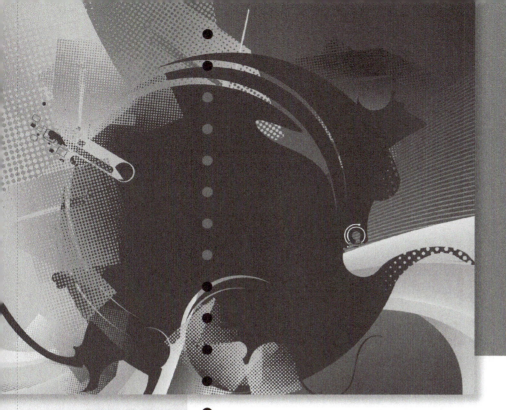

Group Speaking: You Become the *Participator*

KEY TERMS

group resolution

small group

panel discussion

moderator

spoken public statement

plural language

round-table discussion

symposium

oral interpretation (OI)

forum

team presentation

videoconferencing

five-factor approach

"The leader can never close the gap between himself, and the group. If he does, he is no longer what he must be."
—Vince Lombardi

"Individual commitment to a group effort—that is what makes a team work, a company work, a society work, a civilization work."
—Vince Lombardi

When most students think about participation of some kind, they frequently think it may be better to sit back and let others do all the work. Often being in a team or a group can be comforting in that you may be able to slack off and let others take things into their own hands. But today, with the recognition of teams and assemblies of organizations continually on the increase, most college students will stumble upon conditions which require them to work in harmony with others when presenting information in a public manner. It's become a part of the digital age.

Perhaps when working in a more persuasive manner—say, on a student election campaign, or on a sales presentation—you may be required to work with others in a shared group appearance, or before a live audience to help sell a product, or persuade your student body to elect a given candidate as your class president. At other times you may be required to work in a group behind closed doors at your job, or simply be assigned a group project in one of your other classes. Either way you will be expected to work in harmony with others; and to achieve a common group of goals and objectives. Participating in a group usually involves both cooperating with others *within* the group, as well as interacting with those *outside* of the group. As members of a group you must interact with each other and depend upon each other to solve a problem, make an important decision, or merely work together to achieve some common needed objective which will then require definite action. In this chapter we will focus on what it means to further function as a public speaker, but to participate as one within a group setting.

Small Groups in General

In most cases a small group must include at least three people, and for a maximum, roughly no more than twelve people at best. Beyond twelve people it becomes very difficult for members of a group to regularly interact with each other, especially if they are going to make a presentation before a live audience.

> In general, the central objective of small groups is simply to resolve common problems; and to then present those resolutions in a public setting.

What is often referred to as a **group resolution** is a means of finding approaches and effective methods for overcoming obstacles to achieve a preferred goal. Not all approaches to problem-solving follow the same steps. Time for reflective thinking does provide a helpful framework which can reduce the ambiguity which initially exists when groups attempt to solve problems. In short, a **small group** is merely an assortment of personalities who gather together for a common goal. Listed below, for your reflection are a few all-purpose questions for attempting to solve a problem by way of a group.

General All-Purpose Questions for Group Participants

1. What is the actual problem (or goal) or series of questions at hand which concern us as a group?

2. What (if any) ideas, concepts, or technical knowledge do we as a group need to be aware of in order to approach our desired goals?

3. Are any individuals, groups of people, or communities being impaired, disenfranchised, or immediately oppressed by the problem at hand? Do we need to act immediately, or can it wait?

4. If there is an immediate situation of need or harm, under what conditions does it occur, and are we in a position to take action?

5. What is within our actual reach of capability as group which may enable us to take action to solve our defined problem?

6. Is it necessary for our group to speak in public before a live or broadcast audience, or it is possible to meet and work behind closed doors?

The answers to the all-purpose questions should help you and your group to begin planning a strategy which will provide your possible listeners with a high level of awareness toward your common goal, as well as in deciding which of the seven group categories offered in this chapter may best suit your needs.

In many of your other courses, you may have already been expected to work in groups on discussion questions, on solving moral dilemmas, or completing a business project in a marketing class. In your public speaking and communication courses, you may even be required to work in groups on analyzing a taped speech by a professional speaker, or on devising a common topic for discussion with the class. Either way, you will need to choose the most appropriate presentation model to best serve your needs.

● ● ● ● ● Group Presentation Models

"Be still when you have nothing to say;
when genuine passion moves you,
say what you've got to say . . . and say it hot."
http://www.finestquotes.com/quote-id-29261.htm

—D. H. Lawrence

Working in groups in a classroom setting and performing group presentations, help prepare you for participating in business settings, professional organizations, committees, and local government or societal institutions. This brief section will help you prepare for and appraise seven common types of group presentation models: *panel discussions, spoken public statements, round-table discussions, symposiums, forums, team presentations,* and *videoconferencing.* We will now briefly take a look at each of them. All seven are centered on each group being required to perform a presentation within a public setting.

Panel Discussions

Most likely we've all watched lively **panel discussions** on daily TV talk shows, Sunday morning radio news analysis programs, or at our local city hall or scheduled university senate meetings. In most cases a moderator or intermediary asks questions to focus and direct the group's communication, which occurs in front of a live radio or television audience.

> ▶ Most group members in a panel are specialists or authorities on the subject at hand, and most are acquainted beforehand with which topics or questions will be discussed.

The **moderator** in most cases provides an introduction, thus providing an overview of the topic or topics, and then states the purpose and goal of the discussion for the audience themselves to clearly focus upon. In most cases the moderator will briefly present each participant's credentials, or in some cases invite them to introduce themselves to the audience.

Even though panel discussions are rarely rehearsed, at the same time they are not completely improvised either. Participants rely upon prepared notes, and in some cases live computer information to access new data at their fingertips. A few questions are often asked which are spontaneous and at the whim of the moderator. All participants, of course, must be prepared in the event that they are thrown an unexpected curveball question.

Panel participants often prepare well in advance, have a very good grasp beforehand of both the scope and direction of the discussion, and are rarely expected to be spontaneous and off-the-cuff in their remarks. Today some presidential debates may take this form, especially during primary season, when perhaps as many as five or six candidates may be interested in becoming a party's nominee.

On a more local note, an example of a panel discussion occurs when universities sponsor financial aid strategies for students at the end of each school year or during the summer semester. Here, experts provide firsthand information for students within a public setting, about what they can do with the financial opportunities available to them by their state, federal, and local governments, as well as local banks and lending institutions. The university at hand invites several financial aid experts and banking or loan officials to speak about lending options, debt, and sometimes even grant and scholarship opportunities. A university official usually moderates the discussion in an orderly manner. After the formal discussion, audience members composed of both students and parents, may direct their questions to various panel members.

Spoken Public Statements

When a group presents a **spoken public statement**, one participant from the group offers the entire statement on behalf of all involved. This is often the case with formal organizations and work teams, as well as governmental committees. In most cases various members of the organization develop and shape the public statement, then one of the group participants is carefully selected to present the findings or results to upper management (in the business world), the university or school administration (in the educational world), or to legislators (in the sphere of government). Such effective oral presentations clearly acknowledge the involvement of all those in the group.

When speaking in public, the group's representative often speaks not on his or her own behalf, but as if a group entity. He or she uses **plural language** to reflect the entire group's involvement, by means of such phrases as "we," "they," and "us," all to deemphasize the action of any one individual. To recognize everyone's involvement, the designated speaker must be well acquainted with all characteristics of the report, and be to ask group members for clarification and illumination if necessary.

> ▶ Spoken public statements should always remain clear of internal interruptions associated with various group members individually commenting or speaking, unless they are specifically invited to do so.

It is important that the public be connected to the group *via* one representative and not various speaking styles, approaches, or attitudes. This provides order, focus, and a strong sense of group consensus. Audience members need only focus upon one symbolic representative of the group, for their public connection. Oftentimes in a psychology or history class you may be asked to answer questions in a group, then your groups answers are publicly presented by one individual in the form of a class or public statement.

Round-Table Discussions

Contrasting to panel discussions, which we mentioned earlier, round-table discussions do not involve an observing or listening audience. Only group members are in attendance, and each participates in a **round-table discussion,** which may not require a moderator, discussion leader, or lead spokesperson on any level. Most responses are spontaneous, since those involved are experts, and need not be specially prepared to speak before a public assembly of listeners or observers. Nevertheless each participant must be adequately prepared, aware of the latest developments on the topic, and ready to engage in any unexpected debate or questioning. In most cases this dialogue is informal and conversational in nature, while allowing room for interruptions, long pauses and, even light quarreling.

If a formal facilitator or host is present, he or she will first explain the reason for the round-table, outline a basic approach, and perhaps set some simple communicational and time limits for approaching the topic at hand. At the conclusion of the round-table (usually all of this is done behind closed doors), the facilitator will summarize the main points that came forward from the gathering and states how such results will be utilized.

▶ In many cases a round-table discussion is recorded or videotaped, and a designated secretary will take notes so as to preserve the information for future discussions and historical documentation.

The strength of round-table discussions is that they provide a safe, confidential outlet for individuals to exchange information and ideas about a topic of common importance. All members are expected to participate, and no one is expected to simply listen or observe, since the purpose is to make the best use of everyone's differing or common points of view. Frequently, round-table discussions are serial and continue over a protracted amount of time to gather more evidence, keep participants up on further developments, and stimulate further and deeper involvement.

Most larger and, more importantly, many smaller cities and towns often bring together local experts to present strategies for encouraging the local business economy by way of panel discussions. Local and sometimes outside business professionals, are brought to a round-table discussion in order to chat about promoting private enterprise, small business growth, and possible new start-up commerce in the local area. Oftentimes within university settings, faculty members within a given department may hold a round-table discussion about possible new course offerings, or new academic majors which the department may consider adopting into its expanding curriculum. In the end, round-table discussions provide a safe, private atmosphere away from the viewing and listening public.

Symposiums

In a symposium, the group selects a topic, and then partitions that topic into disconnected areas for special group focus. Each member of the group then presents a small speech on his or her focused contribution, or subdivision of the whole topic. In general, a **symposium** is a public discussion in which several participants each give individual speeches, on different facets of the same topic. Each participant typically follows a formalized sequence pattern, in order to provide the audience with a sense of connection and overall consistency among the divided speeches.

▶ Once the ground plan for the overall topic is organized, symposium members act separately in preparing their individual section of the main topic.

As the day of public presentation approaches, group members then come together to rehearse, connect, make necessary adjustments, and attempt to present themselves as one cooperating public presentation. Clearly planning and developing a solid format, is essential to a successful symposium.

Distinct from participants in panel discussions, symposium participants usually provide fully prepared speeches which are then formally presented. The participants are most often experts in a given area, so as to provide the audience with an opportunity to learn about many aspects of the single topic at hand. A moderator usually introduces each separate participant, states his or her particular offering, and then also facilitates any audience questions and comments should they arise.

In general: a symposium may feature from three to five speakers with each one speaking from ten minutes, to as long as one half hour. In general, a typical symposium may last from roughly one solid hour and a half to two and a half hours or more.

A typical example may entail a group of space engineers and radio astronomers holding a symposium in which they discuss the significance of the search for extraterrestrial intelligence (SETI), in our galaxy and beyond. They may present the advantages and disadvantages of conducting a search, ranging from the economic consequences, to the possible societal and religious implications involved. Each scientist would offer his or her focus on the subject, and then the audience would have the opportunity to react and respond. One scientist may discuss the costs involved, along with the possibilities of little or no successful results. Another may discuss the risks involved with encountering the possibility of unsympathetic intelligent life. A third may focus on: the religious and ethical implications upon religion, sacred texts, and the possible disruption upon global society, and its ordered structure as we know it. After the presentations are made, the observing audience will have been exposed to a wide range of viewpoints, and in turn have a fuller perspective on this controversial and fascinating topic.

> ► Unlike other forms of public speaking, most participants in a symposium use a clearly defined manuscript for their spoken text.

Being able to read aloud, at an even pace, and of course clearly, is a prized skill in any symposium. We refer to this ability to read effectively as **oral interpretation,** or **(OI)**. When reading in public, symposium members often "interpret" a detailed structure, and rarely diverge from their highly prepared presentation. They are expected to stay within their given time limits, so that the entire event remains as fresh as possible, and all other participants receive their fair amount of allotted time.

In most cases a moderator will actually time each presentation, and then provide indications to the speaker of any time constraints. There is often a question-and-answer (Q & A) session after each participant concludes his or her prepared speech; and this is also coordinated through the chosen moderator.

Forums

In most cases the Q & A sessions following any model of group presentations may be conveniently labeled: a **forum**. In short, group members in symposiums, panels, round-tables, public statements, and other forms of group presentations most often will be expected to handle Q & As from their respective audiences. As such:

> ► Group members must listen attentively to each other, and always be prepared to answer audience questions in a thorough and all-embracing manner.

They should be prepared to respond in the same efficient style which they employed in their own individual speeches. Dealing with questions from audience members is in many ways a fine art all its own. Managing group members' responses can prove challenging in a forum, since it is important not to emerge before an audience as disorganized, unconfident about answers, and contradictory to previously discussed information.

It is important before any group presentation occurs, that group members agree upon which members will address which question areas. Also, choosing one individual to facilitate the forum is best done beforehand. In symposiums, anyone who participated may lead the Q & A forum. Following a panel discussion, that same individual would most likely be the moderator; while for public statements the group may assign the presenter, or request that another group member coordinate the forum with the audience.

Here are a few guidelines to help you and other participants in a group setting, create a better question-and-answer relationship with your audience. We call these the A, B, Cs for better Q & A sessions.

Your **A**, **B**, **C**s for Better Q & A Sessions

While **conducting** questions you should *always:*

A Approach your topic with sensitivity and respect.

B Maintain good eye contact with those asking the questions.

C Smile and use nonverbal signals to make the questioner feel valued.

While **listening** to questions you should *always:*

A Acknowledge any immediate concerns the questioner may have.

B Refer to others in the group if you cannot respond with expertise.

C Repeat the question so as to be sure you heard it correctly.

While **responding** to questions you should *always:*

A Remain calm and collective even if the questioner is not.

B Not bolster your argument by becoming defensive and cynical.

C Respect the questioner and his or her position on the topic.

While **counter-responding** you should *always:*

A Graciously thank the questioner for their offered position.

B Acknowledge anything you may not have been clear about in your remarks.

C Let the questioner know, in a courteous manner, that you agree or disagree.

Team Presentations

Team presentations are more common in university settings, and are popular among classroom assignments in public speaking courses. A **team presentation** is a collective talk made by several members of a group, with each participant presenting a different speech on a single topic. Each of the speeches is formal, with participants attending to diverse elements of a topic or problem, with each speaker using a largely similar style and approach. There is usually a relaxed flow of energy from one speaker to the next. In most cases, to help ensure a smooth overall presentation, one of the participants serves as a general moderator, but this is not a necessity.

When obligated to give a team presentation, in either your speech classes or some other course such as history, sociology, or one of the other humanities or social sciences, be sure to arrive well organized, and prepare your part of the presentation as thoroughly as possible. Don't feel you have to always speak up, even when you have little to say. In most cases, with team presentations, the instructor will often provide specific guidelines, as to how your various teams should both operate and eventually present your work in class, or before a small audience.

Videoconferencing

Today videoconferencing has become more fashionable, and certainly more convenient when conducting small group events over larger distances. With web-cameras readily available on most standard office and home computer systems, along with other forms of online video capabilities, video communication is becoming more standard. It has become a viable choice for all forms of public communication and group presentations, including panels, round-tables, symposiums, and the like.

In **videoconferencing**, group participants are located at a variety of remote physical locations. They are, by nature of this technology, capable of communicating both orally and visually in real time (as if present together) in the same physical location.

In an article entitled "Videoconferencing sees record growth" (2007) in *Business Communication Review* [37(8), 6)], we are told that videoconferencing has become increasingly more economical and more commonplace among business, educational, and public events. Videoconferencing may be done using a personal or industry computer, along with specialized interactive software, to enable various types of group discussions between individuals in different states or provinces and across international borders.

Many universities which have various branch campuses are now able to conduct faculty meetings, administrative conferences, and student-sponsored events between campuses, without having to meet at any one designated campus.

> ▶ When you are on camera, always be sure to speak clearly, and to pace your words so as to be seen and heard adequately by the technology involved. Always keep in mind that you are being seen and heard across time and space!

Effective Group Participation

In order to be an effective *participator* in a group, it is essential to understand how to manage the problem-resolution course of action. But devising and being acquainted with procedures and approaches to your problem, is not sufficient, since each member has to be responsible for personal preparation for regular meetings and any research which may be necessary. Knowing *how* and *when* to analyze evidence is crucial, as is summarizing information, and also reviewing the group's progress. Everyone in the group should be able to resolve disagreements and conflicts; and be adept at listening to everyone else in the group. Be sure to take an important look at the Always Rules which follow for group member participation. These rules in general will be helpful in the most basic of group settings, from classroom assignments to government committees and executive board rooms.

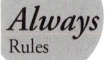

Always Rules ## Group Member Participation

- *Always* be prepared with any beforehand information, and have it at your fingertips. Prime yourself for group discussions by researching the necessary issues for each meeting.

- *Always* support and encourage the ideas of others. When you like something someone else says, tell them so in an honest, clear fashion before the entire group. Create a positive rapport with everyone, even those you may disagree with on some of the issues at hand.

- *Always* convey sincerity to other group members, to help them feel at ease about expressing their views openly and honestly. Try to be genuine and offer criticism and praise which is honest and not patronizing toward others.

- *Always* attempt to reconcile differences between group members; and always seek to relieve any tension when differences of opinion which may have become heated. Remember to clarify misunderstandings in meaning, and to keep your emotions in check.

- *Always* be willing to adjust your opinion; and reconcile any previous statements or positions to new ideas and input from others. Never remain obstinate in your point of view. Constantly be willing to incorporate new and developing ideas.

- *Always* make every effort to keep the group on the subject at hand, and cooperate to keep the group moving toward its goal. Never give in to the temptation to diverge from the topic at hand.

- *Always* be sure not to dominate the group with your own input and excessive speaking time. Let others take over after you've had your say. When there seems to be no one else who wishes to speak, ask a few questions to others.

Effective Group Leadership

As with any social gathering, small groups generally necessitate a leader. As noted earlier, a leader helps the group to collaborate effectively, and also to work more efficiently. Most groups need someone they can follow and rely upon regularly throughout the group process. Many groups rely upon one individual whom they delegate to work and direct the group toward their ultimate goal. In actuality, the heart of successful group leadership lies in group leadership which is shared equally among members by virtue of their individual capabilities and talents. In general, an effective group leader should be adept at dealing with questions, good at summarizing new and developing information and data. An effective leader continually keeps members of the group equally involved and reminded about their responsibilities and tasks. Below are some twin-rules for effective group leadership.

TWIN RULES — Being an Effective Group Leader

Questioning

A. **Remember:** Ask questions, open-ended questions help make possible the exchange of ideas and opinions which promote interesting discussion.

B. **Your goal:** Ask "yes" and "no" questions to help the group eventually arrive at clear choices or some closure on various points of discussion.

Summarizing

A. Remember: When the energy of an important point or thought starts to lose its strength or power, summarize what has been discussed and learned, before prompting the group to move on to another point.

B. Your goal: Engage everyone to focus on the discussion at hand, by creating a relaxed environment in which all participants understand where the discussion currently is going. By reviewing things frequently, help keep the group refreshed and on target.

Involving

A. Remember: Some participants will be more interested in sharing their thoughts and ideas than others, so involve everyone as equally as possible in the discussion.

B. Your goal: Offer a practical and safe set of conditions for all to feel comfortable to participate equally. You may at times need to invite certain members to participate if they remain uninvolved.

Reminding

A. Remember: Remind group members of the task at hand by using language which reminds everyone to continue on the topic at hand.

B. Your goal: Continually shift the group toward problem-solving and; not merely theoretical concepts and ideas.

Leadership Styles

Every type of small group, independent of the leader, will function by using some form of shared or single-person leadership. In turn, a *leadership style* will eventually emerge within the group by the actions of a single dominating individual, or perhaps two or three at most. This, of course, depends upon both the size and the goal of the group. A leadership style can and will eventually bring about a given group spirit, create a comfortable working atmosphere, and evolve a particular type of productivity in the end. Both experience and research have shown repeatedly, that three basic styles of leadership generally emerge within most small group settings.

● ● ● ● ● Flow of Leadership Styles

If you are a controlling leader, you most likely will approach things with a direct and more controlling style of management. You are not fond of sharing power and prefer to do most of the speaking and planning. This style is effective and efficient under specific circumstances. It works well for groups which will meet only one major time, or with a leader who is more knowledgeable and experienced than the other group members.

You may use this style by utilizing verifiable facts, figures, documented examples, and the personal talents of experts in the area of their topic.

A few common examples of controlling leaders are: coaches, sports team captains, dance leaders, military officers, seminar leaders, and business project leaders.

If you are a hands-off leader, you are more moderate in your approach to control, and you rely upon more directive and passive means to guide others. You are comfortable with permitting the group to move forward toward its goal, without working out the specifics ahead of time.

You may use this style by relying upon the more prepared, more advanced, and experienced members of the group, and by promoting a sense of self-direction and self-motivation among group members. You are not a doer as much as a motivator, and are one who likes to inspire others.

A few common examples of hands-off leaders are: community organizers, religious group leaders, environmental activists, some political group leaders, and musical and arts project leaders.

If you are a nominated leader, you are more instructive, while at the same time not overly direct or inflexible. You do not crave power and you realize that others have elected or nominated you to your task by their approval.

You may use this style by tending to support all members in taking on inventiveness; and making their own informed decisions. You permit others to troubleshoot and to solve their own problems, and will not intervene unless requested to do so.

A few common examples of nominated leaders are: union leaders, community organizers, educational leaders, property/condominium association officers, and all elected officials in both local and state government committees, *etc.*

Organizing Your Group Presentations: Five Simple Factors

Once your assigned or chosen group undertakes a mission, such as coming up with a solution to a given problem, the group then of course must put together some sort of public presentation. Group presentations can be more challenging, because group participants must bring together their speeches as one public event, as opposed to acting as an individual. Oftentimes when students are asked to work together on group projects for their public speaking courses, or in other university course assignments, they may react with a measure of resistance or at times frustration.

Some students do not want to have to depend upon others for information, or have to schedule time to meet with new people. They may be reticent about exchanging e-mails or having to depend upon someone else for their final grade. Some fear that they may have to put up with the behaviors and opinions of others in a manner which may be displeasing to them, while others are concerned that perhaps one or two people will attempt to control the entire group project. As we have seen, there are a number of ways to approach these potential anxieties. When you are ready to prepare your group presentation, one possible way of organizing things into a simple yet effective manner, is to consider the following simple **five-factor approach** to group presentations:

Factor 1: Share your chosen topic to see how it may be portioned into various areas of responsibility for each member of your group. Each member should be responsible for organizing and researching only one specific area of content, which then should be rendered as one main point of the overall project. If there are more participants in your group than there are main points, then you may have two participants per main point, or have one person work on information while the other works on presentation, using charts, tables, diagrams, and so on for presentation *via* PowerPoint.

Factor 2: Each participant should put together an outline for his or her main focus of the topic (main point) area for the entire project. Even though each individual outline is for only part of the overall presentation, it still should be comprehensive and well organized. The better each participant is prepared, the stronger the group presentation will be.

Factor 3: Form a general group outline by combining each individual member's outline. Each participant should share his or her individual outlines and then later, as a group, broaden the transitions by connecting main points, and finally make any other modifications needed for continuity and uniformity which may be more representative as a combined group. You should also decide which participant (you may have more than one) will be in charge of the introduction, the summary, and the concluding remarks. At this point, if your group desires to use visual aids, PowerPoint, or any other printed or hands-on artifacts, these should be integrated into the preparation as well.

Factor 4: Complete the delivery elements by deciding who is going to speak what, and when they will be presenting it. Since the group will be presenting as a whole, the manner and organization of the presentation must look and sound organized and strong—you are a team! Selecting the right *presentation model* such as panel, symposium, or forum, is essential to a successful group dynamic. Be sure to think about every detail. Who will do what and when is essential. You should have a well-organized seating order, a time for handing things out to your listeners, and someone to be in charge of any visual aids or audio needs. Nothing is worse than looking and sounding disorganized or underprepared.

Factor 5: Be sure to rehearse your group presentation. Like any public production, a group presentation should be rehearsed both on an individual level, and then of course together as a group. This helps avoid any unforeseen surprises, creates confidence among each participant, and also helps fashion an early and strong team spirit. Even minimal rehearsal and trial-sessions of your presentation can help immensely. Rehearsal helps you to better focus upon those areas which may need more focus, and also upon who may be perceived as more or less effective in the overall presentation. Sometimes rehearsal helps to reorder things, and can cause your presentation to take on a new and improved approach. One which may have been quite different on paper or in theory. The more you work together, the more you become seen and heard as one.

Summary

In this chapter we have explored what it means to be a *participant* within a group setting, both behind closed doors and before the general public; namely to offer a effective speech or speeches as a defined group in a successful team effort. We have learned that groups may give several types of presentations within various settings, such as: spoken public statements, panels, symposiums, or round-table discussions, and learned that any group may offer their presentations by way of videoconferencing.

In addition to all of the necessary qualities which are important to public speaking, group participation must be presented as an effective, unified whole before an audience. No one dominates in a group setting, so a team attitude and team spirit are vital. The interrelated nature of a group's overall presentation depends upon serious preparation, both as an individual and as a group member.

Always keep in mind that all participants have definite responsibilities to the group in general. More importantly, all participants need to be committed to the group goal(s) at hand. It is the responsibility of participants to keep the discussion on track, and to complete any and all individually assigned tasks. It is also important that everyone in the group help manage conflicts and disagreements in a timely and courteous manner, while encouraging equal input from all participants.

Discussion Questions

1. What do we mean when we offer the saying "the purpose of a small group is for everyone to participate, and in turn no one to dominate"?

2. What do you think constitutes a helpful and smooth moderator in a group public presentation? In light of your textbook's formal definition, do you think that more than one moderator could also be effective in certain situations? Why or why not?

3. There are several types of group presentation categories in this chapter. Which do you think requires the most research, preparation, and challenging skills overall, and why? Is each approach to preparation of equal importance? Why or why not?

4. What is meant by the term "Videoconferencing?" When is it often a better choice for group/audience interaction? Do you think there are any limitations on its effectiveness? Is it always preferable for participants (including the audience) to be at the same geographical location? Why or why not?

5. In what ways might you go about making sure your group conducts an effective and helpful Q & A session for an audience? What may be the best approach, should an argument or heated exchange break out during your group presentation? How may it be best handled? How may it best be avoided?

● ● ● ● ● Quick Quiz

Match the following capsule sentences with the correct letter which seems to best describe the key terms or phrases discussed in this chapter.

1. ____ Presentations which have anywhere from three to fifteen participants involved.

2. ____ Structured discussions facilitated by a moderator before a live audience.

3. ____ A group where each participant offers a different speech on a single topic.

4. ____ Words used in public, such as "we," "us," and "they," within a group setting.

5. ____ A group where participants give speeches on diverse aspects of the same topic.

6. ____ The coordinated use of Q & A after any group presentation before the public.

7. ____ He or she introduces speakers, and then facilitates the audience in Q & A's or comments.

8. ____ Bringing distant groups and audiences together *via* technology.

9. ____ Speech given by a single individual on behalf of a group and its findings.

10. ____ Expert participants discuss a topic behind closed doors without an audience.

A. Round-table discussions	**B.** Symposium	**C.** Forum
D. Moderator	**E.** Small groups	**F.** Spoken public statement
G. Plural language	**H.** Team presentations	**I.** Panel discussion
J. Videoconferencing		

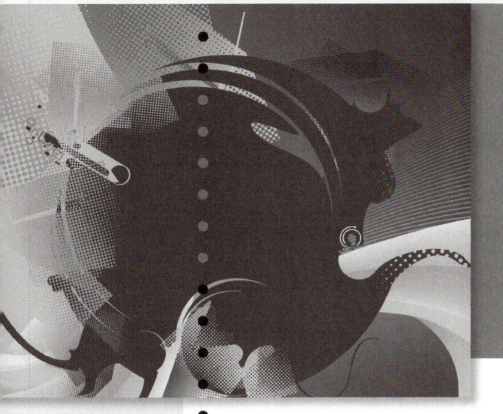

Ceremonial Speaking: You Become the *Presenter*

"At the Academy Award dinners all the actors and actresses in Hollywood gather around to see what someone else thinks about their acting besides their press agents."
—Bob Hope, entertainer and comedian

". . . In the name of the hungry, of the naked, of the crippled, of the homeless, of the blind, in their name . . . I accept the award."
—Mother Teresa, Nobel Peace Prize speech, 1979

Whether it be a graduation speech, a talk at a memorial service, an acceptance speech for an award, or a few words given at a retirement celebration, each speech requires carefully chosen words of inspiration and encouragement on behalf of you, the public speaker.

Presenting appropriate words at a public ceremony or a special occasion is an honor and a privilege. In fact, most public speaking students are given this opportunity more often than any other form of speech, after having taken a public speaking course in a college or university. Of course, saying the *wrong* thing or being *mistaken* about the facts, figures, local history, or even about the ceremony at hand, could lead any presenter to serious feelings of awkwardness and embarrassment, not to mention the possibly of hurt feelings and resentment by others.

By preparing carefully, and then effectively practicing your special-occasion words beforehand, you can approach your role as a *presenter* (or even a receiver) at any event, fear-free and with a genuine sense of self-confidence.

Ceremonial Speaking

From *weddings, eulogies, retirements,* and established holidays and remembrance events (such as *Veterans' Day, Fourth of July, Arbor Day, Holocaust Remembrance Day,* and the *anniversary of 9/11),* to the dedication of new buildings, monuments, portraits, or sculptural works, ceremonial or special occasion words by a public speaker are expected and required.

Ceremonial or *special occasion* speeches should always sound and feel as if relaxed and *conversational.* Although they require definite preparation and a level of creativity and innovation, it is your job to remain interesting in the eyes and ears of your listeners at all times.

> ▶ Ceremonial speeches include: addresses of honor, tribute, festivity, and the reception of awards. They are designed to pay tribute to a person, group, institution, thing, special event, or even an idea such as freedom or women's rights.

When honoring individuals or groups, ceremonial speeches consist of far more than the supplying of basic information, such as personal achievements, distinguished accomplishments, past awards, and interesting historical background. Ceremonial speeches depend upon *admiration, inspiration,* and *passion* being focused on the subject at hand.

> ▶ Your main goal is to inspire your audience: to enhance their regard for the person, group, institution, event, thing, or idea being honored or celebrated.

Although you should present adequate information about your subject, a ceremonial speech is unlike an *informative* speech in that its main goal is to *communicate feelings, rouse sentiments,* and *encourage* or even *inspire* your gathered audience. In short, ceremonial speaking requires the public speaker to be either a presenter or a receiver. In many ways it is a form of public CELEBRATION, and can be either a joyous or a solemn occasion.

Basic Types of Ceremonial Speaking

When asked to offer a ceremonial speech, knowing some basic directives can help make certain that you leave a helpful and lasting impression. In addition, such occasions usually require someone, and oftentimes more than one person, to address an audience with a festive attitude appropriate to the circumstances. When you are called upon to deliver a ceremonial or special occasion speech, if you are familiar with these directives, you will be equipped to deliver an effective, perhaps unforgettable speech. A ceremonial or special occasion speech may be one of any eight basic types, which generally consist of the following:

1. Celebrating by INTRODUCING a guest speaker.

Time:	Roughly **2–3** minutes

Intentions:	Keep in mind that you are *not* the main speaker here. The audience has gathered to hear someone else, so *keep it brief.* In fact, *speeches of introduction* normally should last only two to three high-energy minutes.	Be sure to state the *purpose of the occasion* in the first few opening sentences; in the remaining sentences, establish the speaker's credibility; and then conclude by repeating the speaker's name and announcing the *title* of his or her speech.

2. Celebrating by TOASTING to others.

Time:	Roughly **2–3** minutes

Intentions:	A *toast* is a ceremony in which a drink is taken as an expression of honor or goodwill. The term may be applied to the person or thing so honored, the drink taken, *or* even the verbal commentary accompanying the drink.	The *toast* may be elaborate and formal; but merely raising one's glass toward someone or something and then drinking is in effect a toast as well! Your message should be one of kindness and thoughtfulness toward the person or event toasted.

3. Celebrating by HONORING others.

Time:	Roughly **5–7** minutes

Intentions:	This is a speech *honoring* someone, either living or dead. Be sure to address three to five areas concerning the individual and his or her accomplishments.	Be sure to include anecdotes by illustrating personal historical achievements and gentle humor within your speech of honor.

4. Celebrating by ROASTING others.

Time:	Roughly **3–5** minutes

Intentions:	A *roast* is an event in which an individual is subjected to a public presentation of affectionate insults and praise. Jokes are offered in good humor and not as serious criticism or insult, and therefore show the speaker's fondness and admiration for the subject. Oftentimes at the end of a roast, the roasted individual has the final say and gets to retaliate.	You may adapt and personalize humorous material from other sources. Deliver jokes and humorous stories in a kind but honorific manner. You may even offer a skit, wear a silly costume, or show slides or doctored photos.

5. Celebrating by PRESENTING an award.

Time:	Roughly **3–4** minutes	
Intentions:	Always present an award with dignity, style, and poise. Acknowledge the contributions of the recipient; briefly offer any personal tribute; and thank them on behalf of yourself or others.	Be sure to explain the reasons for the award in general, what the award is, and why and when it is given. You may wish to inform your audience about the past recipients of the award, and how the current recipient is worthy to be among them.

6. Celebrating by ACCEPTING an award.

Time:	Roughly **5–7** minutes	
Intentions:	*Accept* the award with dignity, polish, and sincerity. Never flatter yourself. Humility is always in order. If you cry, do not be ashamed, for it will be an honor to those who are bestowing the award upon you.	Always acknowledge and thank the presenting organization; and recognize any other nominees or fellow recipients of the award if you are among several recipients at the same event.

7. Celebrating by ACKNOWLEDGING others at retirement.

Time:	Roughly **5–7** minutes	
Intentions:	Retirement it is a very special celebration: being the termination of a career. Retirement speeches are typically given at a party, and need not be lengthy. If you are the main speaker, your tribute should include humor as well as testimonials about the person's character or contributions to the company or organization.	Conclude with something both serious and humorous; and always be sure to point out how much the retiree has contributed to their profession and how their presence will be greatly missed.

8. Celebrating by MEMORIALIZING or eulogizing.

Time:	Roughly **5–7** minutes	
Intentions:	A *eulogy* is a way to celebrate and remember a dead person's life. It is also an opportunity to provide consolation to those who are hurting. Also, keep in mind the deceased's personality, any achievements, and your personal connection to him or her.	Bear in mind that you do not have to remain serious at all times. Humor can be a welcome relief and even helpful at a memorial service. It is appropriate to recall fun and even humorous times with the person you are memorializing; albeit a more solemn occasion, eulogies can also be seen as a celebration of life.

Five Quick Directives to Keep in Mind

1. **Inscribe across the top of your note cards,** or in bold print on your computer screen, your main overall intention or goal as the presenter (or receiver).

   ▶ Ask yourself: *"What is it I want my listeners to know, appreciate, be aware of, or believe by the time I have concluded my words?"* Be sure to focus upon one *main goal*. This goal should summarize all you hope to present to your listeners in a simple *thesis statement*.

   Example: "Retirement is the first step in making a new beginning in life."

2. **Now support your goal or main thesis with no more than three or four supporting points.** Each of the supporting points must give evidence that what you stated in the thesis statement is evident, accurate, and true. Every supporting point must be distinctive and must provide support which the others did not.

   ▶ Demonstrate each supporting point with a short illustration from life experience, literature, or other cultural sources. Be sure to be practical and universal in your approach.

3. **Know your audience.** Once you know who your audience will be, you can appropriately adjust your overall *approach, attitude,* and *manner of addressing your listeners.* You can choose words and ideas which will speak powerfully to your particular audience. Always connect your audience to the ceremony at hand; never go off on a tangent.

   ▶ Competent ceremonial speakers are responsive to the fact that there may be others outside the principal audience who may hear their message as well. Depending on the nature of the ceremony, or the number of these visitors, it may be essential to direct a few kind words to all of them.

   Example: A speech directed toward a retiring individual may include a few brief comments recognizing the employer, other employees, or any special guests, such as a spouse, children, or grandchildren of the retiree.

4. **As your speech approaches its conclusion, pause and rephrase your thesis statement in a refreshing, new way.** This reminds your audience about the purpose and theme of what you have told them, and reinforces your words within the context of the special occasion.

   ▶ Your conclusion is the place to make any personal statements about how you, the speaker, relate to the purpose or theme of the speech, the ceremony itself, or the special occasion.

5. **After you have given the main points and the conclusion,** be sure to add any introduction last, even though you will present it *first* to your audience.

   ▶ Again, remember the nature of your audience, take into account the ceremony at large, and then address everyone in an attitude and tone appropriate to the time, place, and energy of the occasion.

<u>Sample</u>: Welcome and Toast Speech from the Father of the Bride (1–2 minutes)

Good afternoon, friends, relatives, and special guests. On behalf of my lovely wife, Sarah, I would like to welcome you all, and graciously thank you for coming to this very special occasion with us to celebrate the marriage of our daughter Linda to David.

Unfortunately I am not a very seasoned speaker—I think I received a grade of "C" in my public speaking course way back in my college days—so please bear with me.

Firstly, I would like to say what a pleasure it is to welcome John and Karen, David's parents, along with his brothers Simon and Sean David, and of course all the friends and relatives of both families, some of whom traveled from the nearby Chicagoland area, and from as far as San Francisco and Seattle, just to be here today.

A big, big thank-you also goes to John and Karen, who had very definite wedding ideas and suggestions on how to help best make this day a memorable one for all. Through their thoughtful planning and tireless efforts they have made today a tremendous success for everyone. Let's give them a hand.

Sarah and I are very proud of our daughter Linda and pleased to see her looking so beautiful and joyful today. Linda, this is the time that almost every bride fears. . . . "What is he going to say to everyone?" "Is he going to embarrass me?" And "Oh my God, will he talk about when I was a baby or way back in grade school?"

Relax. I won't tell of any of those times, but I'm going to say thank you for being you, and for choosing the best groom ever to give to me and your mom as our son-in-law! This is indeed an honor for me and your mom. When you and I shared our little smile at one another as we were ready to start our walk down the aisle, that was a moment I will cherish forever. Thank you!

Ladies and gentlemen, Linda is a wonderful daughter. She has provided us with so much joy and laughter, and over the years we have always been proud of her. In everything she does, she always makes good, responsible choices and is a fine teacher.

My simple advice today to both David and Linda is that older married couples know that the mystery of a successful marriage is found in patience, open-mindedness, and regular bouts of forgiveness.

Now at this time I would like to take this opportunity to formally welcome David to our family, as well as his parents as our new and welcomed in-laws. My final duty and very great privilege, is to propose a toast to our daughter and our new son-in law.

Please stand and raise your glasses and join me. And so: "Linda and David: Here's to the past, for all that you have achieved. Here's to the present, for all that you will share together. Here's to the future, for all that you will look forward to together.

Ladies and gentlemen, I give you Linda and David—today's new bride and groom." Thank you.

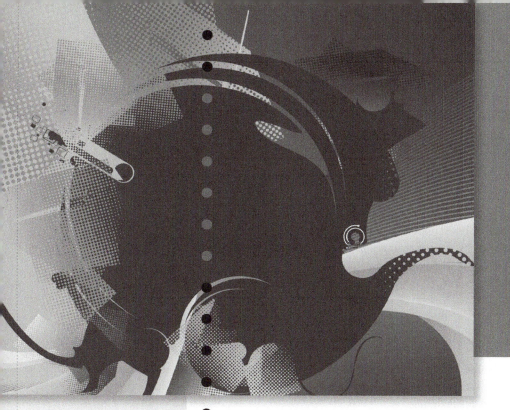

Sample Speeches: You Become the *Analyzer*

"A people without the knowledge of their history, origin and culture is like a tree without roots."
—Marcus Garvey

"Over one's mind and over one's body the individual is sovereign."
—John Stuart Mill

"If women want rights more than they got, why don't they just take them, and not be talking about it."
—Sojourner Truth

For the student of public speaking, analyzing sample speeches can be an excellent foundation for preparing your own successful speech. By examining and detailing how others have put together their own speeches, you can be inspired, and can also observe firsthand how to refine the overall structure and content of your speech. It is possible to build upon a tradition of successful speeches which have preceded your own. You have an opportunity to observe, through *analysis,* the whole content of another's speech in terms of its use of *clever tales* and *anecdotes, humorous stories or jokes, direct quotations,* or the asking of *rhetorical questions.*

If you feel clueless as to how you should begin molding your own speech, then oftentimes a *brief analysis* of sample speeches can be an inspiring step toward providing you with confidence. You may begin *via* a sample speech that you find attractive, using it as your core or foundational centerpiece by putting it in the form of an *outline.* You may then progressively remove, add, adjust, and modify various elements by replacing them with creative and more developed elements you discover on your own topic of interest. You may add those special ingredients which have come from your own research and experience, coupled with your own unique approach and creative adaptation.

When Analyzing a Sample Speech:
Re-explore Your Five Senses

Always keep in mind that all of the *five senses* may be utilized when it comes to analyzing and molding your speech based upon a sample speech. *Taste, touch, smell, seeing,* and of course *hearing* can all be enhanced by the creative incentive to readapt and analyze someone else's speech. All you need is a bit of enthusiasm, coupled with your own imagination. But first, always ask yourself these three quick questions:

1. How can I best use all of the five senses, inspired by another's speech, as a touchstone for creativity, originality and imagination?

2. Which of the five senses can I emphasize to help my audience experience my speech more truthfully in a way which will enhance my words, and that will go beyond what is presented in the speech I am analyzing?

3. What careful measures should I take to help my speech be even better than the speech I am analyzing, while not succumbing to any plagiarism?

Directives for Analyzing Sample Speeches

There are primarily two basic approaches to analyzing sample speeches to the advantage of molding and crafting your own unique and successful speech. It is important to create a speech that is *solely your own*, and is conscience-free of any copying or plagiarizing. If you feel you have found a speech which is attractive to you, then use that speech as a foundation for your own, and affix various parts of it by molding and shaping them into your own approach and style. Your analysis should include the following five observations:

1. Study the entire speech as a whole. Enjoy it in its entirety, as if you were only the *listener* and not the *analyzer.* Then attempt to put it in the form of an *outline.*

2. Pay close attention to the *introduction* and *conclusion,* as well as the *main points* and *subpoints.* Notice how they are crafted and then presented. What do you think the *thesis statement* of the speech may be?

3. As mentioned earlier, be sure to explore how the five senses may have been used. Ask yourself how you may be even more vivid and employ more vivid elements by making use of digital technology.

4. Pay close attention to concise word usage and phrasing. What words are used? And *how* and *when* are they used by the speaker? Is the speech primarily informative or persuasive?

5. Pay close attention to the use of *statistics, facts,* and any *quotations* or *rhetorical questions.* How does the speech make use of building arguments in favor of its *thesis statement?*

If your sample speech uses humor, you in turn may want to use *sound* or *photos* to be humorous in your speech. If your sample speech makes use of *quotations,* you may wish to make use of reading *quick, short excerpts* or to give your audience a brief handout, which you then read along with them. You may update any *quotes, humorous stories,* and *old jokes,* and may of course switch *visual elements* for *sound elements* and vice versa.

▶ What is important about analysis, is that it should help you personalize your speech. So be sure to add those elements that only *you* can provide by your own knowledge, insight, research, and personal experience.

Remembering Visual and Sound Resources from Chapter 9

Keep in mind that *visual* and *sound resources* help you present your speech in a manner well beyond your own spoken words and language. They are enhancements that your audience will see and hear, in addition to or beyond you, the speaker, in front of them. These visual resources may include objects or artifacts such as *clothing, rocks, coins, flags, personal relics,* and *even food items.*

▶ No matter how excellent an orator you may be, audiences generally enjoy something beyond your words to help them visualize those words.

Sound resources help you focus on the use of sound literally beyond your own words and language, and will often involve the use of recordings such as: *conversations, interviews, music, sound effects, animal noises,* and even *clips* and *bits of speeches by other speakers.* Both *sound* and *visual* resources may now be downloaded *via* laptop for actual (real-time) use during your speech.

By enhancing your words and actions, sound and visual resources help make your ideas and your approach to your sample speech more tangible, and readily more comprehensible for your audience. Some public speakers also make effective use of sound and visual elements by temporarily darkening or lowering the lighting level of the room.

▶ Always ask yourself "what can I, by way of alternative sound resources, do to help my audience *hear* my sample speech beyond the use of my own voice?"

You may recall from Chapter 9 that the use of computer-generated slides, accompanied by music, poetry, or a more detailed narrative, may be quite effective as well. At other times, presentations may be best served by the use of videotapes (DVDs and VCRs), which may include excerpts from movies, TV, cable commercials or home-made videos.

We discussed in Chapter 9 that both visual and sound resources help amplify the natural limitations of using only spoken language as a sole means of communication. As powerful as your spoken language may be, it can often be abstract and loaded with concepts, ideas, and even intangible impressions. Thus, making use of spoken language alone can produce a sense of incomplete communication. Since that is the case:

▶ Additional visual and sound resources give your audience a more instinctive connection with your overall message. They can strengthen sample speeches in many different ways which words alone cannot do.

Six Reasons for Utilizing Digital Resources Beyond What You Analyze in Sample Speeches

The following are six general reasons every speaker should keep in mind when seeking to use digital visual or audio resources. The use of other resources should always be carefully considered.

1. To help make your own new analysis and observations even more tangible and immediate for your listeners . . .
   Consider that: a *visual example* may be worth far more than what is provided in any sample speeches that you may analyze, no matter how famous the speeches may be.

2. To help add a sense of variety and diversity to your overall spoken message beyond a sample speech . . .
   Consider that: *sound resources* can help eliminate monotony and possible boredom, no matter how "classic" or effective you may analyze the sample speech to be.

3. To help reduce fatigue and anxiety on you as the central communicator . . .
   Consider that: digital, visual, and sound resources give you a short break from speaking, and in this digital age many listeners are more comfortable with other sense resources beyond mere human words.

4. To help increase the audience's memory of your newly reworked and reanalyzed speech . . .
   Consider that: when things are re-presented with additional resources, it promotes retention in the hearts and minds of your listeners.

5. To help increase a sense of power toward the credibility of your personally chosen sample . . .
   Consider that: other digital visual and sound resources help reinforce a sense of authority and persuasion by reawakening the senses to listeners, who today are digitally more tuned in to visual and sound elements that suggest information. These resources can build a strong argument for you.

6. To help address a multiplicity of new information, new learning methods, and other possible approaches beyond what your sample speech may provide . . .
   Consider that: people understand and learn differently in this *digital age*—the more resources you use, the better you can likely speak to your gathered listeners.

Sample Speeches for Your Consideration and Analysis

As an exercise in crafting another's speech through analysis, consider the following three classic American speeches: (a) *Who and What Is a Negro* by Marcus Garvey, (b) *On Liberty* by John Stuart Mill, and (c) *Ain't I a Woman?* by Sojourner Truth.

Keep in mind as you re-think and re-craft each of these speeches, that all three of them once depended entirely upon live spoken words, and only the actual speaker delivering them. Each of these speeches was delivered completely unaided by any digital or sound technology; and only by pure inspiration in the classic rhetorical style first advocated by the ancient Greeks and Romans we learned about in Chapter 2.

After your own close analysis, attempt to re-shape any one of them of your choice, in a contemporary 21st century manner. By using your own approach and original style, you may incorporate any visual and sound resources; along with any other technological and digital elements which you feel may "re-create" each classic speech into an engaging contemporary rhetorical presentation. These may include: the re-shaping and updating of any antiquated words or phrases; and the adding of any visual and sound technology. You may add and delete words and phrases as you see fit. Make the speech your own! One based upon and inspired by the speech author you chose to analyze. Be sure to come up with a basic outline which will include both an effective attention getter (AG), and a clever attention-retainer (AR).

● ● ● ● ● Who and What Is a Negro
by Marcus Garvey

The New York World under date of January 15, 1923, published a statement of Drs. Clark Wissler and Franz Boaz (the latter a professor of anthropology at Columbia University), confirming the statement of the French that Moroccan and Algerian troops used in the invasion of Germany were not to be classified as Negroes, because they were not of that race. How the French and these gentlemen arrive at such a conclusion is marvelous to understand, but I feel it is the old-time method of depriving the Negro of anything that would tend to make him recognized in any useful occupation or activity.

The custom of these anthropologists is whenever a black man, whether he be Moroccan, Algerian, Senegalese or what not, accomplishes anything of importance, he is no longer a Negro. The question, therefore, suggests itself, "Who and what is a Negro?" The answer is, "A Negro is a person of dark complexion or race, who has not accomplished anything and to whom others are not obligated for any useful service." If the Moroccans and Algerians were not needed by France at this time to augment their occupation of Germany or to save the French nation from extinction, they would have been called Negroes as usual, but now that they have rendered themselves useful to the higher appreciation of France they are no longer members of the Negro race, but can be classified among a higher type as made out by the two professors above mentioned. Whether these professors or France desire to make the Moroccans other than Negroes we are satisfied that their propaganda before has made these people to understand that their destiny is linked up with all other men of color throughout the world, and now that the hundreds of millions of darker peoples are looking toward one common union and destiny through the effort of universal cooperation, we have no fear that the Moroccans and Algerians will take care of the situation in France and Germany peculiar to the interest of Negroes throughout the world.

Let us not be flattered by white anthropologists and statesmen who, from time to time, because of our success here, there or anywhere, try to make out that we are no longer members of the Negro race. If we were Negroes when we were down under the heel of oppression then we will be Negroes when we are up and liberated from such thraldom.

The Moroccans and Algerians have a splendid opportunity of proving the real worth of the Negro in Europe, and who to tell that one day Africa will colonize Europe, even as Europe has been endeavoring to colonize the world for hundreds of years.

Negroes Robbed of Their History

The white world has always tried to rob and discredit us of our history. They tell us that Tut-Ankh-Amen, a King of Egypt, who reigned about the year 1350 B.C. (before Christ), was not a Negro, that the ancient civilization of Egypt and the Pharaohs was not of our race, but that does not make the truth unreal. Every student of history, of impartial mind, knows that the Negro once ruled the world, when white men were savages and barbarians living in caves; that thousands of Negro professors at that time taught in the universities in Alexandria, then the seat of learning; that ancient Egypt gave to the world civilization and that Greece and Rome have robbed Egypt of her arts and letters, and taken all the credit to themselves. It is not surprising, however, that white men should resort to every means to keep Negroes in ignorance of their history, it would be a great shock to their pride to admit to the world today that 3,000 years ago black men excelled in government and were the founders and teachers of art, science and literature. The power and sway we once held passed away, but now in the twentieth century we are about to see a return of it in the rebuilding of Africa; yes, a new civilization, a new culture, shall spring up from among our people, and the Nile shall once more flow through the land of science, of art, and of literature, wherein will live black men of the highest learning and the highest accomplishments.

Professor George A. Kersnor, head of the Harvard–Boston expedition to the Egyptian Soudan, returned to America early in 1923 and, after describing the genius of the Ethiopians and their high culture during the period of 750 B.C. to 350 A.D. in middle Africa, he declared the Ethiopians were not African Negroes. He described them as dark colored races . . . showing a mixture of black blood. Imagine a dark colored man in middle Africa being anything else but a Negro. Some white men, whether they be professors or what not, certainly have a wide stretch of imagination. The above statements of the professors support my contention at all times that the prejudice against us as Negroes is not because of color, but because of our condition. If black men throughout the world as a race will render themselves so independent and useful as to be sought out by other race groups it will simply mean that all the problems of race will be smashed to pieces and the Negro would be regarded like anybody else—a man to be respected and admired.

● ● ● ● ● On Liberty

by John Stuart Mill

The object of this essay is to assert one very simple principle, as entitled to govern absolutely the dealings of society with the individual in the way of compulsion and control, whether the means used by physical force in the form of legal penalties, or the moral coercion of public opinion. That principle is, that the sole end for which mankind are warranted, individually or collectively, in interfering with the liberty of action of any of their number, is self-protection. That the only purpose for which power can be rightfully exercised over any member of a civilized community, against his will, is to prevent harm to others. His own good, either physical or moral, is not a sufficient warrant. He cannot rightfully be compelled to do or forbear because it will be better for him to do so, because it will make him happier, because, in the opinions of others, to do so would be wise, or even right. These are good reasons for remonstrating with him, or reasoning with him, or persuading him, or entreating him, but not for compelling him, or visiting him with any evil in case he do otherwise. To justify that, the conduct from which it is desired to deter him, must be calculated to produce evil to some one else. The only part of the conduct of any one, for which he is amenable to society, is that which concerns others. In the part which merely concerns himself, his independence is, of right, absolute. Over himself, over his own body and mind, the individual is sovereign.

It is, perhaps, hardly necessary to say that this doctrine is meant to apply only to human beings in the maturity of their faculties. We are not speaking of children, or of young persons below the age which the law may fix as that of manhood or womanhood. Those who are still in a state to require being taken care of by others, must be protected against their own actions as well as against external injury. . . .

But there is a sphere of action in which society, as distinguished from the individual, has, if any, only an indirect interest; comprehending all that portion of a person's life and conduct which affects only himself, or it is also affects others, only with their free, voluntary, and undeceived consent and participation. When I say only himself, I mean directly, and in the first instance: for whatever affects himself, may affect others through himself; and the objection which may be grounded on this contingency will receive consideration in the sequel. This, then, is the appropriate region of human liberty. It comprises, first, the inward domain of consciousness; demanding liberty of conscience, in the most comprehensive sense; liberty of thought and feeling; absolute freedom of opinion and sentiment on all subjects, practical or speculative, scientific, moral or theological. The liberty of expressing and publishing opinions may seem to fall under a different principle, since it belongs to that part of the conduct of an individual which concerns other people; but, being almost of as much importance as the liberty of thought itself, and resting in great part on the same reasons, is practically inseparable from it. Secondly, the principle requires liberty of tastes and pursuits; of framing the plan of our life to suit our own character; of doing as we like, subject to such consequences as may follow: without impediment from our fellow creatures, so long as what we do does not harm them, even though they should think

——————————

From *Utilitarianism* by John Stuart Mill, London, 1859.

● ● ● ● ● Ain't I a Woman?
by Sojourner Truth

Several ministers attended the second day of the Woman's Rights Convention, and were not shy in voicing their opinion of man's superiority over women. One claimed "superior intellect," one spoke of the "manhood of Christ," and still another referred to the "sin of our first mother."

Suddenly, Sojourner Truth rose from her seat in the corner of the church.

"For God's sake, Mrs. Gage, *don't* let her speak!" half a dozen women whispered loudly, fearing that their cause would be mixed up with Abolition.

Sojourner walked to the podium and slowly took off her sunbonnet. Her six-foot frame towered over the audience. She began to speak in her deep, resonant voice. "Well, children, where there is so much racket, there must be something out of kilter. I think between the Negroes of the South and the women of the North—all talking about rights—the white men will be in a fix pretty soon. But what's all this talking about?"

Soujourner pointed to one of the ministers. "That man over there says that women need to be helped into carriages, and lifted over ditches, and to have the best place everywhere. Nobody helps me any best place. *And ain't I a woman?*"

Sojourner raised herself to her full height. "Look at me! Look at my arm." She bared her right arm and flexed her powerful muscles. "I have plowed, I have planted and I have gathered into barns. And no man could head me. *And ain't I a woman?*"

"I could work as much, and eat as much as man—when I could get it—and bear the lash as well! *And ain't I a woman?* I have borne children and seen most of them sold into slavery, and when I cried out with a mother's grief, none but Jesus heard me. *And ain't I a woman?*"

The women in the audience began to cheer wildly.

She pointed to another minister. "He talks about this thing in the head. What's that they call it?"

"Intellect," whispered a woman nearby.

"That's it, honey. What's intellect got to do with women's rights or black folks' rights? If my cup won't hold but a pint and yours holds a quart, wouldn't you be mean not to let me have my little half-measure full?"

"That little man in black there! He says women can't have as much rights as men. Cause Christ wasn't a woman." She stood with outstretched arms and eyes of fire. "Where did your Christ come from?"

"*Where did your Christ come from?*" she thundered again. "From God and a Woman! Man had nothing to do with him!"

The entire church now roared with deafening applause.

"If the first woman God ever made was strong enough to turn the world upside down all alone, these women together ought to be able to turn it back and get it right-side up again. And now that they are asking to do it the men better let them."

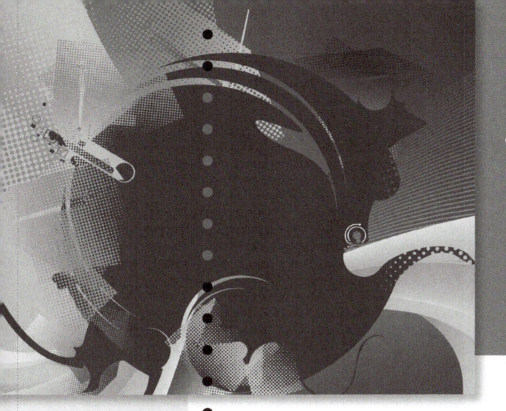

Comprehensive Glossary

age of instant information: the notion that the 21st century will be largely characterized by the capability of individuals to transfer information freely all over the world; and to have immediate access to it instantaneously. It is also known by the phrase: *the digital age.*

all-purpose words: the use of language or words which are of a general nature; and offer the listener no real concrete sense of any meaning. All-purpose words will always weaken the power of a speech because they are *ineffective* in telling an audience exactly what the speaker feels, thinks or even believes. All-purpose words such as *good, bad, wonderful* or *nice* do not help an audience see, feel or understand anything in a specific manner.

anecdote: a personal story or narrative which a speaker may use to serve as an *attention-getter.* Anecdotes are most often short accounts or narratives of interesting or amusing incidents, they are intended to help a speaker illustrate or support the main points which will follow in the body of a speech.

argument: the degree to which a persuasive speaker furnishes balanced reasons for claiming his or her point of view. These normally include: facts, figures, statistics, testimonies, and the speaker's capacity to challenge counter-arguments held by opposing viewpoints. A strong argument is akin to the rendering which an architect may utilize in constructing a new building; and gives a persuasive speech its structure and power. All strong arguments must be based upon sound evidence. There are three basic varieties of evidence, these include: rational evidence (or *logos*), emotive evidence (or *pathos*), and credible evidence (or *ethos*)

Aristotle: The Greek philosopher (384–322 B.C.E.) who was the first to passionately disapprove of the ideals and practices of *sophistry.* Aristotle was very displeased at the exploitation of public speaking; and was able to see the great and powerful potential it had in helping those gathered in large crowds to understand informational truths, and to pursue honest means of persuasion.

artifact: is considered anything which is *not* directly related to a speaker's speech, but which nonetheless does emotionally connect the speech to the audience. Artifacts are a very broad category and may include virtually anything the speaker wishes to show the audience.

attention-getter (AG) a speaker's introductory device for gaining; and hopefully keeping the attention of every member of an audience. An AG may be the first spoken, unspoken or visual cues a speaker gives an audience. These may include anything from personal stories, jokes and quotations to: live music, video clips, and even attention-grabbing photos.

attention-retainer (AR): A clincher which a speaker uses to help remind an audience of his or her speech topic sometime in the future, long after the actual speech has ended Retaining the attention of an audience can be a challenge, but also an opportunity for personal invention, creativity and originality just as with an *attention-getter* or AG.

attire: the overall physical appearance of a public speaker. Attire options should be adjusted to an audience and *not* only of the speaker's own choosing. A speaker should always dress in a manner which is characteristic of his or her audience, unless he or she wishes to wear clothing which is directly relevant to the speech. When speaking about a particular ethnic institution or culture, a speaker may prefer to wear clothing unique to that set of cultural traditions.

attitude: a learned disposition or mind-set which an individual or an audience inherits from their parents. Attitudes are not genetically inherited, but are a product of socialization. Attitudes regularly subscribe to a consistently constructive or fault-finding temperament. This temperament may be with respect to an *individual,* a *thing,* a specific *idea,* or even a particular *incident.* Attitudes come in a variety of different shapes and appearances.

audience adjustment: tailoring a speech to offer a message which identifies with a speaker's intended audience; one which will resonate with them, and speak to their special needs, desires, and interests.

audience assessment: how a public speaker approaches a speech, and then successfully tailors it to the specific, time, place, and demographic of his or her audience.

audience preview: a speaker's sample of what his or her main points will be as presented in the body of his or her speech. An audience preview should briefly and concisely list or discuss the speaker's main points for an audience in a conversational manner. Because of the audience preview, there should be no surprises later in the actual content of the speech. The audience preview simply offers the speaker's plan or organization before launching into the detailed body of the speech.

audience: a group of people gathered together to experience an event in a public setting. For public speakers, this simply means the live assembly of people gathered together to see and hear what a speaker has to say about a given topic. Public speakers should take the time to get to know the nature of their audience by first viewing them as communal collaborators. A speaker should always know and understand the nature of his or her audience before actually speaking to them.

audiotapes: sound effects and music preserved on CDs, or MP3 files which may be quite useful as an enhancement to a speaker's presentation. Insect sounds, animal calls, rare whale and exotic bird songs, and even bits and pieces from the speeches of famous individuals can all be offered as an audiotape enhancement to any speech. Sometimes a speaker may even choose to make use of commentary from friends and relatives as a part of his or her own self-created sound enhancement. Often times recorded music which simply accompanies or underscores a speech can provide quite a powerful and enjoyable enhancement for an audience.

audiovisual resources: resources which make effective use of computer-generated slides which then may be accompanied by music, poetry or a more detailed narrative to be used during a presentation. The use of such technologies may also include the utilization of videotapes

(DVDs and VCRs) which may comprise: excerpts from movies, TV, cable commercials, or even home-made videos.

auditory arts: all forms of *experimental sound, music, acoustics, theatre, spoken narratives,* and *sound literature* which have today taken on a new role which is beyond that of being only aural. Each of these art forms can be effectively incorporated into public presentations and creative speech formats. The auditory (hearing) arts can greatly enhance and boost audience interest for any speech, by being united with other major speech elements such as an attention-getter, attention-remainder or as part of a summary.

biased-pigeonholing fallacy: a fallacy which categorizes people or groups by placing an unfair marker on them. Pigeon-holing includes such monikers as: "religious fanatic," "raging liberal," and "fascist" which are often bantered around among political supporters during various local and national campaign seasons. It is important for the speaker to avoid such unfair labels at all costs. Pigeonholing individuals or groups may result in hurting speaker credibility in the end. A speaker should always let an audience decide how to mark a person or group, it is not the responsibility of the public speaker to label or pigeonhole anyone.

blackboards: green or black erasable boards made of carbon most often used in classrooms, which enable a speaker to write or draw at freedom; and then to erase any non-permanent information with ease.

body: the very informational center of any speech. It includes all of the *main points* and *sub-points* which a speaker hopes to convey to an audience. Each of these points must be clear; and then listed in a logical, connecting sequence. The body of a speech is both the informational and also the argumentative core of what every speaker hopes to communicate.

brainstorming: a general technique which encourages free association of thought in a fun game-like manner. Brainstorming encourages a speaker to seek out an interesting and informative topic not only for his- or herself, but also for the benefit of the intended audience.

broad goal: a speech's *general intention.* A broad goal may be to *enlighten, inform* or even *persuade* an audience. It may be to *motivate* them into taking some form of action. Or it may be to solemnly persuade them of a specific viewpoint. A broad goal may be as simple as *introducing* a speaker for an important public presentation, or to *memorialize* a significant event, or serve as the occasion for someone to *accept* an award or citation.

canon: a basic rule or foundational principle to be memorized; and then to be put into regular practice. *Quintilian's* standard notion of ancient Roman rhetoric included the following five canons: *Invention, Arrangement, Style, Memory,* and *Delivery.*

channel: the means by which communicators go about sending and receiving messages. There is a multiplicity of channels available in the early 21st century—everything from simple *face-to-face* and *telephone* conversations, *text* messages, and *e-mail,* to all forms of *social media* found on the Web. Before the advent of social media, the dominant channels of technology were radio and television. Before those, they were postcards, telegrams, letter writing, flyers, advertisements, and various types of memos and reports.

charts: visual resources which are helpful to public speakers in that they offer visual reviews of connections and associations which are not readily visible by words themselves. Oftentimes charts can be detailed and quite complex in nature. It is best for a speaker to use a series of simplified charts presented in an ordered sequence, rather than one highly detailed or visually-busy chart. An audience should be able to understand and decipher all charts easily with the help of the public speaker as their guide.

civic duty: the moral and ethical obligation to help enlighten, educate, and promote a more just an opportune society by a public action. In the specific case of public speaking before a live audience, this includes being open, honest, and not resorting to any deceptive or unethical informational or persuasive tactics.

class status: a public speaker's perceived worth and sense of social power of his or her audience based upon such factors as: income, occupation, neighborhood location, and even level of education.

coercion: an approach to public speaking which attempts to *persuade* an audience by forcing them to think or behave in a certain manner by which they are made to feel obligated to believe in a particular way. Coercion forces listeners to listen or act under pressure or threat. *Brainwashing, intimidation,* and *coercion* are each unethical forms of persuasion. All good persuasive words should inspire. Persuasive speakers should help stir their listeners into wanting to pay close attention to what we have to say, think; and hopefully even want to do.

collaboration: the mutual process of working together as a team. This begins and ends with understanding the joint nature between a speaker and his or her audience. Collaboration is the key to public speaking success.

communication: the means by which humans transport ideas and information to each other from one location to another. Animals also communicate, but only by sending information; and not by the transmission of thoughts and ideas.

communicational relationship: an honest sense of give and take between a speaker and his or her audience. This relationship in turn may cause an audience to laugh, cry, chuckle, moan, applaud or even be respectfully silent. A communicational relationship must be maintained throughout the duration of the entire speech.

computer-assisted resources: (also called presentation graphics programs) are computer software packages used to display information, normally in the form of an attractive slideshow. Such resources normally include three major functions: an editing capability which permits a speaker to insert and format content, a method for inserting and manipulating graphic images, and a slide-show system to display the entire content before an awaiting audience. A computer-assisted program should assist the speaker in more easily accessing his or her ideas; and any other participants with visual and sound information. Computer-assisted resources should only complement the spoken presentation at hand, and never be at the center of a presentation.

conclusion: the place toward the end of a speech where a speaker *signals that he or she is concluding,* and *summarizing the main points* of his or her speech, and then offers the *attention-retainer* (AR). The conclusion should provide an *emotional sense of closure* by offering a final dismissal to the listeners. It should be brief and tight; and has to be emphatic, dynamic, and confident. The final *thank you* to an audience should draw honest, unforced applause (not to mention at times: a bit of vocal affirmation as well); thus leaving an audience with a sense of enjoyment and appreciation for a speaker taking the time to talk to them.

conscious choice: a selection whereby a speaker personally *chooses,* rather than just includes his or her research ideas at random or by impulse. Making conscious choices uniquely tailors a speech to each individual speaker, and in turn helps an audience focus upon a particular viewpoint or unique perspective on a given topic. In a good speech, nothing should be presented which is not of a conscious nature.

contemporary rhetoric: the art of bringing information and persuasive meaning not only through traditional public speaking, but also through visual language, sound technology, and embodied performances. As they were in the past, colleges and universities are once again on the forefront of developing and promoting rhetorical growth. Contemporary rhetoric explores new and experimental ways in which speakers may more effectively communicate in the *digital age.*

contrast blueprint: a plan for an informative speech which correlates an unfamiliar subject to something an audience is already acquainted with, or for the most part has a basic knowledge or understanding. Oftentimes when a speaker makes such comparisons they are usually *factual, symbolic,* or *actual* contrasts. For instance, contrasting the structure of a complex scientific principle with that of commonly found household objects.

controlling leader: a management style whereby a leader will most likely approach things with a direct and more controlling approach of supervision. Controlling leaders are not fond of sharing power, and prefer to do most of the speaking and planning themselves. This style is effective and efficient under specific circumstances. It works well for groups which will meet only over one time period, or with a leader who is more knowledgeable and experienced than the other group members. A few common examples are: acting coaches, sports team captains, dance leaders, military officers, seminar leaders and business project leaders.

convictions: deep-rooted *beliefs, opinions,* or *ideologies* that an individual or a group may strongly adhere to; and to the point of little negotiation or discussion. A public speaker needs to be aware of audience convictions, whether those opinions or ideologies are accurate or not. True or untrue, obstinate convictions can be a major barrier to a public speaker's reception by an audience.

credible evidence (*ethos*): the level of trust which a speaker creates during his or her speech. It is important that a speaker create for an audience the impression that they are not someone who is subject to distorting the truth or over accentuating the facts. The moment a speaker begins to speak, he or she will be judged by an audience. Speaker credibility may increase or decrease depending upon a speaker's ability to appear and sound trustworthy throughout the duration of the speech.

culturally perceptive: the insightful ability to appreciate other cultures and acquire the necessary skills to speak successfully to them in public while being sensitive to their diverse racial, ethnic, and nationalistic backgrounds.

decoding: fully receiving and understanding the message(s) sent by an encoder. Readers, listeners, and anyone who observes gestures or receives a text message takes on the role of a decoder. If the decoder is not clear about the code, he or she who attempts to decode the message will become confused, and the information will be partially or even completely lost.

delivery: the manner by which a speaker looks, sounds, and moves his or her body, along with the very level of confidence and preparation each of these offers before a gathered audience. *Delivery* involves the fact that a speaker knows the he or she is on stage, and enjoys being there. It involves both a speaker's wants and needs to be seen and heard as a confident and prepared individual.

digital age: often seen beginning in the early 21st century as the that age where almost all peoples everywhere, have the potential or actual capability to communicate and send information in an open free manner.

economic status: a public speakers' perceived worth and sense of social power of his or her audience based solely upon income, material ownership and investment portfolios.

educational significance: the amount of information an audience gains about a given topic by attending a public speaking event. The educational significance of a speech is measured by how much innovative and supportive information, as well as further awareness a public speaker provides for his or her audience.

emotive evidence (*pathos*): the emotional tone a speaker sets while delivering a speech which helps to effectively connect him or her to an audience. Emotional connection is particularly important when needing to call an audience to immediately respond on some level. Emotional evidence works well when it gently taps into an audience's present beliefs and genuine needs. It is quite powerful in that it can strengthen *or* even seriously alter their point of view. More importantly, emotional evidence or *pathos* can inspire and stir an audience into taking direct action.

encoding: the ability to send information simply and clearly while anticipating and eliminating likely causes of confusion and misunderstanding in the process. Writers, speakers, and anyone who *sends* gestures or signals or instant texts is by definition an encoder.

ethical word choices: word choices by a speaker which center around rightness and wrongness in public presentations. For a speaker to choose words with a sense of ethics in mind is far more than being sensitive to religious values, sexual orientation, gender or political sensibilities *etc.* Such awareness does not guarantee that a speaker will be ethical in his or her attitudes or approach toward our audience. None the less, ethical word choices do promote as sense integrity and good intentions toward an audience.

ethnocentrism: a perspective that one's own culture is dominant and that other cultures are not quite as significant or well-developed. This unspoken (and in most cases) subconscious attitude, is the direct opposite of being *culturally perceptive*. All public speakers must avoid the trap of being ethnocentric.

event: an historical happening which may be used as the basis for a speech topic. Events may be taken from either U.S. or world history; and are either formally or informally recognized and commemorated by others. The most straightforward and informal of events may simply be a speaker's own birthday, Abraham Lincoln's or say the prophet Mohammed's; and may be spoken of on a much more commemorative and public scale. During Christmas, July 4th, and at the anniversary of a tragic incident, events take on a powerful meaning.

excerpt: quoted passages directly from letters, sacred texts, novels, plays, and even poetry collections which can serve as a form of *attention-getter*. Excerpts may be in the form of quotes from business and more academic literature; and not just from noted literary works *per se.*

exhibition speech: speeches which focus on an activity which an audience is encouraged to perform themselves. Performing an activity is at the center of exhibition speeches. They include the ability of a speaker to *demonstrate* a procedure, a specific process or a proper manner of doing something. The important element in the exhibition speech, is to exhibit or visually *display* before an audience, the very essence of what a speaker wishes to tell them or show them how to do themselves.

extemporaneous delivery: sometimes designated as *ex tempore*, is a delivery approach where by the speaker presents his or her speech from an *outline, note cards,* or from an assemblage of key words, phrases, or from concisely written comments or a series of short sentences. Extemporaneous delivery is the preferred mode of most public speaking instructors; and it is most often used for guest speaking events. Extemporaneous delivery is the public speaking approach generally preferred by most audiences since it permits a sense of natural spontaneity between both speaker and audience.

eye contact: the manner by which a speaker monitors an audience while speaking to them. Eye contact directly connects the speaker to his or her audience. Generally speaking, eye contact is a skill which tends to grow with public speaking experience. It lets listeners know that a given speaker is interested in them, in addition to the words actually spoken to them.

fallacy: a speaker's error in valid, logical reasoning. Fallacies in reasoning will immediately weaken a speaker's argument. Fallacies may come in many sizes, shapes, and forms. The test for effective persuasive speakers and their audiences rests in properly recognizing fallacies. On the surface fallacies often seem legitimate and at best, quite sensible. Upon closer inspection they are clearly erroneous, and in the end are evident upon reflection. Fallacies in a speech, even if they are not willful, are unacceptable; and will cause the speaker to no longer be credible.

feedback: a clear indication that *decoders* have received and understood any messages sent through *verbal, written,* and *nonverbal* responses. Oftentimes feedback may be delayed, or even conveyed through public media. Radio sports channels offer call-in feedback opportunities for fans, while some religious broadcasters even offer spiritual Q and A sessions to live listeners about the Bible or contemporary moral topics. For public speakers, feedback includes any and all verbal and non-verbal responses from the listening audience.

figurative words: words a speaker uses which offer something more dramatic and dynamic as opposed to the literal meanings of words. They are more poetic in nature; and are frequently used by artists, musicians, playwrights, poets, and preachers. Figurative words force imagination, stimulate thought, and create depth in a speech.

five-factor approach: a five step approach to a group presentation whereby: (1) each member shares a portion of a chosen topic to see how it may be portioned into various areas of responsibility for each member of the group; (2) each participant then puts together an outline for his or her main focus of the topic (main point) area for the entire project; (3) a general group outline is formed by combining each individual member's outline; (4) the delivery elements are then completed by deciding who is going to speak what, and when they will be presenting it; and (5) the group then rehearses the outline and prepares it for a public presentation as one overall group project.

forum: the question-and-answer (Q & A) sessions following any variety of group presentations. Group members in a symposium, panels, round-tables, public statements and other forms of group presentations, most often will be expected to handle Q & A from their respective audiences. As such, group members must listen attentively to each other, and be prepared to answer audience questions in a thorough and all-embracing manner.

gender: a culturally constructed and psychologically based perception of one's self as either *feminine* or *masculine.* An individual's gender-role identity, which wavers on a sliding scale from highly masculine to highly feminine, is learned or socially reinforced by one's surroundings, as well as by one's own personality and life experiences. Of course inherited genetics will also help determine and shape an individual's gender role identity: a role identity biologically defined as male or female. Over the centuries the understanding and description of gender has continued to evolve.

genres of rhetoric: Aristotle identified three types of rhetoric which include *forensic,* (or judicial), which was concerned with determining the truth or false nature of events; *deliberative,* (or political), which was concerned with determining whether or not particular actions *should* or *should not* be undertaken in the future; and *epideictic* which was concerned with either honoring or faulting others, and with acclaiming right and wrong, as revealed in each present age.

gestures: a speaker's actions determined by the public movement of his or her arms and hands as well as the body as a whole. Efficient gestures make a distinction between outstanding and dynamic speaking; and boring or commonplace speaking. Gesture should always contribute to highlighting a speech and never detract from it.

get-with-the-program fallacy: a fallacy which encourages an audience to believe or even do something because that's what everyone else is doing. This fallacy is about encouraging listeners to get-with-the-program and be trendy. Advertisers adore this approach to selling their products and services. Persuasion here is simply based upon being stylish or hip, and it's all about what's fashionable. For example: "If you are sexy, intelligent and know how to be a successful woman who knows what she likes, then you buy and use X regularly." And during election season: "Morally responsible people of faith, and those who are true Americans like our country's founders once were, are all voting for Y this presidential election."

global plagiarism: extracting a speech entirely from a single source and passing it off as one's own personal presentation. This is more frequently done than most speakers are aware of, and will most assuredly result in ethical problems, possible legal action, and for students in a classroom situation: a failing grade, if not removal from a college or university.

goal: a desired target(s) which a public speaker desires to reach or achieve by offering a speech in public. It is a focused objective which nudges a speaker to move on and reach it to some form of satisfaction. In public speaking there are *broad goals* and *narrow goals*. Without a topic goal, a speaker is at risk of rambling on with unorganized information which will eventually distract and turn off an audience.

graphics: visual resources which may include *sketches, charts,* and *maps.* Graphics should always be displayed for only short amounts of time during a speech, and then (as if on a blackboard) they should be quickly removed. Each graphic should focus upon one concept or idea. All images and colors should be intense, all lettering should be bold, and everything should be in razor-sharp contrast to the background at hand.

great noun: a universal category of person, place, thing or idea. As public speakers think about great nouns which interest them, they can devise a *noun inventory*. Great nouns should consist of simple broad nouns which should first interest the speaker; and then will in turn be of appropriate interest to a gathered audience.

grounds blueprint: a plan for an informative speech which shows how one circumstance creates, or is possibly created on the grounds of another. This blueprint is often utilized in speeches of *clarification*, where a speaker may express a topic either as a result of certain grounds, or on the grounds of a certain outcome. Usually the speaker initiates a *grounds blueprint* by recounting the topic and its significance, and then either questions how it came about, or what its end result may be like if actually carried through.

group blueprint: a pattern of speech organization which focuses upon the inherent or routine divisions within a topic. Divisions and categories help an audience mentally classify information so that they may discover a better understanding in the end. Most listeners find order and comprehension of the world around them, by seeking ordered divisions within it or by finding effective ways to partition it. A *group blueprint* should provide information about items, and show how they are commonly thought to constitute a group or category for some useful motive or end.

group resolution: the means by which a group goes about finding various approaches and effective methods for overcoming obstacles to achieve a preferred goal. Not all approaches to problem-solving follow the same steps. Time for reflective thinking does provide a helpful framework; it can reduce the ambiguity which initially exists when groups attempt to solve problems.

handouts: printed information which a speaker literally hands out to an audience before, during or after a speech. Handouts are quite useful when a speech topic is complicated or difficult to fully communicate by the use of words alone, or if the speech requires a lot of statistical information or scientific inquiry. In most cases, handouts may serve a speaker quite well by increasing the overall impression of a speech, while at the same time endorsing the information which the speaker has personally provided.

hands-off leader: a management style whereby a leader will most likely approach things with a more restrained or moderate approach of control. Hands-off leaders rely upon non-directive and passive means to guiding and directing others. They are generally more comfortable with permitting the group to move forward toward its goal without working out the specifics beforehand. They rely upon the more prepared, more advanced and experienced members of the group, by promoting a sense of self-direction and self-motivation among group members. Common examples are: community organizers, religious group leaders, environmental activists, some political group leaders and musical and arts project leaders

hyperbole: a figure of speech which uses an exaggerated or extravagant statement to generate a strong emotional response. As a figure of speech, hyperbole definitely is not intended to be taken literally. Sometimes it is used to create humor, or lightheartedness in a speech. Hyperbolic statements are not literally true, but speakers like to make use of them in order to: command attention, emphasize a main point, create absurdity, or even cause a shocking reaction. Hyperbole can be fun and most often promotes a sense of *speaker-audience bonding.*

impromptu delivery: presenting a speech with the least amount of preparation, and consequently the least amount of homework or time involved. Most often minimal planning and research is involved or required for this mode of delivery. *Impromptu delivery* is centered on the speaker simply taking the time to quickly focus and organize his or her thoughts, and to then efficiently arrange important points and goals without the concern of detailed preparation. In most cases only highly experienced speakers succeed at this approach to speaking in public.

incremental plagiarism: plagiarism whereby a speaker fails to give recognition for explicit quotations and paraphrases which are borrowed from other individual works, pieces of literature, or of any resource which is not original to the speaker. Whenever a speaker presents a speech, he or she must be sure it represents his or her own work entirely; and always give public credit or written citations for another's work.

inspiration: the ability of a speaker to emotionally enable an audience to connect with his or her point of view. Inspiration should motivate and cause an audience by their own prompting, to desire and truly feel that they need to take action in manners which the speaker may suggest to them. Persuasive speeches which more directly incorporate inspiration, are ones which occur at: places of worship, sports and political rallies, national events, and leave-taking or graduation speeches.

interpersonal communication: the combination of both *nonverbal* and *verbal* forms of communication which serve as a primary tool for expression between two or more people. They are an essential ingredient in fostering good relationships with other individuals or with a listening audience. Interpersonal communication lies at the intersection of all cultural understanding and construction of world society. Without them, modern life would have *no digital age* which consists of using cell phones, instant messaging, e-mails, Twitter and the Web.

interrupters: words or phrases in which the speaker unconsciously interrupts him- or herself. We often interrupt ourselves in daily informal conversation with filler expressions such as: "yah know?", "uh-huh", "ummm", "uhhhh", "let's see now", "Okay, okay?" These are fine for daily informal conversations, but not for a more prescribed conversation with an audience in a public setting. A speaker's interrupters can cause an audience to experience a disconnection; and in turn may even make both they and the speaker appear insignificant or even trivial.

introduction: that part of a speech which communicates preliminary information to an audience. It helps them become familiar with a speaker's chosen topic, and why it should be important to them as an audience. A good introduction should indicate how the speaker plans to proceed with his or her public conversation with an audience.

it's-so-simple fallacy: a fallacy which welcomes words and phrases which embrace some highly accepted positive norm or virtue. The *it's-so-simple* fallacy invites an audience to approve of an idea without examining any thought-out plan or forms of evidence. Politicians during election season and on heated televised debates, make every government problem seem so easily solvable. For example: "All this current president needs to do to quickly end this prolonged war is to: X, Y, Z." and "Our country needs to stop doing X and, then unemployment will drop suddenly within the next quarter or so." Such simple statements misuse the very positive desire to see political development and change, without acknowledging or analyzing the complexities involved.

jargon: the technical vocabulary which professionals, such as scientists, lawyers, and various artists rely upon to communicate with each other. Jargon may refer to specific ideas, specialized processes and even tools or instruments. Unless a speaker defines each piece of jargon for an audience, he or she may sound and appear intimidating and cause them to stop listening.

level of unawareness: the standard of topic alertness by those watching and listening to a public speaker. It is the task of the speaker to not only repeat information the audience may already be aware of, but also to raise their information and knowledge of a topic to new levels of understanding and consciousness.

liberal education: Liberal education entails being equally acquainted with world history, politics, ethics, the basic sciences; and finally, literature and the arts. *Cicero* believed that by having a liberal education, anyone who spoke in public would be able to bond with any audience at any time or location. For him a liberal education was the key to being an effective public speaker.‐

literal words: words which express exactly what a speaker means, are centered on the facts and in turn are designed to directly inform an audience. Literal words are most often the first meaning offered in a dictionary. Literal words give an audience unembellished, factual meanings. They are accurate clarifications or statements; and they help with truthful communication of information.

magnified language: word choices a speaker makes which are inflated or which seem to indicate his or her intention to make a good impression on an audience. A magnified vocabulary makes a speaker look and sound counterfeit, and will often cause an audience to view the speaker as not being authentic. It is always important *to be* a speaker, and not merely try *to sound* and *appear* as one.

main points: the very key points of information which comprise the *body* of a speech. Main points should sustain the *thesis statement* and never diverge away from it. It is essential that all three to five main points communicate the essence of a thesis statement, and not meander away from it in different directions. Just as a good pilot makes sure his or her air craft never diverges from its planned route, so too, a speaker must never divert from his or her main points.

manuscript delivery: offering a presentation in public with a fully written out statement—virtually: word-for-word. In essence, it is a skilled and authoritative manner of reading in public—yet it is *not* memorized, although the speaker must be very familiar with its entire contents. A manuscript is appropriate when the information being offered must be *specific, accurate and avoid all error,* since in the end the speaker will be *accountable* for every word offered in public. High-level business speeches, sermons, diplomatic, and presidential speeches often-times will resort to this format of delivery.

maps: geographical photos and drawings which have been around since ancient times. Today commercially prepared maps include far too much information and detail for effective use in public speaking. The most successful maps are those which focus specifically upon a given topic. Maps ideally should be used to put questions or problems into perspective, or simply illustrate for an audience geographically where events of interest included in a speech were historically or even currently happening. Once again like with charts: the simpler a map, the more helpful it usually becomes.

mark of agreement: a *path marker* which suggests that everything a speaker offers in a speech should continuously communicate the same overall intent and purpose. This helps the speaker to remain on target and not succumb to the temptation of wandering way from his or her goals. The mark of agreement implies that if any information offered to an audience does not communicate *or* contribute directly to those goals, then it should be eliminated from the speech.

mark of consistency: a *path marker* which suggests that the connections among the various parts of a speech should always remain understandable and logical to a listening audience. This helps maintain listener interest, and creates speaker credibility, while helping the audience to never become lost during the speech.

mark of equilibrium: a *path marker* which suggests that the three basic elements of a speech: *Introduction, Body, and Conclusion* should be largely proportional; and they should be in a comfortable relationship to each other; and that there must be a sense of proportion and *equilibrium* among each of them.

mark of major focus: a *path marker* which suggests that a speaker must always be aware of both his or her major points in a speech; and focus upon them appropriately. This also implies that a speaker clearly emphasizes and focuses only upon the main points as declared in the outline and does not diverge from that intended plan.

mark of minor focus: a *path marker* which suggests that a speaker must always be aware of his or her minor points in a speech and focus upon them appropriately. Keeping them in center builds a stronger emphasis of priorities among listeners, and in turn supports the content of the main points of the speech.

memorized delivery: a speech format by which a speaker has memorized *everything* about a prepared speech. Not only everything in the sense of word-for-word, but this also includes gestures, pauses, and even when and where to look up and make eye contact. This may also entail any smiles, frowns, and dramatic use of loud and soft volume. For the most part everything is planned and memorized. A memorized delivery is not uncommon among political speakers.

message: in its most basic form, a message is the central item of communication. It is a container of information which provides those who communicate with the means they need to *send* or *receive* information. Classes of messages include: *nonverbal, verbal,* and *written.* The first two are also part of the animal world, particularly of mammals and primates such as gorillas, orangutans, and chimpanzees. These classes of messages include those that encompass body movements, gestures, words, phrases, and even sound signals. Only humans have true verbal messages *per se.*

moderator: a selected individual who in most cases provides a public introduction for a small group discussion. The moderator provides an overview of the topic(s); and the purpose and goal of the discussion for a listening or viewing audience. In most cases the moderator will briefly present each participant's credentials or in some cases invite them to introduce themselves to the audience.

monotone: The opposite of *vocal pitch* is monotone, or the lack of vocal variety on the part of a public speaker. Nothing is more boring to an audience than feeling held hostage to a speaker who is monotone.

mythos (or mythology): a form of proof which bonds a persuasive topic to a given cultural, societal or traditional set of narratives (or stories) to a given audience. Such narratives may remind them of their forgotten heroes; and just who their enemies might or should be; and perhaps prompt them of who their adversaries were all along. When presenting a persuasive speech it is often quite powerful and appealing to make direct use of religious values, religious faith, societal identity and good old traditional beliefs. The use of *mythos* can be quite effective at unifying an audience and will almost always strike an emotional chord with them.

narration speeches: speeches which focus on description. They directly tell an audience about something. Daily we hear narrations on the radio, see them on television, and even read them on the internet. They may describe or *narrate* to an audience information about activities, persons, places, objects and even ideas. A narrative speech provides listeners with a clear, concrete and colorful description of a *person, place, thing,* or *idea* which is of importance to the gathered audience.

narrow goal: a goal with a more specific and focused purpose, one which identifies precisely what a speaker wants to accomplish with his or her speech by its final conclusion time. Narrow goals are the core and substance of a well-prepared speech.

noise: any obstacle(s) to communication which might be present and may hinder or even stop a message intended by an encoder. These obstacles may include any barriers to the listeners' experience and understanding of the context of the message, their psychological state, the time and place of reception, as well as many other potential factors which may contribute to confusion.

nominated leader: a management style whereby a leader will most likely approach things with a more instructive attitude, while at the same time not being overly direct or inflexible. They usually do not crave power, and realize that other people either elected or nominated them to their task, and are a leader by virtue of elected approval.

nonverbal messages: those forms of communication, other than verbal (spoken) or written, which create or transmit meaning to others. These may include facial expressions, general body movements, sound, visual signals, and even simple gestures. Nonverbal messages communicate without directly speaking by way of spoken words

noun inventory: a speech topic list which consists of simple *great nouns* which should first interest the speaker, and which will then in turn be of appropriate interest to his or her listeners. Making a noun inventory is an important part of *brainstorming*.

olfactory messages: communication propelled by animals in the form of what are called *pheromones*; and are sent into the air and received by way of smell. They play an important role in reproduction and other social behavior, but are quite primitive when compared to any other form of human communication. In humans scents a smells do play a role in communicating, but are ancillary to any other form of communication.

oral interpretation (OI): the art of skillfully reading clearly and audibly before a gathered audience. This includes reading with an even pace; clear enunciation of words and the ability to keep or maintain minimal eye contact while reading. Excellent oral interpretation skills are vital when reading poetry, drama, personal memoirs or children's literature in public.

orator: an individual who delivers an eloquent *oration* (or speech). An orator is distinguished for his or her skill and power as a public speaker. Cicero is famous for having said: *"Great is our admiration of the orator who speaks with fluency and discretion."* For the Romans, a proper rhetorical education should create a politically active, publicly-minded citizen who is both confident and distinct. Contemporary speakers, often considered to be orators, include: Martin Luther King, Jr., Ronald Reagan, John F. Kennedy, and President Barak Obama.

order blue print: a blueprint for speeches which visually or verbally moves an audience through an *order* or time. Informative speeches designed around an order blue print characteristically present steps for listeners to follow in a clear and defined succession. This type of blue print is most effective for *exhibition speeches,* which attempt to display or demonstrate a concept or a "how to" progression of steps. The speaker initiates things by identifying the needed steps; and then carries them out in the required order in which they should be taken.

organization: the placing of gathered information and research data in helpful order for both the benefit of the public speaker, and his or her audience. Organization will be different for each speaker. The key to successful organization is all about making *choices* as to which elements to include (and *where* to include them) and of course which elements to *exclude* entirely. A successful speech must embrace some of the research information available, and at the same time consciously exclude perhaps even a larger percentage of it.

outline: a general plan of what a speaker actually hopes to present to an audience. It should include the arrangement and order of the speaker's general purpose, audience demographic, actual location, time of day, and any time constraints involved... *etc.* Further, an outline should include the general approach to both the *introduction* and the *conclusion.* In more specific detail, it should also delineate what each of the *main points* (anywhere from three to five) and subsequent *minor points* are, along with any visual or sound resources the speaker may hope to utilize.

panel discussions: a *small group* comprised of specialists or authorities on a particular subject at hand. Most panel members are acquainted beforehand on what topics or questions will be discussed by the entire group or viewing audience. In many cases a moderator or intermediary asks questions to focus and direct the communication, which may occur in front of a live, radio, or televised audience. Even though panel discussions are rarely rehearsed, they are at the same time not completely improvised either. Panel participants often prepare well in advance, have a very good grasp beforehand of both the scope and direction of the discussion, and are rarely expected to be spontaneous and off-the-cuff in their remarks.

patchwork plagiarism: patching a speech together by copying more or less word-for-word from a number of individual or separate sources. Whenever a speaker presents a speech, he or she must be sure it represents their own work entirely. Patchwork plagiarism is the most common form found among public speaking students.

path markers: logical and emotional uniformity in the organization of a speech. They are akin to passing landmarks while on a road trip. Path markers let both the speaker and audience know that the goals of the speech are heading in the right direction as previously stated in the *introduction.* The most important path markers include: *mark of equilibrium, mark of agreement, mark of consistency;* and also *marks of major* and *minor focus.*

performance arts: those art forms which can be either visual, auditory or a combination of the two; and are then performed live before an audience. They are unique to the late 20th century and have been further developed into the 21st century as well. *Performance art* blends rhetorical history and theory, with movement and performance to explore how information and persuasive techniques can communicate new and powerful meaning to audiences.

persuasive speech: a type of speech which *argues* or *convinces*. A persuasive speech is essentially interested in influencing an audience's thoughts about a given topic or awareness. More significantly, persuasive speeches often are interested in attempting to change audience behaviors as well. A successful persuasive speech will hopefully provide listeners with challenging arguments, and even answer many of the thorny disagreements which were in the back of their minds before and during the delivery of the speech itself.

photographs: photos or pictures (such as paintings or sketches) chosen by a speaker for their particular significance to the topic of the presentation. All photographs ought to be displayed only as the speaker discusses them, and then be taken out of view from the audience. All photographs should visually amplify a speaker's words and not *vice versa.*

plural language: the use of language by a speaker before a *small group* or large audience to reflect the entire involvement of others beyond oneself. Plural language includes such phrases as: "we", "they", and "us" to de-emphasize the action of any one individual. To recognize everyone's involvement, a speaker must be well acquainted with all characteristics of a given topic, or report; and be ready to ask group members for clarification and illumination if necessary.

position of partiality: a situation whereby an individual or group speaker deliberately presents information that unevenly favors or discredits one side of a topic over another. Such speakers are considered to be presenting a biased or partial viewpoint. Although it is more or less impossible for any speaker to be completely objective, there must at minimum, be a conscious effort by all public speakers to be as objective and impartial as is possible.

posters: (an old fashioned visual aid) which can still be used quite effectively to exhibit pictures, photos, and even textual graphics. For the average classroom speech, an effective poster size should be roughly about 14 by 17 inches in width and length. Posters are great in that they are quite easy to handle and manipulate. Posters are also convenient because a speaker can paste note cards behind them, as a reminder about what he or she needs to emphasize and point out about the given image(s) at hand.

PowerPoint: a *computer-assisted resource* program developed by Microsoft Corporation. It is part of the Microsoft Office system, and runs on Microsoft Windows and the Mac OS computer operating systems. PowerPoint has become quite a popular visual and sound resource for a number of good reasons. It should always be utilized as a guide for an audience, and never a substitute for the public speaker.

Q & A session: the opportunity for questions and answers which follow a speaker's public presentation. By offering a Q and A session, speakers are more likely to leave a speech without misinterpretations or any misconceptions about the information or ideas which were delivered. Further, a good Q and A session most often strengthens and reinforces the overall goals and purpose of a given speech.

rational evidence (logos): those elements in a persuasive or informative speech which are essentially rooted in facts, figures, statistics, and documented information. Facts and figures alone do not guarantee the persuasion of an audience. A speaker must have conviction combined with an order and strategy. None-the-less, good sound facts are quite hard to take issue with when they are passionately presented to an audience.

relic: any object directly related to a speaker's topic which may be used to bring attention to his or her speech. This tangible object should help an audience both *see* and *feel* another dimension of the speech beyond the words themselves. A relic should be convenient to handle or observe, and simple for an audience to see or touch without much effort or care.

repetitive language: the excessive use of the same or very similar words and phrases in a speech. Repetition is far more than boring; it creates an opportunity for an audience to turn-off a speech entirely. Repetition highlights a speaker's failure to understand all the information being presented, and to see all the angles of an argument. It often is considered to be a sign of a speaker's lack preparation.

rhetoric: the ancient Greek and Roman art of using language honestly and effectively to inform and persuade an audience. Today modern rhetoric has become focused upon discovering creative approaches to using speech, developing personal styles, and making effective use of current digital technology to develop and enhance public presentations.

rhetorical analysis: a constructive awareness in the relationship between rhetoric and civic responsibility; and its connection to all of written and sound literature in general. Today rhetorical analysis has helped unite the learning of public speaking skills with the broader humanistic tradition of how students, teachers, and citizens in general, address their shared desires and goals in a highly diverse and information-driven society.

rhetorical appeals: public speaking petitions designated as: *pathetic, logical-ethical,* and *stylistic.* The goal of rhetorical appeals is to both inform and persuade an audience that a speaker's ideas are valid, or more suitable than alternatives offered by other speakers on the subject. Rhetorical appeals have their origin in the rhetorical philosophy found in ancient Greece and Rome beginning with Aristotle, Quintilian, and Cicero.

rhetorical purpose: the overall rationale for giving a speech. Whether for a class assignment, marketing a product, a scientific lecture or even a religious teaching, a *rhetorical purpose* must be designed to accomplish some clear goal. Trained professional speakers spend a great deal of their time thinking and planning how to reach their goals by making their chosen topic engaging, appealing, and if necessary, capable of persuading their audience for or against a position.

rhetorical question: a question which is largely philosophical, and requires no expected answer. If a speaker chooses, he or she may ask more than one rhetorical question, but they should be short and sweet, be very involved or give the impression that the speaker is honestly seeking an answer from the audience.

rhetorical situation: a multifaceted state of affairs which public speakers encounter while giving a speech. It includes the gathering of persons, events, objects, and relations presenting an actual or potential situational dialogue with each other. The *rhetorical situation* dictates the significant physical and verbal responses, as well as the sorts of observations to be made by the public speaker, and influences the *feedback* given by the audience.

rhythm: the tempo or pace of a presentation. In a speech, rhythm most often starts out measured and slow, then starts to build as the speaker becomes more involved in his or her topic. Oftentimes we refer to *tempo, rhythm,* and *pace* as the same commodity: namely the speed of a speaker's words and phrases. After a short time the speaker should find his or her "sailing speed" for the speech, a rhythm which is natural and comfortable for both the speaker and audience.

room blue prints: a blueprint for speeches which develops a topic within a geographical setting, not unlike the arrangement of a room in a house or office building. The arrangement of the speech is based upon the geographical relationship of things arranged in space. Room blue prints are quite useful for *speeches of narration* in which they assist an audience in visualizing the physical relationship of objects to one another.

round-table discussion: a *small group* event in which only group members are in attendance, and each participates freely in all discussions. If a formal facilitator or host is present, he or she will first explain the reason for the round-table, outline a basic approach and perhaps set some simple communicational and time limits for approaching the topic at hand. At the conclusion of the round-table (usually all of this is behind closed doors) the facilitator will summarize the main points which came forward from the gathering, and then state how such results will be utilized. In most cases, a round-table discussion is recorded or videotaped; and a designated secretary will take notes to preserve the information for future discussions and historical documentation.

search engine: use of electronic technology to help a speaker further *brainstorm* for possible topic ideas. Search engines consist of on-line sites which help a speaker find a word, topic or idea available by simply entering data *via* that given site.

shooting-from-the-hip: when a speaker makes the choice to speak off of his or her prepared and memorized words. When this happens, more often than not, the speaker often gets into trouble and will make the headline news if he or she is a well-known celebrity. As for politicians and public servants: shooting-from-the-hip sometimes leads them to offering a public apology.

signpost: a specific transition which indicates progressive movement in a speech, and points toward the speech's final conclusion. Signposts indicate to an audience where a speaker is in a speech, where the speaker hopes to go, and also helps bridge thoughts and ideas in a smooth, logical manner.

sketches: free-hand or simplified illustrations of what a speaker is speaking about. Sketches should always be simple and direct. They should lack detail, and be used for the straightforward illustration of a basic concept or idea. Simple sketches of common objects and ideas can make a clear and profound impression on an audience.

small group: an assortment of individuals who gather together for a common goal. This may include various individuals in the group preparing reports, short talks and informational data for the entire group at hand. In most cases a small group must include at least three people (minimum), and for a maximum, roughly no more than twelve people at best. Beyond twelve people it becomes very difficult for members of a group to regularly interact with each other, especially if they are going to make a presentation before a live audience.

sophistry: the deliberate use of fallacious reasoning, intellectual deceit, and ethical corruption to mislead individuals by way of public speaking. Sophistry is not concerned with what is helpful, truthful, or virtuous, but rather seeks to achieve power and control by public means. Both Plato and Aristotle challenged the philosophical foundations of sophistry, which later gave rise to *rhetoric.*

sound resources: resources which help a speaker aurally present a speech in a manner well beyond spoken words and language; and are enhancements which an audience will hear in addition to or beyond the speaker in front of them. These may include the use of recordings such as: conversations, interviews, music, sound effects, animal noises and even perhaps clips and bits of speeches by other speakers. By augmenting a speaker's words and actions, sound and visual resources help make a speech tangible and more comprehensible for an audience.

speaker-audience bond: the intellectual and emotional relationship created between a speaker and his or her audience throughout the course of a speech. This involves trust, intimacy, and the minimal level of openness involved for communication to honestly take place. The audience-speaker bond is like a two-way boulevard, and goes in both directions. It is the task of the speaker to maintain a strong and continual bond with his or her audience throughout the duration of the speech.

speech blueprint: a structure which will help frame a speech in an effective pattern which in turn will best enable listeners to receive it. A blue print, not unlike the rendering which an architect may utilize in constructing his or her new building, is what gives an informative or persuasive speech its foundation. There are several categories of blue prints available to the public speaker. Blue print patterns may include: *Room, Order, Time, Group, Contrast,* and *Ground blueprints.*

speech dynamics: how a speaker regulates his or her eyes, voice, and body movements while delivering a speech. Namely, how a speaker controls every aspect of a speech, apart from the actual words and content. Speech dynamics involve all which is *nonverbal,* and is concerned with everything from *eye contact* and suitable attire to exact pitch, volume, rhythm, and pacing.

speech of clarification: a speech which provides information about a meticulous subject, a complex situation or an abstract idea. The purpose of a clarification speech is to provide an audience with a comprehension, explanation, or clarification of a topic by way of clear definitions of ideas and terms, along with plentiful examples and illustrations.

spoken public statement: the speech or prepared statement from a participant involved in a group who offers his or her declaration on behalf of all involved. This is often the case with formal organizations and work teams, and governmental committees. In most cases various members of the organization develop and shape the public statement, then one of the group participants is carefully selected to present the findings or results to upper management (in the business world), the university or school administration (in the educational world), or perhaps to legislators (in the sphere of government). Such effective oral presentations clearly acknowledge the involvement of all those in the group.

stereotypes: fixed beliefs or opinions about people of a particular social or ethnic group. This may also include political and intellectual, to economic, sexual and regional stereotypes as well. Stereotyping neglects individual differences and often causes people to make decisions based on flawed reasoning. The best way to avoid stereotyping, is to learn as much as possible about an audience by using personal research instead of relying upon preconceived notions of any given race, culture, gender, or sexual orientation.

sub-points: the focused examples, embellishments, and details about each *main point* found in a speech. If a speaker has a clear *thesis statement* and useful *main point* headings, adding the *sub-points* should be fairly straight forward, almost like filling in the colorful details.

symposium: a public discussion in which several participants each give different speeches on different facets of the same topic. Each participant typically follows a formalized sequence pattern, in order to provide the audience with a sense of connection and an overall consistency among the divided speeches. In a symposium, the group selects a topic and then partitions that topic into disconnected areas for special group focus. Each member of the group then presents a small speech on his or her focused contribution, or subdivision of the whole topic.

tangible words: words or language which is very specific or concrete to the listener. The more tangible the word, the better for an audience. Even colors, sizes, and dimensions can be made more tangible and vivid by choosing to be more detailed. Making use of *bright turquoise* for *blue, a 1968 Lincoln Continental* in place of *an older car,* and *a high-rise Chicago apartment* in place of: *an urban home* are powerful and tangible word choices, which create an honest sense of what a speaker hopes to describe to an audience.

team presentation: a collective talk made by several members of a group, with each participant presenting a different speech on a single topic. Each of the speeches is formal, with participants attending to diverse elements of the topic or problem at hand, with each respective speaker using a largely similar style and approach. There is usually a relaxed flow of energy from one speaker to the next. In most cases, to help assure a smooth overall presentation, one of the participants serves as a general *moderator,* but this is not a necessity. Team presentations are more common in university settings, and popular among classroom assignments in public speaking courses.

thank you: The very final words of a speech which expresses the speaker's sincere and heartfelt gratitude to an audience. A "thank you" let's an audience know that indeed the speech has ultimately concluded, and that there are no more ideas, intentions or surprises which will follow.

thesis statement: a verbal nutshell of exactly what a speaker hopes to speak about; and how he or she proposes to do it. A *thesis statement* should be established early in the speech itself, and be noticeably articulated to an audience. In many ways a thesis statement in a speech is similar to a *topic sentence* or a central statement in a written essay or perhaps a term paper. A thesis statement always reveals the general direction and content of a written paper or public speech.

thinking-in-a-circle fallacy: a fallacy which utilizes two unproven propositions to provide evidence for each other. When a speaker argues in a circle, he or she repeats the same tune over, and over and essentially attempts to argue one thing by defining it by another. An example would be: "Marijuana should be outlawed because it is a harmful drug. Harmful drugs are never legal, they are controlled, or are deemed as crime by those who use or sell them, therefore Marijuana should not be legalized…"

this-because-of-that fallacy: a fallacy stemming from a Latin phrase often employed by lawyers: *post hoc; ergo prop hoc* which simply translated means: "after this; therefore, because of this." This popular fallacy attaches adversity and disaster to a given event or circumstances which occurred before such misfortunes themselves. Even though there is no evidence of any connection, a connection is assumed. Fundamentalist preachers of all religions often times attribute storms and natural calamity to a specific group or individual's public or private actions which they may find undesirable or immoral. Just because two things appear to be occurring closely together, does not mean that one caused the other to take place.

this-or-that fallacy: a fallacy which assumes that all issues are binary or polar opposites; and that every issue has two clear and opposite positions. It erroneously proposes that everyone must be on one side *or* the other. Politicians and advertisers alike love to suggest: "You are either on our side or not" or "It's either America—*love*: it or America—*leave*: it." Such fallacies delete any possibilities for growth or change in any situation. The heart of this fallacy lies in the fact that it does not recognize that most issues are far more complicated than they appear; and are subject to numerous points of view.

timbre: the very tones, qualities, and vocal characteristics which are unique to a given speaker. Homer Simpson, Mickey Mouse, and well known celebrities each have a *timbre* which is quickly identifiable at an instant. The timbre of a speaker is what makes he or she (among others things) a unique communicator. Like a thumb print, timbre is unique to each public speaker, it is the vocal element which makes each individual distinctive from all others.

time blue print: a pattern of speech organization which follows a succession of important events in a historical pattern. Using this blue print for a speech, the speaker may begin with the earliest history of a subject, and trace it up to the very present moment, or simply *vice versa*. In order to keep such a speech interesting and easy to follow, the speaker must be selective in the order and particular number of points chosen for presentation.

topic goals: a speaker's main objectives for wanting to speak about a chosen topic before an audience. A speaker's topic goals should be rooted in his or her own individual motivation, inspiration, and level of personal experience. A topic goal is always a goal which is not previously unfamiliar to the speaker.

totems: the unconscious movement of the body by a speaker in a public setting.. These may include the following: constantly straightening a tie, excessively adjusting eye glasses, fixing ones hair continuously, the tapping of feet, scratching the nose; and even bobbing up and down in front of the podium. Totems are distracting and could indicate to an audience that a speaker may not be prepared, is unfocused or really not in control of his or speech. To say the least, totems may indicate a high level of nervousness in a speaker as well.

transition: the emotional and informational change a speaker makes from one main point to the next, which continuously *signposts* the direction of a speech. Transitions help bridge thoughts and ideas between main points in a smooth, logical manner. Transitions should assist the audience in thinking easily about a topic from one point to the next.

vague language: unclear and neutral language which does not indicate apparent ideas, thoughts or intentions. Vague words and phrases will make a speaker's message weakened and stale. It is important for a speaker to say exactly what is meant, and in turn: to mean exactly what has been said at every point throughout a given speech.

values: relatively firm loyalties which individuals or groups may hold about the worth or advantage of material items, actions or ultimate aspirations. These may incorporate both religious values and moral values which may include: equality, fairness, justice or even loftier values concerning the appropriate religious attitude to a topic such as traditional marriage as opposed to say gay or lesbian marriage. Compared to *beliefs,* values are surprisingly more difficult for a public speaker to influence or change in an audience. They are developed over a long span of time, are often rooted in experience, and take root at a very early age.

verbal messages: messages which utilize vocal sounds and language to communicate. Such messages include all communication which can first be spoken and then heard. *Verbal messages* serve as a powerful means for expressing human thoughts, ideas, inspirations, needs, and impressions.

videoconferencing: a meeting or group discussion whereby participants are located at a variety of remote physical locations. They are by nature of this technology, capable of communicating both orally and visually in real time (as if present together) in the same identical location. *Videoconferencing* may be done using a personal or industry computer, along with specialized interactive software; and it has become increasingly more economical and more commonplace among business, educational and public events.

videotapes: are recorded information which can provide a great added visual-sound experience which will enhance a speech. Using foreign films and Hollywood movies, can be a powerful emotional and narrative resource to help underscore any presentation. Short clips from videotapes often make an excellent *attention-getter (AG)* or *Attention-retainer (AR)* when a speaker wants to be visually striking, provocative, or simply entertaining.

visual resources: resources to help a speaker present a speech in a manner well beyond spoken words and language; and which will serve as enhancements which an audience will see in addition to or beyond the speaker in front of them. These may include objects or artifacts such as: clothing, rocks, coins, flags, personal relics, and even food items. Other visual resources may include: photographs, design models, diagrams, sketches, charts, and even actual art work. On the whole, audiences enjoy some level of visual stimulation beyond that of the central speaker.

vocal fluency: the smoothness of a speaker's words, and the ease with which he or she speaks to an audience. A fluent public speaker never stumbles over words or phrases. Vocal fluency can be accomplished by: practicing the correct intonation of foreign words and phrases, checking on the correct pronunciation of technical, scientific, and medical terms; and also by being sure how to articulate words which are new to a speaker's vocabulary.

vocal pitch: is the relative highness or lowness of a speaker's voice or the downward or upward intonation of that voice. In many ways vocal pitch is the musical nature of the spoken word. A competent public speaker is never *monotone*, but explores the variations in pitch at various points in his or her presentation. Appropriate pitch can illustrate the difference between a question and a declarative statement, or the difference between being gravely serious about a topic, or simply speaking about it in a light or joking manner.

vocal projection: how a speaker properly adjusts his or her speaking volume to both the audience and the situation at hand. Management of volume can be a powerful communicational tool. Controlling one's voice can convey solemnity, stress certain important points, and even add a level of humor to any speech. A speaker's voice must carry at all times; and he or she must always speak loudly and strongly, and not be afraid to ask the audience if they are being heard by all present.

whiteboards: erasable glossy white boards most often used in classrooms, which enable a speaker to write or draw with colored markers at freedom, and then to erase any non-permanent information with ease.

word choices: the means by which a speaker expresses his or her thoughts and beliefs when communicating to an audience. All of a speaker's words should be carefully chosen. Word choices are the nouns, verbs, adverbs, and adjectives selected by the speaker to present his or her audience within the context of the *main points* and *sub-points.*

word confidence: the conscious effort a speaker makes which implies that he or she intends to use the very words which the audience is hearing. Word confidence implies that the speaker knows and understands the words which are being used, and is always in command of them. A speaker should never stumble over words, nor use any word or phrase with a sense of trepidation, or with a sense of uncertainty. Word confidence always creates speaker confidence and *vice versa.*

written messages: any type of communication which makes use of written symbols, words, and written language *per se.* Written messages do not have to be delivered instantaneously or be even in real-time before a crowd as in a public speech. They can be corrected and revised numerous times before they are sent to those who will receive them; and in the end provide a permanent record which may be set aside for later study and review by those who receive them.

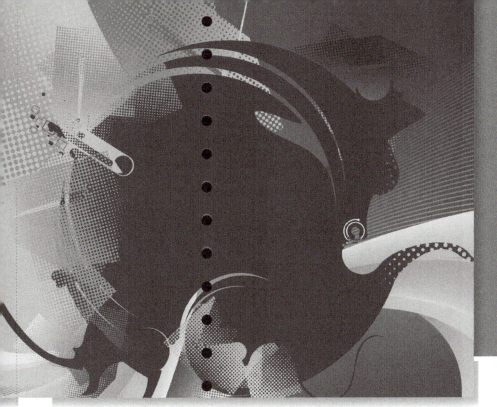

Index

CPSIA information can be obtained at www.ICGtesting.com
Printed in the USA
LVOW02s1933271214

420473LV00002B/2/P